Symbian for Software Leaders

TITLES PUBLISHED BY SYMBIAN PRESS

❑ Wireless Java for Symbian Devices
Jonathan Allin
0471 486841   512pp   2001   Paperback

❑ Symbian OS Communications Programming
Michael J Jipping
0470 844302   418pp   2002   Paperback

❑ Programming for the Series 60 Platform and Symbian OS
Digia
0470 849487   550pp   2002   Paperback

❑ Symbian OS C++ for Mobile Phones, Volume 1
Richard Harrison
0470 856114   826pp   2003   Paperback

❑ Programming Java 2 Micro Edition on Symbian OS
Martin de Jode
0470 092238   498pp   2004   Paperback

❑ Symbian OS C++ for Mobile Phones, Volume 2
Richard Harrison
0470 871083   448pp   2004   Paperback

❑ Symbian OS Explained
Jo Stichbury
0470 021306   448pp   2004   Paperback

❑ Programming PC Connectivity Applications for Symbian OS
Ian McDowall
0470 090537   480pp   2004   Paperback

❑ Rapid Mobile Enterprise Development for Symbian OS
Ewan Spence
0470 014857   324pp   2005   Paperback

Symbian for Software Leaders

Principles of Successful Smartphone Development Projects

David Wood

Reviewed by
Richard Harrison

Head of Symbian Press
Phil Northam

Managing editor
Freddie Gjertsen

John Wiley & Sons, Ltd

Other Wiley Editorial Offices

John Wiley & Sons Inc., 111 River Street, Hoboken, NJ 07030, USA

Jossey-Bass, 989 Market Street, San Francisco, CA 94103-1741, USA

Wiley-VCH Verlag GmbH, Boschstr. 12, D-69469 Weinheim, Germany

John Wiley & Sons Australia Ltd, 42 McDougall Street, Milton, Queensland 4064, Australia

John Wiley & Sons (Asia) Pte Ltd, 2 Clementi Loop #02-01, Jin Xing Distripark, Singapore 129809

John Wiley & Sons Canada Ltd, 22 Worcester Road, Etobicoke, Ontario, Canada M9W 1L1

Wiley also publishes its books in a variety of electronic formats. Some content that
appears in print may not be available in electronic books.

Library of Congress Cataloging-in-Publication Data:

Wood, David, 1959–
Symbian for software leaders : principles of successful Smartphone
development projects / David Wood ; Head of Symbian Press, Phil Northam ; Managing Editor,
Freddie Gjertsen.
    p. cm.
Includes bibliographical references and index.
ISBN-13: 978-0-470-01683-1 (cloth : alk. paper)
ISBN-10: 0-470-01683-3 (cloth : alk. paper)
1.   Operating systems (Computers) 2.   Cellular telephone systems – Computer
programs. I. Northam, Phil. II. Gjertsen, Freddie, III. Title.
   QA76.76.O63W658 2005
   005.4'3 – dc22

                                                                   2005012177

British Library Cataloguing in Publication Data

A catalogue record for this book is available from the British Library

ISBN-13 978-0-470-01683-1
ISBN-10 0-470-01683-3

Typeset in 10/12pt Optima by Laserwords Private Limited, Chennai, India
Printed and bound in Great Britain by TJ International, Padstow, Cornwall
This book is printed on acid-free paper responsibly manufactured from sustainable forestry
in which at least two trees are planted for each one used for paper production.

To software leaders in the smartphone revolution

– the creators of outstanding products which will yield high value to hundreds of millions of mobile users

Contents

Introduction: projects, projects, projects

I dedicate this book to everyone interested in the exhilarating task of creating smartphone products using Symbian OS. That task is exhilarating because it is, at times, both truly hard and truly rewarding. My goal with this book is to make the task less hard, and even more rewarding.

My target audience comprises project managers, product managers, development managers, design authorities, system architects, quality managers, software engineers, technical consultants, and industry analysts – everyone involved in creating smartphone products (whether these products are complete smartphones or applications or services designed to be used in close conjunction with smartphones). The book should be particularly valuable to the people who assemble and run an overall development team, as well as to their advisors, and the people who aspire to this level of responsibility.

In the chapters ahead, I condense key practical learnings from my own helter-skelter experience of breakthrough product development and market development at Symbian and Psion (the original parent of Symbian). For the best part of two decades, I have lived through one demanding "urgent and important" project after another, assisting the creation of numerous connected mobile devices – laptop organizers, handheld PDAs, and (over the last nine years) more than one hundred different mobile phones. The experience has been fraught with challenges, but rich in lessons learned.

I had the good fortune to be recruited into the software development team at Psion in early 1988. Since then, I have been successively immersed in virtually every department in Psion and Symbian:

❑ In the early 1990s, I managed teams that created highly successful software for SIBO, the 16-bit predecessor of Symbian OS *(see the glossary in the appendix for help with acronyms)*

❑ I went on to lead the build and integration team for version 1 of Symbian OS (then known as "EPOC32"), and created the architectural framework for its UI and applications. Many of the source code files for Symbian OS still contain references to me as their originator – identified either as "DavidW" or "DWW" or sometimes "dw2"

❑ As a founder director of the Psion Software division in 1996, I took part in numerous sales and strategic review meetings leading in turn to the formation of Symbian in July 1998, when I was one of the founding team of four EVPs (along with Stephen Randall, Bill Batchelor, and Juha Christensen) reporting to Colly Myers, Symbian's first CEO

❑ From 1998 to 2002 I headed Symbian's Technical Consulting department, building and directing teams that worked with Symbian's customers to create the world's first smartphones

❑ During 2002 and 2003 I held the position of EVP of Partnering, supervising the rapid growth of Symbian's partnering programs, working with companies throughout the emerging Symbian ecosystem to help them lay strong foundations for technical and commercial success

❑ Since 2004 I have been Symbian's EVP of Research, responsible for a series of collaborative cross-functional research projects, focused on improving the competitiveness and value of Symbian's overall offering. This position gives me the chance to indulge my passion for education and knowledge sharing – including taking the time to write this book.

The book covers material that is one or more levels up from the purely technical. I avoid discussing specific APIs (Application Programming Interfaces: the programming methods of the C++ classes that make up Symbian OS), since there are already many fine books covering that level (see *www.symbian.com/books*). Instead, I cover the general principles governing:

❑ The use of these APIs
❑ The design of these APIs, and the philosophy behind them
❑ The way to organize teams to make best use of these APIs
❑ The methods that are most likely to deliver commercial success when using Symbian OS
❑ The wider significance of Symbian OS skills and expertise in the evolving mobile marketplace.

Symbian OS is designed for phones – actually for a new kind of phone, called a smartphone. The story of Symbian OS starts with the story of smartphones.

Part 1

Symbian in context

1 At the heart of the smartphone revolution
- ❑ The phenomenon of smartphones
- ❑ Taking advantage of the smartphone opportunity
- ❑ The role of the smartphone operating system
- ❑ Regarding APIs and operating systems
- ❑ Why Symbian OS?
- ❑ Aside: from organizers to smartphones
- ❑ Coming to terms with Symbian OS

2 The big picture of a Symbian OS project
- ❑ High-level components of a smartphone
- ❑ Providers of integrated solutions
- ❑ The commercial model of a smartphone project
- ❑ Some conclusions from the smartphone commercial model
- ❑ Typical smartphone project timescales
- ❑ Warning regarding timescales
- ❑ Factors influencing project timescales
- ❑ The big picture: beyond timescales

3 Involving ISVs
- ❑ ISV smartphone opportunity and risk
- ❑ Beyond technical skill-sets
- ❑ Different routes to market
- ❑ Symbian endorsements
- ❑ Companion Technology Program
- ❑ Symbian Signed

Part 1 (continued)

4 Twenty reasons why smartphones will win
- ❏ Two kinds of battle
- ❏ Multitasking
- ❏ Messaging and entertainment
- ❏ Mobile knowledge access
- ❏ Organizers and finance
- ❏ Pocket consolidators
- ❏ Social tools
- ❏ Personal development
- ❏ Phones win
- ❏ Openness wins

1

At the heart of the smartphone revolution

1.1 The phenomenon of smartphones

Mobile phones are phenomenal. Today, one quarter of the earth's population owns a mobile phone. But only a few years ago, mobile phones were the stuff of science fiction. As such, mobile phones are arguably the most successful item of consumer electronics in history.

Mobile phones owe their phenomenal success to the fact that they satisfy some deep-seated human needs:

❑ First, they provide extra means for people to communicate – to explain, to speculate, to chat, to inform, to plan, to replan, to inquire, to instruct, to entreat, to woo, and to give thanks. We humans have a great deal to communicate; the amount of money we collectively spend on mobile phones shows that we are heartily grateful to them for increasing our communications power

❑ Second, mobile phones boost their owner's sense of safety. Their owners strongly appreciate that, in times of major or minor emergency, they can connect to people and services that are important to them

❑ And third, mobile phones have become veritable objects of fashion, which their owners can show off, complete with their customizable covers, chart-topping ringtones, wacky homespun messages, and personalized image backgrounds. We all like to be unique; our phones increasingly help us to stand out from the crowd.

Each new generation of mobile phone meets the above needs in ever richer ways, for example adding text messaging to complement voice calls (or predictive text input to ease the creation of text messages), or new kinds of audio and graphics. At the same time, each new generation improves the portability, robustness, reliability, and basic usability of the phone. Batteries last longer, the phones themselves are lighter and smaller, the voice of the remote caller sounds clearer and louder, and the phone is increasingly resilient against misuse. In short, mobile phones are becoming better and better.

But the best is yet to come. Our current favorite mobile phones, valuable though they are, are dumb and impotent when compared to the new types of phone that will become increasingly commonplace over the remainder of this decade.

These new phones provide much greater levels of intelligence to their users. This intelligence resides partly in the phones themselves and partly in the ever-smarter networks into which they connect. This intelligence is a potent combination of hardware and software – a compelling mix of data and algorithms. In recognition of this increased intelligence, these phones are collectively described as "smartphones".

Smartphones are phones – great phones – but they are also much more than phones. Smartphones are rich mobile personal gateways into the digital universe – a universe that keeps on expanding and growing in importance. It is a universe that combines content, commerce, computing, and community. It is the home of google.com, ebay.com, amazon.com, yahoo.com, bbcnews.com, slashdot.com, aol.com, msn.com, espn.com, expedia.com, multimap.com, playboy.com, pokerroom.com, everquest.com, friendsreunited.com, lastminute.com, and much, much more. You can access this universe through a mobile web-browser – as provided on smartphones – but you can also access it through dedicated smartphone interfaces that make the experience more intuitive, more engaging, and more valuable. And just as the digital universe is steering the evolution of smartphones, the increasing prevalence of smartphones will steer the next phase of the evolution of the digital universe.

Smartphones occupy the tumultuous intersection space where four powerful contemporary trends collide.

❑ The first trend is that software is becoming ubiquitous. Inanimate objects all around us are becoming smarter and smarter. Highpowered software, once found only in stationary computers, now flourishes inside all manner of mobile devices

❑ Second, levels of communication keep on rising. More and more types of message are being sent between more and more people – and between more and more devices. Mobile smart devices are constantly joining dynamic networks that potentially make their users into even smarter individuals

❑ Third, users are increasingly demanding an external simplicity in the devices and tools they use (even though these devices abound with inner complexity). Users have lost the patience to bother with tedious operating manuals. Users want power, but they want it easy

❑ And fourth, users are demanding additional abilities to customize, personalize, and adapt the devices and the tools that they use. They want to be creators and innovators, not just consumers. They want their devices to be unique and distinctive. This brings programmability to the fore. It's where software becomes really soft. It's where smartphones become really personal.

Because smartphones accompany their users almost everywhere they go, they are the natural repository to adopt and then augment functionality which previously required numerous different pocket-sized devices. Wallets, tickets, keys, maps, cameras, PDAs, dictionaries, phrase books, entertainment centers, and business communicators are all in the process of being superseded by smartphones with converged functionality. These "always on" devices become ever more central to the way users interact with the world. The consequences will be phenomenal.

1.2 Taking advantage of the smartphone opportunity

It's no surprise that the commercial market for smartphones has grown by at least 100% in each of the last three years. There are good reasons why this growth should continue throughout at least the next three years – reasons grounded in technological progress, networking dynamics, and market evolution:

❑ Moore's Law means that, for the same cost, more and more powerful hardware can be supplied; tomorrow's smartphones will have as much computing power as yesterday's PCs

❑ New generations of phone networks (3G, 3.5G, 4G, and so on) will allow the speedy transmission of ever larger amounts of data, both satisfying and whetting still more user demand

❑ More powerful devices and more powerful networks jointly enable the provision of attractive add-on services, created by third parties, which in turn increase the market pull for devices capable of supporting such services

❑ The cumulative operation of software means that new services and applications can piggy-back on the functionality and power of previous services and applications, with striking, innovative results

❑ Many of these services are community-oriented: the more people who take part in these services, the more valuable these services become (this is sometimes called Metcalfe's Law)

❑ As people discover the benefits of mobile online gaming, mobile commerce, and so on, they will spread this message by word-of-mouth, so that the communities of smartphone users swell in size

❑ Phone network operators have a strong interest in ensuring that phone users are attracted to make regular use of services that involve greater amount of data transfer (and which therefore attract higher fees).

In short, smartphones are at the heart of a powerful virtuous cycle (see Figure 1.1). Improved phones, enhanced networks, novel applications and services, increasingly savvy users – all these factors drive yet more progress elsewhere in the cycle. Applications and services which prove their value as add-ons for one generation of smartphones become bundled into the next generation – much the same as happened for PCs in the 1980s and 1990s (except that the market for mobile phones is an order of magnitude larger than that for PCs). The cycle is so vigorous that we can call it a revolution: the smartphone revolution.

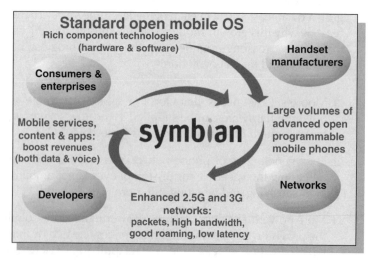

Figure 1.1   The smartphone market virtuous cycle

No wonder, therefore, that there is such a strong interest in the question of how best to add new functionality and new services into these awesomely powerful devices.

This is a question with a lot riding on the answer. It is the central question that I address in this book. The answer will allow companies and individuals to take full advantage of the smartphone opportunity.

The answer has two parts:

❑ The first part of the answer is Symbian OS – the de facto standard operating system for the emerging generation of advanced mobile phones

❑ The second part of the answer is the set of skills and expertise necessary to successfully complete projects using Symbian OS.

1.3 The role of the smartphone operating system

The single most important factor to appreciate, when contemplating the ongoing growth of smartphone opportunities, is the role of Symbian OS. Although invisible to the majority of end-users, Symbian OS is the internal plumbing that enables the fruitful collaboration of countless smartphone technologies. Its combination of efficiency and sophistication make it both future-proof and highly fit-for-purpose. At the time of writing, there are already more than 32 million phones in the world that run Symbian OS. By the time you read this, the number will be significantly higher.

It often comes as a surprise to people that operating systems are important in mobile phones. Most consumers have bought mobile phones without giving a moment's thought to what (if any) operating system might be included in the phone. However, like any device with a significant quantity of software, mobile phones do have operating systems.

Briefly, on a smartphone, the operating system has to fulfill the following requirements:

❑ To make it easy for the applications on the smartphone to take advantage of the power of the phone hardware and the phone network

❑ To avoid different applications clashing with one another – preventing, for example, two applications from drawing to the same part of the screen at the same time, or storing data to the same part of memory storage, or interfering with each other's network communications.

Without an operating system, all the different applications would have to delve into the lower levels of the phone hardware and phone network, and would need a huge amount of knowledge of these elements. They would also need to know about all the other applications, in order to coexist peacefully with them.

The greater the number of applications on a phone, the greater is the need for a sophisticated operating system. This is especially important when you consider that any given smartphone will in general contain applications from a number of different sources:

- ❑ Applications provided by the supplier of the operating system
- ❑ Applications provided by the phone manufacturer
- ❑ Applications provided by the network operator
- ❑ For phones used in a business setting, applications provided by the corporate IT department
- ❑ Applications sourced from third parties by the phone manufacturer, the network operator, and the corporate IT department
- ❑ Applications downloaded by end-users, or purchased in retail outlets.

The numerous different authors of these different applications generally have little interest to delve individually into the lower levels of phone hardware and phone networks. On the contrary, these authors are keenly interested to have their applications running on numerous different phones and different networks (so they don't want to become specialists for just one phone). It is much more productive for these authors to be able to write to the application programming interfaces (APIs) provided by an operating system, confident in the knowledge that the same APIs will work on a wide range of different phones and networks – even though these phones and networks vary among themselves in many ways. It is the role of the operating system to deal internally with the variations between the different phones and networks.

I spoke earlier of the powerful virtuous cycle involving smartphones. However, this virtuous cycle depends on the APIs being common between many different phones. Without this commonality, it takes everyone much more effort to develop applications: the marketplace is too fragmented. With this commonality, applications that are originally developed for phones by manufacturer A can be used, as well, on phones by manufacturers B to Z, frequently without any changes being required.

1.4 Regarding APIs and operating systems

Strictly speaking, the arguments I've just outlined do not (yet) demonstrate the need for a single preeminent smartphone operating system. To be accurate, the conclusion of these arguments is that there need to be lots of common APIs for use by writers of smartphone applications. In principle, this need could be met by the existence of multiple layers of APIs, with the operating system itself being of little interest to the application writers. Examples are Java APIs, BREW APIs (popular on phones with Qualcomm chipsets), graphics APIs such as OpenGL, and Internet standard APIs such as TCP/IP.

In this way of thinking, the actual operating system has less importance: some smartphones will use one operating system, others a second, yet others a third, and so on. The names of the operating systems will be no more likely to enter the public consciousness than the names of the diverse operating systems which have been used to create non-smart mobile phones.

There is some merit in this way of thinking. The sets of APIs mentioned – along with many others – do have a vital role to play. They make it easier for developers to write certain types of application (and certain parts of other types of application). However, these API sets, by themselves, are not sufficient to enable the full flowering of smartphones. More is needed – namely a programmable operating system that underlies and embeds these API sets. As I'll explain in a moment, there are three main reasons for this: performance, scale, and openness.

To make this easier to discuss, here are two definitions:

❑ Phones are "natively programmable" if application writers can access (relatively easily) the same set of APIs as are used by the operating system itself

❑ In contrast, phones are "restrictedly programmable" if application writers are in practice restricted to higher levels of standard APIs (such as those mentioned earlier).

These definitions are fuzzy ("... relatively easily" and "... in practice restricted") since an application writer can, *with sufficient effort*, find out how to program at the native level of virtually any phone. To that extent, all mobile phones are natively programmable. However, the key question is the degree of effort required, and whether that effort can be reapplied with profit on lots of different phones. If the effort required to access the native APIs is broadly the same as to access the functionality at higher levels of the phone (graphics, UI, TCP/IP, etc.), and if the same APIs exist on a wide number of different phones, then (by my definition) the phone is natively programmable. In contrast, phones whose main APIs are Java APIs or BREW APIs are restrictedly programmable.

Here are the principal benefits of native programmability versus restricted programmability:

❑ *Performance*: native programming delivers greater speed and power, since it bypasses the need for conversion layers or intermediate virtual machines over lower level software. For many types of software, restricted programmability gives sufficient speed. However, in many other types, the additional speed of native programming is required. Suppliers of virtual machines unsurprisingly point out the increases in performance available from their virtual machines, from one version to the next. Indeed, these improvements are real. However, at the same time, the amount of data needing manipulation also increases, owing to screens having higher resolution, wireless networks having higher throughput, and users becoming accustomed to storing and accessing more data on their phones, etc. The result is that, for the foreseeable future, there will remain plenty of examples where owners of restrictedly programmable phones will find some of the apps on these phones to be annoyingly sluggish in performance

❑ *Scale*: a native API set contains many more functions than restricted ones. So long as an application is simple and well-defined, a restricted API set is often sufficient to implement it. However, competitive pressures (from the market, from enterprises, and from end-users) keep identifying new requirements for applications to meet. For example, there is often competitive pressure for add-on applications to behave in certain aspects "the same way as built-in apps". It is much easier to add in the new functionality when programming at the native level. Otherwise, the developer has to wait until the intermediate APIs have been extended

❑ *Openness*: this is an important expansion of the previous point. The best new applications frequently combine together, in unforeseen ways, functionality from two or more different components of functionality in the phone. Or, they may provide new domain expertise, for a subject matter previously not expected to feature on a smartphone, and combine this with aspects of the core functionality of the smartphone. This requires programming at several different levels at the same time. This is where an open, unified set of APIs has great advantage.

1.5 Why Symbian OS?

To recap: because the number and scope of applications on smartphones is substantially increasing, there is great benefit in there being a set of natively programmable APIs, common across a wide range of phones, for the authors of these applications to use. For optimal results, these APIs should dovetail smoothly into the lower levels of the operating system, providing applications with power, wide capability, and a strong measure of being future-proof.

That's the case for there being an operating system used across many different smartphones. Now it's time to state the case for this operating system being Symbian OS – as opposed to some of the other operating systems that have from time to time been proposed for this same role.

The simplest argument refers to the size of the installed market. Worldwide, there are around five to ten times as many phones running Symbian OS as running any competing open operating system. Each of the top six phone manufacturers (as measured by volume sales) have launched Symbian OS phones, or are in the process of doing so: Nokia, Motorola, Samsung, Siemens, LG, Sony Ericsson. Other phone manufacturers who have successfully launched Symbian OS phones include Fujitsu, Panasonic, Mitsubishi, Sendo, and BenQ. Sales volume is the biggest driver of platform confidence: the value network ("ecosystem") naturally invests in volume platforms (refer to Figure 1.2). Volume drives value, and in turn, value drives volume. The platform with the largest sales experiences a "tipping point" and comes to strongly lead the whole market.

So, in very practical terms, Symbian is at the heart of the smartphone revolution.

It is important to understand the factors responsible for Symbian attaining this leading position. These factors apply long-term,

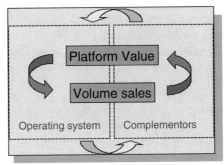

Figure 1.2 The Symbian OS open virtuous cycle

and mean that Symbian's leadership position has every chance of continuing throughout the foreseeable future:

- Symbian was created by the phone industry, for the sake of the phone industry

- The roots of Symbian OS are in connected handheld devices (Psion organizers). Symbian OS was forged in an environment where the following principles had the highest priority: data integrity, high software performance on hardware with limited power, efficient usage of memory, long battery life, the robustness of the overall software system even in the face of potential errors in individual applications, the preparedness of applications for new event sources (such as communications input), and user enchantment (enchanting the user was always much more important than technology for technology's sake). These principles were far more than mere words; I remember countless unscripted discussions over coffee or at the water cooler where engineers agonized (out of their own volition) over how best to follow these principles through actual software development

- Symbian avoids dictating the user interface or basic phone design to customers. Symbian's customers can create products that are very far from being clones of each other. However, the resulting differentiation of products is achieved without fragmenting the underlying software system. Profound attention to architectural principles has resulted in a platform that supports the holy grail of "differentiation without fragmentation"

- As far as it is ever possible to trust other companies within the phone industry, Symbian is trusted by its customers. It is clear to our customers and partners that Symbian plays at only one point of the value chain: Symbian has no aspirations to make money from server-side technology, from tools, from add-on applications, from PC applications, etc. Symbian's revenue is dominated by income from licensing; Symbian's focus is entirely on the operating system. Our customers have no fear that we will start to encroach on their part of the value chain

- Another important mark of the trust between Symbian and the companies within the Symbian ecosystem is the very significant extent of sharing of source code that takes place. This accelerates the understanding, debugging, and optimization of software components, and makes it easier for partners and customers to create variant innovative solutions

☐ Because of this formidable degree of trust, Symbian's customers feel comfortable to share with Symbian their own sober assessments of the evolution of the phone industry, together with their own planned product roadmap, and the technology requirements of forthcoming products. In this way, Symbian has in effect by far the largest product management group in the industry, working on its behalf. This mega-grouping provides extraordinarily useful guidance on how to evolve Symbian OS, which in turn further benefits our customers and the whole smartphone industry

☐ Symbian's learnings from customers go beyond the formal learning from official roadmap reviews and the like. They involve numerous nuggets of practical insight gained in the heat of actual project engagement. In each phone implementation project, there are aspects of the development that are awkward or particularly demanding. By reflecting on these issues, Symbian has constantly evolved Symbian OS, with each new version incorporating literally hundreds of major and minor improvements arising from previous projects. Step by step, year by year, Symbian has built up a tremendous body of knowledge embodying unprecedented intellectual capital and collective experience of smartphones

☐ As a result of the foregoing, Symbian OS has become much more than simply "an operating system". It contains around 10 million lines of source code, and delivers an astonishing variety of telephony middleware – software that provides rich APIs enabling add-on applications and services. Perhaps this is the biggest single difference between Symbian OS and competing candidate smartphone operating systems: the depth of the functionality provided (over and above the core operating system), that meets the needs of present and future smartphone applications

☐ Symbian has been focused since even before its inception on the subject area of smartphones. Unlike other companies, there is no distraction from semi-related areas, such as PC software, standalone PDAs, other embedded software, and so on. Symbian has always been able to deploy the "A team" on the key smartphone issues, rather than a B team or C team. Smartphones are significantly different from all these other kinds of product, and deserve the highest quality of attention. That's what Symbian has been able to supply, consistently, for nearly a decade. No other company in our space comes close to this level of dedication

☐ Other companies may seek to catch up with Symbian OS, but Symbian OS itself continues to leap forward with giant strides. At the last count, Symbian has just over 1000 in-house personnel, all focused on improving Symbian's product offering. So far, more than one quarter of a billion UK pounds has been invested in the development of Symbian OS. The result shows!

1.6 Aside: from organizers to smartphones

Before there were smartphones, there were smart organizers. During the 1980s, Britain's Psion was the world-leader in the creation of handheld electronic organizers. Due to wide press coverage in the UK, I was well aware of the Organiser II even before I started work at Psion in June 1988. I confess that, initially, I was not keen on the product concept. Somehow I had picked up the idea that electronic organizers were for "yuppies" (the pejorative name given at the time to young, upwardly-mobile professionals) – a set of people who (in contrast to the "hippies" of a previous generation) were said to be thrusting and self-interested. I did not care to become a yuppie.

But since I had taken a job at Psion, I thought I should find out more about their product, and I started keying my address book into a brand new Organiser II. It did not take me long to realize the considerable benefits of the electronic organizer over the paper-and-pencil version that I had previously used:

❑ The paper-and-pencil version was full of messy crossings-out and duplicate entries

❑ The electronic version could be searched, instantly, in numerous ways – just type "Plumber" even if you forgot the actual name of the plumber, or "Restaurant" to find all restaurants listed.

Although the Organiser II had a swathe of other applications available, it was the contacts application that made the really big impact on me. (Later, I also came to rely heavily on the alarms app.)

A few weeks later, one of my colleagues pointed out that I ought to backup my organizer. He pointed out that it was much easier to backup an electronic organizer than to laboriously photocopy every page of a paper-and-pencil address list. That made sense to me. Apparently electronic backup would require a "comms lead", to connect the organizer to a desktop PC.

Alas, although my first experience with an organizer was good, my first experience with comms was bad. After a bit of squirreling around, I found a comms lead and plugged the organizer into a PC. A few moments later, everything froze. The organizer would no longer respond to keypresses.

Another colleague, noticing my predicament, stopped by my desk and helped me out by resetting the organizer. After it restarted, there was no data to be seen on it. "I hope you had a backup of that" was the advice I received. Whoops.

So I learned three lessons:

❑ Backup is important!

❑ Comms is hard!

❑ Take care over configuration management: you need to know what versions of hardware/software you're using (apparently the comms lead I had picked up was known in the department to be defective, but it was still kept around for testing purposes).

Anyway, I typed in my data again. Seventeen years later, I still carry some of the descendants of that data with me, everywhere I go. I know which entries are seventeen years old because these are the ones typed with all letters in upper case. I only learnt to switch data entry into lower case when I upgraded my Organiser II from a two-line version to a four-line version in the following year.

Even before the Organiser II there had been an Organiser I, with just a one-line display. Amazingly, lots of applications were written even for these restricted screen sizes, including a spreadsheet application.

The evolution of organizer screen size (one line, two lines, four lines, and then a full graphics display) mirrored the subsequent evolution of mobile phone screen size. The two device families had lots of other things in common: small batteries, deliberately under-powered hardware, highly demanding users (hence the support for add-on applications), always-on fast start-up, hard requirements of connectivity, and especially tough requirements on mobile data integrity. The rare skill-set acquired by Psion along the way was one of the key reasons that made Psion's next generation software uniquely suited to be the core of Symbian OS – at the heart of the smartphone revolution.

1.7 Coming to terms with Symbian OS

Symbian OS provides the framework to develop advanced new mobile phone solutions, and has the potential to dramatically accelerate the development of advanced mobile phone projects. However, this acceleration only takes place if the leaders of these projects first take the time to deeply appreciate how best to use Symbian OS.

It is crucial to realize that Symbian OS requires special skill and experience to use well.

There is no escaping the reality that the world of the new mobile phones is tremendously complex. The goal of Symbian OS is to tame the complexity and hide it from users, but that doesn't make the complexity go away (in fact, it actually makes the development task even harder). For companies that wish to develop new mobile phone solutions, a solid knowledge of the technicalities of Symbian OS is an excellent starting point, but it's by no means sufficient. Sadly, without the right overall set of skills and understanding, even great endeavors with Symbian OS can lead nowhere.

This book covers the missing set of skills and understanding. It is based on my experience with literally hundreds of Symbian OS development projects and hundreds of partner companies within the smartphone space. Some of these projects have been shining successes, whereas others have, frankly, fared poorly. Over that time, I have more clearly identified the issues that are key to determining whether a development project with Symbian OS will be successful or unsuccessful. The book you now hold in your hand highlights and explains these key issues.

As it happens, the most significant of these issues is the caliber of the people who are leading the software development process. It's not a matter of the quantity of the resources or the size of the team; it's a matter of the quality of the team leaders. Accordingly, I especially dedicate this book to all software leaders. It is my earnest desire that these leaders can take good advantage of the advice in the following pages, in order to create truly outstanding products which yield high value both to their companies and (in time) to hundreds of millions of mobile smartphone users.

2
The big picture of a Symbian OS project

2.1 High-level components of a smartphone

A product based on Symbian OS typically includes, and interfaces with, numerous software and hardware components. This is true whether the product is:

- An entire smartphone
- Designed to be used in conjunction with existing smartphones, as an "add-on"
- Designed to be incorporated in forthcoming new smartphones, as a "build-in".

In all three cases, it is important to understand the relationships between the high-level components that make up a smartphone. From the point of view of a Symbian OS project, these components include the following:

- The silicon chips on the phone – including the "application processor" (AP) and the "baseband processor" (BP); note that these are sometimes combined into a single chip

- A wireless signaling stack, running on the baseband processor, which talks to the wireless network and implements the GSM and/or CDMA protocols

- Symbian OS itself, running on the application processor

- Communications between the two main chips (often known as "ISC" – "Inter Systems Communications")

- Graphics, audio, and other multimedia components (often including many software plug-ins to implement specific items of multimedia functionality)

❑ Other aspects of the hardware design of the phone – including keypad, antenna, battery, etc.

❑ The UI system – such as UIQ, Series 60 from Nokia, or the FOMA UI used by NTT DoCoMo phones

❑ Third-party applications

❑ Third-party software that *enables* extra applications.

Upwards of a dozen companies can be involved as suppliers of the above components. From this fact, two important principles follow:

❑ One of the fundamental tasks in a smartphone project is that of *integration* – making sure that the individual components work well together

❑ Another fundamental task in a smartphone project is *management of relations with suppliers.* This covers both technical and commercial aspects of the relationships.

Conversely, here are two of the principal *mistakes* that leaders of Symbian OS projects can make:

❑ Putting too much focus on innovation (writing new software) whilst neglecting to apply the effort required to ensure that the new software and all the old software work together harmoniously

❑ Putting too much effort into managing the internal team, without also attending to managing external suppliers – neglecting to finalize important contractual details, which end up delaying the project.

2.2 Providers of integrated solutions

A major service that can be provided by a small number of third parties is that of providing an "integrated solution" for a smartphone project. In this idea, the provider of the integrated solution takes care of the majority of work of integration and supplier management, leaving it to the original project team to concentrate more on the provision of innovation and style.

See ***www.symbian.com/partners*** for a list of companies that can act as integrated solutions providers.

Some providers of integrated solutions base their solutions on "smartphone reference designs". These designs allow companies with limited prior experience with Symbian OS to bring smartphones to the market quickly. See Chapter 14 for more details.

Deciding whether to contract an integrated solution provider (and if so, which one) is one of the key choices that the smartphone project leader needs to make. A good integrated solution provider can make a great difference to the effectiveness of project delivery. Here are some points to keep in mind:

❑ In view of the complexity of the overall technology, it is hard to find a single company that can provide expertise in all aspects of smartphone project delivery

❑ Some companies may be experts in some choices of silicon, but not in others; likewise they may be experts in some UI systems, but not in others; likewise for their degree of knowledge of different major versions of Symbian OS. So check them out carefully, before signing contracts

❑ Any company that is interested in carrying out a series of different Symbian OS smartphone projects may prefer (over time) to grow Symbian OS expertise in-house, rather than becoming dependent on an external company; this argues for a partnership model of working with an integrated solutions provider, rather than a dependency model

❑ It is important to achieve a good cultural fit between any selected integration solution provider and the main project team

❑ In general, you get what you pay for: if you skimp on the costs of the integrated solutions provider, by selecting one with lower charge rates, you are likely to get poorer quality.

2.3 The commercial model of a smartphone project

Smartphone projects vary greatly, on account of their scope and ambition. For example, a project that incrementally extends an existing, successful smartphone product requires many fewer resources than a project to create a smartphone product platform from scratch.

Here are some illustrative figures describing a reasonably major innovative smartphone development project.

At peak times during development, there may be up to 120 full-time equivalent (FTE) people working on the project (including employees, contractors, and consultants). If the project goes well, the

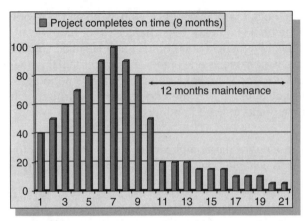

Figure 2.1   Resourcing profile I (percentage of peak)

main development phase might last nine months, with a resourcing profile as in Figure 2.1.

So, in this profile, there are 120 FTEs assigned to the project in month 7 (that is, 100%), but only 48 FTEs in month 1 (that is, 40%).

Figure 2.1 also shows the continuing assignment of people to the project throughout the twelve months after the product reaches the market. These resources are needed for support and maintenance purposes (defect triage and fixing, mid-life silent updates, and so on).

If the project goes less well, the development phase might be considerably extended (see Figure 2.2). In this case, the development takes an additional five months (all clocked at 100% of peak effort). The maintenance period is shorter – only seven months instead of twelve – since (other things being equal) the sales window for the

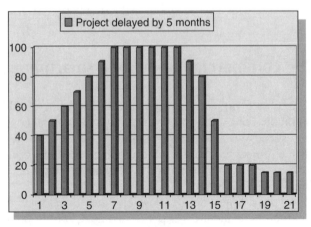

Figure 2.2   Resourcing profile II (percentage of peak)

product will be shorter, as the product has missed its intended market slot.

Let's assume that the average fully-loaded cost of one FTE is $150,000. This results in the following range of development costs (including also the maintenance period):

Number of months delay (from intended schedule)	Total development cost (USD)
0	12,825,000
1	14,250,000
2	15,675,000
3	17,025,000
4	18,375,000
5	19,725,000

So, the development cost ranges from around 12 to 20 million US dollars.

Next, let's consider the income expected to be realized from this project. Suppose that the resulting smartphone can sell 500,000 units, providing it hits its intended market window. (As with the estimate of development effort, the estimate of sales units will vary very considerably, depending on numerous factors. Here, I'm assuming a modest middle-of-the-road outcome.)

Typically, sales ramp up over the initial sales period, as production takes some time to reach full speed. Then sales drop off, as the product loses its novelty factor, and on account of competition from newer products. Figure 2.3 illustrates such a unit sales profile.

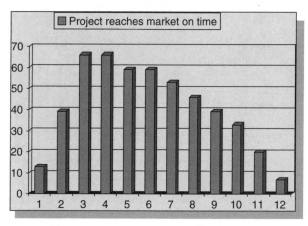

Figure 2.3   Sales profile I (thousands of units monthly)

In case the product launch is delayed, assume that the sales in a month are the maximum of:

- ❏ *The figure above* – which represents the "market threshold" for the product at any time
- ❏ *The time-delayed version of the above figure* – representing the time taken to ramp up production.

So, for example, if the product is five months late in reaching the market, the unit sales would be as in Figure 2.4. (There are only seven months of sales in this case, instead of the twelve months if the product reaches the market on schedule.)

The final factor to model is the income to the phone manufacturer for each unit sold. This will also vary over time, with higher prices being possible at the beginning of the sales period. Let's assume that the possible sales price (in USD) varies throughout the sales period as in Figure 2.5. (This is the fee paid by the network operator to the phone manufacturer. In general it differs from the price charged by the retailer to the end-user, on account of subsidies, which the network operator expects to recover through call charges over the contract period.)

If each phone unit costs $150 to manufacture, this translates into a profit per unit of $150 for a phone sold in the first three months, a profit of $135 in month 4, and so on, down to a profit of zero in month 13 (matching the fact that sales stop at this time). If the phone is late to reach the market, the profit per unit drops off

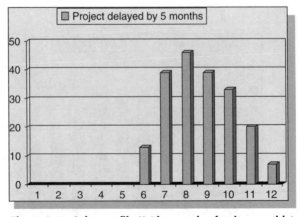

Figure 2.4   Sales profile II (thousands of units monthly)

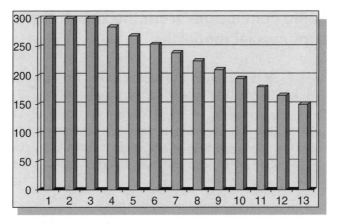

Figure 2.5   Possible selling price, month by month (USD)

accordingly. (This assumes that, on average, other market conditions remain the same.)

Putting everything together yields the following:

Months delay	Development cost	Number of units sold	Earnings from sales	Overall profit
0	12,825,000	500,000	52,697,368	39,872,368
1	14,250,000	434,211	42,828,947	28,578,947
2	15,675,000	368,421	33,355,263	17,680,263
3	17,025,000	309,211	25,460,526	8,435,526
4	18,375,000	250,000	18,453,947	78,947
5	19,725,000	197,368	12,927,632	−6,797,368

Note the following:

❑ The column "earnings from sales" gives the income from sales of smartphones, less their manufacturing cost

❑ This model neglects additional costs such as advertising

❑ The model averages out the effects of seasonal variation and special promotional activities (for example, lowering price to stimulate sales)

❑ The model assumes a fixed manufacturing cost throughout, ignoring the opportunity to secure better component pricing as volumes increase.

2.4 Some conclusions from the smartphone commercial model

Despite its limitations and simplifications, the above model allows significant conclusions to be drawn:

❑ A project that over-runs its intended schedule by five months or more may fail to realize any profit. On the other hand, a project that keeps to its intended schedule can make a very handsome return on its investment

❑ The benefits of maintaining the project schedule more than out-weigh, financially, the incremental costs of some extra personnel (such as consultants, managers, and technical specialists) who can help keep the project running on track.

The following points also need to be stressed:

❑ There is great merit in pursuing an evolutionary model of product development: start by creating an initial product and then keep on refreshing it. Introducing new features and capabilities will prolong sales, for modest additional expenditure, and maintain a high selling price

❑ New product variants to consider include: geographical variants, variants for specific network operators, variants with different styling, and variants for different market segments. In all cases, the idea is to boost sales and maintain high selling prices, without requiring a full (expensive) development cycle

❑ The customizability and platform nature of Symbian OS makes it particularly suited to the creation of variants: phone manufacturers can select numerous add-on products from the huge variety of third-party suppliers within the Symbian ecosystem

❑ Symbian OS itself follows an incremental development model, with the regular release of new versions that contain important additional features and capabilities. Provided that phone man-ufacturers conduct suitable advance planning, they are able to switch over their own development programs mid-stream to take advantage of the new releases, with minimal disruption

❑ The above model assumes that the end product reaches the quality level required by the marketplace (in terms of lack of defects); however, if the development process ends up cutting lots of corners, quality is likely to suffer, with deleterious impact on profits and brand reputation (in turn damaging future sales).

I return to these points at various stages in the chapters ahead.

2.5 Typical smartphone project timescales

Just as the commercial models vary extensively between different smartphone projects, so also do the timescales required for these projects. However, once again, it is useful to consider the potential timescale for a modest middle-of-the-road smartphone implementation project.

As above, if all goes well with the project, the development could be completed within nine months.

This is made up of five months of main development, to the "code complete" point when all features are coded, followed by four months of productization (verification that the product is ready to reach the market – and fixing problems noticed during the verification).

As shown in Figure 2.6, other important activities proceed in parallel throughout the nine months of development.

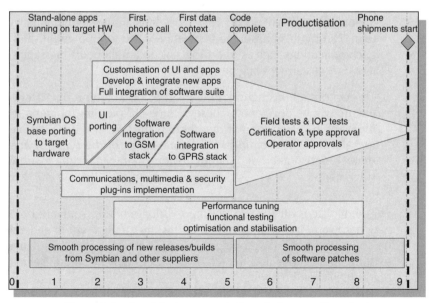

Figure 2.6   Graphical representation of nine-month project

In more detail, the porting phase (lasting five months) breaks down as follows:

❑ The project should allow six weeks for the base-port of Symbian OS onto the target hardware. This assumes that a port of Symbian OS onto electronically similar hardware already exists (otherwise this part of the project will take much longer). These six weeks will involve the tuning of device drivers for specific peripherals, as well as the stabilization of the hardware itself (which typically goes through several iterations at this phase of the project)

❑ The end outcome of this first phase of the project is Symbian OS running with what is known as the "TechView" test user interface. TechView is supplied by Symbian for test and porting purposes. The next phase of the project involves porting an actual commercial UI onto the hardware. Another six weeks should be set aside for this purpose

❑ In parallel with the UI port, the integration of Symbian OS with the telephony stack (GSM or CDMA, etc.) should be taking place. This can take around two and a half months. During this period, the first voice phone calls can be made using the hardware (around two and a half months into the project)

❑ Also in parallel with the UI port, but starting up to six weeks later, the integration of Symbian OS with the data aspects of the telephony stack will occur. This phase lasts around two months in total. During this phase, the first data context will be established, and applications such as web-browsing and multimedia messaging (MMS) will start working properly

❑ Throughout all this period, plug-ins specific to the product architecture will be developed. These include ISC plug-ins for communications between the two main chips (the AP and the BP – *see the glossary for a reminder of the meanings of these terms, and others*), and numerous plug-ins to the multimedia and security subsystems.

The above steps all refer to porting existing working software onto new hardware. In parallel with all of this, the project will in general be sourcing and/or developing new applications, and customizing existing applications and the UI, as software-derived unique selling points (USPs) of the phone.

The final four months of the project are known as "productization" – a set of steps to ensure that the device is a saleable product:

- User tests, involving as many people as possible who are representative of typical users
- Formal field tests, involving the verification department of the company
- Specialized tests, such as inter-operability tests (IOT), stress tests, and tests of binary compatibility (BC)
- Formal certification of individual components, such as Java and Bluetooth, using industry-defined procedures and tests
- Formal Type Approvals (as mandated by, for example, the GSM authorities)
- Tests and acceptance by the operators who will support this phone
- Iterations to the product, arising from items found in the above tests.

Of course, quality is not just something that is injected during this final, productization phase of the project. The quality as verified during this phase reflects the quality of work input throughout the earlier phases. It is for this reason that the following activities take place throughout the duration of the project:

- Functional testing
- Performance tuning
- Optimization and stabilization.

Finally, throughout the project timescale, resources need to be set aside to process incoming new versions (and, later in the project, incoming new patches) of software from suppliers, such as Symbian.

2.6 Warning regarding timescales

I have written the above section with some trepidation. I am well aware, from my experience, that many phone manufacturers (and related companies) hold as a mark of pride a belief that they can always aggressively optimize and improve on "standard project timescales". Because I have written that a typical project could be completed within nine months, there will be many people who:

- Take this nine-month figure as a "worst case outcome"
- Plan on completing a project in a significantly shorter duration.

So let me state again: there are very many factors that can cause projects to last *longer* than this nine-month duration. Recall that in the discussion of the commercial model of smartphone projects, I considered projects that over-ran by between one and five months; I did not consider any projects that completed earlier than this schedule. That was deliberate.

2.7 Factors influencing project timescales

Paradoxically, one of the main factors that can cause smartphone projects to over-run their schedules is over-optimism from the project team. This over-optimism causes the team to cut corners. As in the old saying, "more haste, but less speed", work that is done hurriedly the first time usually takes a lot longer to fix afterwards.

Another old saying (from the poet Alexander Pope) is, "A little learning is a dangerous thing". I mention this because another factor that can cause smartphone projects to over-run their schedules is incomplete knowledge by the project team leaders. Personally, I am a great fan of optimism. Optimism fuels growth and accomplishment. Give me optimism any day, over pessimism. However, when dealing with a product as complex as a smartphone, it's critical to couple optimism with a committed willingness to deeply understand the product domain, including the risks involved.

Having stated these important provisos, I now list some measures that can help a project to keep to its target timescales. (Note: these are not measures which can *reduce* timescales, but are measures which can prevent timescales from becoming longer.)

❑ Keep the product feature-set to an agreed minimum – leave fancier things to follow-on projects

❑ Make sure that all software changes are reviewed by experienced personnel

❑ Make sure that difficult processes are supervised by experienced personnel

❑ Take advantage of technology already developed and hardened by previous projects (this is the principle, "reuse not reinvent"); these previous projects can include reference designs

❑ Take full advantage of the rich experience of personnel in the supplier and partner companies

❑ Provide an optimal working environment for the whole team

❑ Avoid being over-thrifty on costs for consultancy, training, and tools

❏ Keep the project under the direct control of a highly focused senior management review team.

Symbian OS phone implementation projects can be expected to take *longer* than nine months if:

❏ A new UI system is being developed (or there are significant enhancements to an existing UI system)

❏ The project is the test bed (also known as "lead product") for some novel Symbian OS features – with considerable interaction between Symbian and the project

❏ The hardware is particularly novel and ambitious

❏ The launch of the phone is being aligned with forthcoming new features of wireless networks

❏ Unproven state-of-the-art third-party technology is being introduced

❏ The project team is comparatively inexperienced with Symbian OS.

On the other hand, projects can reasonably be expected to take *less* than nine months when they start with an existing phone model, and apply a small number of controlled changes to it. These projects – which are often called "copy projects" – can involve:

❏ Adding extra applications or an additional peripheral
❏ Modifying the industrial design
❏ Upgrading the color density of the screen
❏ Modifying the UI and application styling – for example for operator customization.

2.8 The big picture: beyond timescales

I've spent some time highlighting factors that influence smartphone project timescales. These are weighty factors, and I return to many of them in the pages ahead, explaining them in more detail. Software leaders need to give them very serious thought.

However, it would be wrong to focus solely on reducing project timescale. Project timescale is only one of a matrix of factors influencing the success of a project. The other key factors include:

❏ *Overall costs and resourcing levels*: of course, other things being equal, it would be better to complete a project using an average of 80 FTEs, than to complete it over the same time period using an average of 100 FTEs

❑ *Feature set*: software leaders need to carefully consider the risk that a product reaches the market at the intended time, but lacks sufficient features or differentiation to interest a large enough pool of customers. Alternatively, the product may appeal initially to a small group of enthusiasts, but lack sufficient longevity to appeal to a larger set of customers

❑ *Quality*: another risk to consider is that of the product being found to be unreliable or unusable in various ways: the required features may be present, but they fail to work sufficiently well (for example, being too slow or error-prone)

❑ *Schedule risk*: this is the risk that a project fails to meet its agreed schedule, and ends up missing its market window (note that this factor is independent of the question of the expected project length; you can, to an extent, decide the degree of risk in the schedule separately from the length of the target schedule)

❑ *Platform capability*: a company may successfully bring the first smartphone product to market, but then fail to follow it up sufficiently quickly with subsequent products. In this case, early market leadership will cede to other companies who have a better capacity for repeat delivery. Software leaders need to plan, not just on bringing one smartphone product to market, but on acquiring the capability to bring a series of products to market, based (to maximize the return on their investment) on a common platform.

To an extent, these factors compete with each other. For example, project leaders can decide to cut resourcing levels, but in that case, conventional wisdom says that at least one of the other factors will suffer.

However, it is my contention that project teams that take full advantage of Symbian OS can win on all these dimensions at the same time. The correct application of the key skills reduces project timescale, resourcing levels, and schedule risk, whilst simultaneously boosting features, quality, and platform capability. The core principle is: *Ensure that the project team deeply understands what they should be doing.*

By following this principle, the project team avoids creating "waste" – poor quality software – and avoids losing precious time and effort.

To discover how this works for Symbian OS smartphone projects, please continue reading.

3
Involving ISVs

3.1 ISV smartphone opportunity and risk

The success of the overall smartphone revolution depends upon the success of at least a small number of ISVs (Independent Software Vendors): people who work outside of the phone manufacturers, and who develop innovative new applications and services that significantly enhance the appeal of smartphones.

Many companies see this opportunity. There is no question of the *potential* for companies to achieve striking commercial success in this sector. Users who already spend anything between 30 and 100 USD on their phone bills each month can, in principle, be persuaded to spend anything between another 1 and 20 USD on additional services. Let's start by considering the pessimistic case of an additional spend, on average, of 2 USD per month, for 100 million smartphone users. Let's say that the ISVs manage to hold onto 20% of this (with the remainder being shared among network operators, publishers, retailers, and so on). That means 480 million USD reaching ISVs each year. Finally, let's imagine that the most successful of the ISV companies can each expect one-tenth of this (in other words, that there are around ten similarly successful companies). That makes for annual revenues for the company of 48 million USD.

For an entrepreneurial company, that's just the start. Standard business development theory teaches companies to focus on their potentially biggest customers. 5% of customers can provide well over 50% of the revenues. Keen smartphone users who enjoy the entry-level service of an ISV application can be persuaded to upgrade to a series of more expensive versions.

Here's another way to think about it. Before long, the number of smartphones in the world will be approaching the number of PCs there were in the world a few years ago. Users will spend a lot of time with their smartphone (as their preferred mobile gateway into the digital universe). The amount of money that users spent on applications for PCs in the past therefore serves as a first-order rough estimate for the amount of money that users will spend on applications on smartphones in the future. As smartphones become an ever more important part of corporate information and control systems, and ever more central to personal entertainment and infotainment systems, the flow of revenues to successful ISVs can be expected to drive a considerable number of stellar success stories.

However, as well as the potential upside, there's plenty of potential downside. That's always the case with marketplaces that emerge around new technologies. For each company that is very successful in such a marketplace, there are scores that fail:

- ❏ It's easy to predict the future in general terms, but it's very hard to predict *when* various aspects of the future will take place

- ❏ It's easy to invest too *early* – acquiring expensive capability ahead of the marketplace reaching a critical mass of volume sales

- ❏ It's also easy to invest too *late* – "missing the bus" (when it eventually does arrive)

- ❏ It's hard to predict the specific applications that will create the greatest customer interest – apps that are similar to those that were important on PCs (say), or apps that are quite different

- ❏ After everything else is said, there is a considerable degree of luck that determines which companies are in the right place with the right customer and the right idea at the right time.

Of course, I can't offer any guarantees in this book. I can't say, follow such-and-such steps, and you will develop applications which end-users buy in tens of millions. But I can offer general advice that will increase the probability that:

- ❏ You are able to act quickly and effectively, when a great smart-phone product opportunity does come your way

- ❏ You will avoid many of the common (and not-so-common) mistakes already made by your predecessors as ISVs

- ❏ If, despite your best efforts, your company fails, you will personally be well-positioned to join another new company in the smartphone ecosystem, where you can continue applying your well-honed smartphone project skills.

Most of the time in this book, I address as my primary audience the leaders of teams who actually create smartphones. But most of my advice is also relevant to ISVs. Many of the same issues arise, whether your product is designed to run *on* a smartphone, or whether it *is* an entire smartphone:

❑ Issues of coping with scale and complexity (covered in Part II)

❑ Issues of understanding the underlying Symbian smartphone design philosophy – how to ride with the flow, instead of against it (covered in Part III)

❑ The people skills needed to survive smartphone projects and, indeed, to thrive on them (see Part IV).

What's more, the greater your understanding (as an ISV) of the pressures faced by the teams that create smartphones, the greater is your chance of modifying your work practices to help alleviate these pressures. Your own product deliveries will become part of the solution, rather than part of the problem.

3.2 Beyond technical skill-sets

One of the commonest mistakes made by smartphone ISVs is to focus on technical skill-sets to the detriment of the wider skills of commerce, marketing, management, and leadership. Smartphones are hugely complex, technically, so it's no surprise that technical skills are in high demand. But that's no reason to neglect the other skill-sets.

Sadly, I have often seen fine ISV products pushed aside in the hectic period of rush leading up to a smartphone release. These are products which were fully *intended* to be included in the actual smartphone, as part of a bundle of built-in software. They are ISV products that *seemed* to perform well in their own test environments. But the overall smartphone project leaders found reason to remove them from the smartphone spec at the eleventh hour (see later chapters in this book for more details):

❑ There were problems in integration
❑ There were problems in performance
❑ There were problems with debugging, stability, and optimization
❑ The application turned out to be inconsistent or ill-fitted with the other built-in software
❑ Or, there were unresolved contractual problems.

When it comes to the crunch of the eleventh hour of a major project – the period just before the product is shipped to the market – project leaders often manifest a single-minded focus on "ship at all costs". Anything that gets in the way of this objective is removed. If one of the built-in applications is posing integration problems, the simplest route may be to remove that application altogether. And that is often what happens.

If you are lucky, such an event may just be a temporary setback for you as an ISV. The smartphone project leader may follow up the initial launch with an upgrade release in a few months time, this time including your application. However, I have sometimes seen the phenomenon of "once bitten, twice shy". The smartphone project leader sometimes develops a bias against any application that risked the initial launch, and this bias can prevent your application being included in an update release. Sometimes, indeed, a competitor application is able to win the business at this stage, as a late entrant, taking advantage of the furrow that you were able to plough. So a first stumble could be fatal. To lessen the chance of this happening, I recommend that you work hard on:

- ❑ Relationship management, so that your relation with your customer (the company creating the smartphone) can survive temporary storms

- ❑ Contractual issues, so that your customer is able to understand your contractual terms easily, and so that you can have a signed contract well before any crunch time approaches

- ❑ Making it easy for your customer to integrate your product

- ❑ Mature defect analysis and defect fixing processes

- ❑ Supporting fast customization of your product in line with the design choices of your customer

- ❑ Understanding the difficulties and challenges faced by your customer

- ❑ Being aware of the multiple routes to market that are available for your product, rather than being locked into just one possible delivery channel.

3.3 Different routes to market

A smartphone ISV can bring an application to the market in any of the following ways:

❑ As discussed in the previous section, the application can be built into a smartphone produced by a phone manufacturer

❑ The application can be built into special variants of a smartphone, as commissioned by network operators; in these cases, we can consider the network operator to be the customer

❑ The application can be installed into a range of smartphones being used inside a business, for corporate purposes; in these cases, the customer is the corporate IT department (or perhaps, the team leader inside a vanguard unit of the company)

❑ The application can be distributed at point-of-sale outlets for mobile phones, such as Radio Shack, Circuit City, or Carphone Warehouse (known in mainland Europe as "The Phone House"); in some cases, the application can be included as part of a special sales bundle along with a smartphone; in other cases, the application can be available for purchase as standalone

❑ The application can be downloaded from Internet sales websites, such as Handango.com, MyPhoneGames.co.uk, Symbos.com, and Symbiangear.com; in some cases, the application downloads onto a PC, and is then installed onto the smartphone by local connectivity (USB cable, Bluetooth, etc.); in other cases, the application downloads OTA (over the air) directly onto the phone

❑ As a variant of the previous case, the application can be downloaded OTA from portals maintained by network operators.

In addition to the initial purchase of the application, the ISV needs to plan ahead for maintenance and upgrades – ways for end-users to receive additional value through later releases. This includes:

❑ Defect fixes
❑ New levels for games
❑ Additional audio and graphics "skins"
❑ Additional backup and storage facilities
❑ Extra functionality
❑ Migration onto a new smartphone (including data migration).

The upgrades may reach the end-user through a different channel from the initial purchase. For example, a standard version of the application may be built into a smartphone, with the option for the end-user to purchase OTA an upgrade to a premium version.

So there are multiple possible customers. Some ISVs find this prospect rather daunting, and prefer to take advantage of an intermediary company known as a "publisher". In such cases, the publisher handles the distribution of the application to the marketplace, leaving the original ISV to concentrate on developing the application itself. Some publishers offer extra services to ISVs (in return, perhaps, for a greater share of the revenues), including quality assurance (QA), certification, and localization into different language versions. For a good starting point to find suitable publishers, see ***www.symbian.com/partners***.

3.4 Symbian endorsements

Whichever route(s) to market are chosen, the prospects for the application will generally be improved if the application (and/or the ISV) can display one of a range of endorsements from Symbian. Distribution channels regard these various endorsements as indications of likely quality and reliability. In a fast-moving marketplace, with many hundreds of potential ISV partners, distributors value assistance in knowing:

❑ Which solutions are believed (by Symbian) ready for speedy integration into smartphones

❑ Which solutions are, instead, closer to the "bleeding edge" (hence with a higher risk factor).

It's important to be clear about what the different endorsement levels mean (and what they don't mean).

Membership in one of Symbian's partnering programs (such as Affiliate Partner and Platinum Partner) does *not* necessarily imply that a company has a product that is both ready to ship and easy to integrate onto any given smartphone. Instead, it means that Symbian sees the company as:

❑ Having a *potentially* strong idea for a compelling product or service within the smartphone ecosystem

❑ Having a certain degree of financial backing and stability (so they are unlikely to disappear overnight)

❑ Being sufficiently trustworthy (stable and mature) that they can be invited to attend confidential meetings with Symbian, phone manufacturers, and other partners, where restricted information about future plans is discussed.

Another level of relationship, that is appropriate for some partners, is when the partner acquires a "Developer Kit License" (DKL) from Symbian. This entitles the company to receive more source code, and to access more APIs, than in the standard public Symbian Developer Kits (SDKs). At the same time, the company opens a specialist technical support contract with expert engineers in Symbian. (Don't be misled by the naming here: the "Developer Kit", almost always shortened to "DevKit", is a different product than an SDK; DevKits are restricted to companies with a DKL from Symbian, whereas SDKs are publicly available.) However, by itself, a DKL does not imply that a company has product that is ready to integrate into any given smartphone.

If a smartphone creation team is looking for evidence that a platinum partner company in the device creation space has a product ready to deploy, what the team should look at is the latest version of the Symbian Partner Solution Directory (PSD). This is a confidential directory that is published on a regular basis from Symbian to smartphone manufacturers. At the last count, there were over 360 products and services listed in the PSD, split into the following areas:

Segment	Partners	Entries
Browsing	10	17
Connectivity	27	42
Enterprise	43	58
Games services	1	5
Location-based services	3	3
Multimedia & graphics	47	100
Professional services	15	30
Security	15	25
Semiconductor	11	24
Telephony	5	11
Tools	17	31
UI framework	14	20

Entries on this list are restricted to platinum partners. The information in the directory listings is written by platinum partners, and is subject to review and regular audit by Symbian personnel. Any company that is found to be making exaggerated claims in an entry in the PSD has their entries barred in subsequent editions (thankfully, it has not been necessary to exercise this sanction so far). Each entry contains a general description of the product or service, and indicates:

❑ The versions of Symbian OS which are supported by the technology
❑ The UI systems with which the technology integrates
❑ A website address for further information
❑ An email contact address for follow-up contacts.

Certain sectors of platinum partner have specialist endorsement programs of their own:

☐ See ***www.symbian.com/partners/part-train.html*** for a list of authorized Symbian Training Partners – companies that have access to Symbian OS training materials originally authored within Symbian's internal Technical Training team

☐ See ***www.symbian.com/partners/scc.html*** for a list of authorized Symbian Competence Centers – companies with a proven substantial history of assisting smartphone manufacturers with Symbian OS integration.

There are two other Symbian endorsement programs of particular interest to ISVs: Symbian Signed and the Symbian Companion Technology Program (CTP). These are discussed in the remaining sections of this chapter.

3.5 Companion Technology Program

As its name implies, Symbian's CTP is a program for technologies that are "companion" to the components in Symbian OS. It is suited to what is sometimes called "middleware" – enabling technology at (for example) the comms, networking, graphics acceleration, security, database, or storage levels.

These technologies are liable to integration delays when smartphones are built, on account of close two-way links between these technologies and the lower-level Symbian OS APIs (sometimes called SPIs and HAIs – standing for Service Provider Interfaces and Hardware Adaptation Interfaces). Here's a problem that Symbian observed on several occasions around 2001–2002:

☐ A middleware provider develops a solution on an existing release of Symbian OS (for example, v6.1)

☐ Symbian develops and releases a new version of the operating system (for example, v7.0)

☐ The middleware provider convinces a phone manufacturer to use their solution for a forthcoming smartphone project, based on the later release of Symbian OS

☐ In the course of the smartphone project, it becomes clear that some of the relevant SPIs and HAIs have changed between the two releases – sometimes in explicit ways, but often in subtle ways

❑ As a result, the middleware solution displays many problems on the new smartphone

❑ The smartphone project team bears the brunt of the pain in debugging the resultant problems.

No one comes out of this well. For this reason, Symbian took the decision to put greater priority on supporting this kind of partner. The CTP was one of the outcomes. The idea is to make it easier for suppliers of companion technology to verify (ahead of deliveries to smartphone project teams) that their technology is integration-ready ("pre-integrated") with the relevant new version of Symbian OS. This involves a closer degree of inter-working between Symbian and the partner company (one reason for the name "companion"):

❑ The partner receives early releases of DevKits for forthcoming new versions of Symbian OS

❑ The partner discusses with experts within Symbian about suitable validation software to ensure that the companion middleware works well in the context of the new system software

❑ The result is an extended test framework, providing (as far as possible) a good representation of the environment on forthcoming new smartphones

❑ Once the test framework is agreed, the partner needs to demonstrate that their software does indeed pass the tests.

It sometimes takes several loops round the process before the software passes. But it's better for all concerned that this testing and refinement takes place away from the (often rather turbulent) context of an actual smartphone development project. When the companion technology is in due course introduced to smartphone projects, it has already been through most of the "birth-pangs" associated with a major new version, and can slot into place with much less turmoil.

There is another aspect in which companion technology middleware merits the name "companion". This refers to the distribution mechanism for these technologies (once validated). Phone manufacturer licensees of Symbian OS receive, in parallel with each release of Symbian OS itself, packages of matching companion technology. Depending on the wishes of the partner involved, this package can contain:

❑ The entirety of their software
❑ A demo of their software, with information on how to obtain the remainder
❑ Or, just some information about the technology.

In all cases, ownership of companion technology remains entirely with the partner who creates it (subject to Symbian's standard rules about ownership of any products derived from Symbian OS). When a phone manufacturer wishes to incorporate that technology in their product, they negotiate a commercial agreement directly with the partner. See ***www.symbian.com/partners/CTP.html*** for more details.

3.6 Symbian Signed

Symbian Signed has a different status from the endorsement programs covered so far in this chapter:

❏ The other programs are restricted to official partners of Symbian (such as platinum partners or affiliate partners), whereas Symbian Signed is open to all ISVs

❏ The other programs are mainly targeted to lower levels of software, whereas Symbian Signed is directly suited to applications and services which end-users purchase.

Symbian Signed has wide industry backing from smartphone manufacturers, network operators, and application retailers and publishers. The program has six main elements:

❏ A tamperproof mechanism for end-users of applications to be confident about the origin of these applications; for example, if a Symbian Signed application says it is written by MobiMate, the user is assured that it has not, instead, been written by someone else (presumably with malicious intent)

❏ A defined set of tests which applications need to pass, before they can be granted Symbian Signed accreditation; these tests cover general smartphone usage, and ensure that the application adds to the value of the phone (instead of interfering with the phone's operation)

❏ A cost-effective mechanism for ISVs to prepare for tests and then submit them; this involves a range of third-party test houses

❏ A set of security measures on smartphones, to prevent non-signed applications from being installed, except with the express knowledge and approval of the end-user

❏ The Symbian Signed applications catalog, which publicizes applications that have met the Symbian Signed test criteria; this catalog is available upon request to major distributors of Symbian applications, such as smartphone manufacturers, network operators, publishers, and aggregators

❏ A recognizable logo "For Symbian OS" which can be used in marketing for the application.

Here's an analogy. Symbian Signed is like the official annual road-worthiness test that all motor vehicles over a certain age need to pass. This test does *not* prescribe fashion aspects such as the color of the seat fabric or the precise shape of the car headlights; it does not focus on *style*; instead it looks at matters of core operation, such as whether the brakes work, and whether the lights function. Similarly, Symbian Signed imposes no criteria for taste, artistry, grammar, or similar, but checks that the essential functionality of the phone is unimpaired. For example, tests ensure that:

❏ The application pauses cleanly when there is an incoming phone call
❏ The application in no way interferes with the user's ability to make phone calls, or access any of the other functionality of the phone
❏ The user is aware of any actions of the application that generate billing events
❏ The application supports Uninstall, and the phone is left in a good state after the application has been uninstalled
❏ The application avoids running at an overly-high priority (potentially starving other software on the phone of processing time)
❏ The application shuts down in response to exit messages from the task list on the phone
❏ The application copes well with low-memory conditions and other failure states.

See ***www.symbiansigned.com*** for more information.

The "For Symbian OS" logo of the Symbian Signed program is increasingly being recognized as the mark of a quality add-on application. I strongly encourage all authors of Symbian OS applications to learn about this program, and to follow its advice on best practice. In this way, the industry and end-users alike can grow in confidence that smartphones will be the source of increasing value, rather than (say) a source of increasing confusion and frustration. As more and more companies follow the set of best practices recommended to ISVs, the attractiveness of smartphones will grow and grow. This is the subject of the next chapter.

4

Twenty reasons why smartphones will win

4.1 Two kinds of battle

Press and analysts sometimes write about a battle between vendors of smartphone operating systems – a supposed titanic struggle between Symbian and several other reasonably well-known software companies. This makes for dramatic reading. You've almost certainly seen articles on that theme. However, these articles generally overlook an even greater drama – a battle with much greater significance than that between the smartphone operating systems. This is the battle between two *categories* of phones – between smartphones and feature phones. It's a battle that involves decisions made by hundreds of millions of end-users: will they choose to purchase and use a smartphone, or will they choose to stick with a feature phone? The net outcome of all these decisions determines whether the smartphone market grows over the next few years to hundreds of millions of phones sold annually, or whether it remains an order of magnitude smaller. It's of little interest to me that Symbian's share in the smartphone market is far ahead of any competitor in this space, if the space itself remains small.

Feature phones are one level of sophistication down from smartphones. Feature phones have, well, lots of features, but the primary functionality set of a feature phone is fixed in advance – which is why feature phones are sometimes also called "closed phones". In contrast, for any given smartphone, the functionality is much more open-ended – which is why smartphones are sometimes also called "open phones".

Smartness in phones isn't just about supporting lots of features (more features than a feature phone). It's about the capacity for new features to be added quickly, taking advantage of the ideas of a huge ecosystem of inventors, innovators, and entrepreneurs. Compare the difference between someone who has done a lot of rote-learning, and someone who has the capacity to understand the principles behind the facts learned and who can generate new items of knowledge worth learning in their own right. Only the second person can really be called "smart".

Similarly, smartness in phones isn't just about there being lots of latent intelligence (hardware and software) in the phone. It's about the ability for that intelligence to be programmed and directed. This requires greater sophistication in the phone – an operating system with an extensive set of APIs, and with support for new applications to coexist with the built-in set. This sophistication has a cost. Is it worth it?

In this chapter, I offer 20 representative reasons why smartphones are displacing feature phones. These reasons are "user scenarios", with the following characteristics:

❑ They don't focus on technology – they focus on user benefits

❑ They appeal to a much wider group than just "technology geeks" or "early adopters"

❑ They don't talk in generalities – they talk about specifics

❑ They don't talk about some indeterminate time in the future – they talk about things that can either be done already, or which can reasonably be expected in real phones within a couple of years at the most

❑ They each have the potential to make many people think – "wow, I'd really like to have a phone like that!"

Of course, the list of winning scenarios is by no means exhaustive. But it's enough to establish the flavor. If you conceive of other winning scenarios, you have the chance to implement them quickly, converting your concept into a successful product. After all, that's what open phones are all about!

4.2 Multitasking

Scenario 1 is note-taking, data look-up, and messaging *while in the middle of a phone call*. The technical term for this is "multitasking", which sounds highly theoretical, but we should appreciate the tangible benefits of this to end-users. While using their phones for their primary purpose – making a phone call – users appreciate being able to access other elements of functionality of the device at the same time:

- Looking up a phone number, address, or agenda entry
- Making a note of a new phone number, address, or agenda entry
- Sending a text message to a third party (for example, to answer a question that arises during the main conversation)
- Looking up information on a website
- Perhaps even playing a game (for when the phone call has become boring).

Multitasking requires a sophisticated operating system, and a sophisticated application framework. The phone needs to be able to do several things at once, without pausing or interrupting any of these tasks. This is what you find in smartphones. With a smartphone, users have the extra benefit that all new applications which they buy (for example, a navigation application) automatically also observe the principles of multitasking. So you can consult the navigation system at the same time as you are conducting a phone call.

Multitasking also enables live interaction between applications. For example, an application could prompt users to send messages to friends on their birthdays and suggest suitable gifts, based on information stored on the phone. Or, when you receive a phone call, voice analysis software could display a guess as to the name of the caller (in cases when the incoming phone number has not been recognized), and another application could remind you of the promises you made to that person in previous conversations.

4.3 Messaging and entertainment

The next two scenarios are in the area of additional forms of messaging. **Scenario 2** is animated graphics messaging, and **Scenario 3** is mobile access to Instant Messaging:

- Users (especially young users and the young-at-heart) enjoy sending each other joke messages. If the message has a cartoon attached, so much the better. Increasingly, these cartoons can be animated and incorporate AI (artificial intelligence). Tools such as Macromedia Flash allow end-users to play back cartoons with movement, signs of emotion, action, sounds, and so on. Other enhancements include "buttons" or "hotspots" with a picture message, for additional enjoyment (or even to convey information!)

- Instant Messaging is a kind of rival to SMS (or arguably a complementor to SMS). Very many people log in to at least one Instant Messaging service every time they use a PC, and they chat with their "buddies" at the same time as they are getting on with other work on the PC. (Popular Instant Messaging services include AOL, ICQ, Yahoo!, and MSN.) Instant Messaging has proved invaluable in corporate settings, as well as for connecting users to their friends and family. Support for mobile Instant Messaging on smartphones allows the user to continue to plug into the world of his/her buddies while away from their desktop PC.

Mobile Instant Messaging is an example of how smartphones allow users to continue to access their digital universe while away from their desktop. **Scenario 4** involves the same principle. It's mobile access to multiplayer online games:

❑ Many popular PC games involve individual PCs logging onto a shared online world, where avatars representing the players interact (racing, hunting, killing, bombing, trading, searching for buried treasure, etc.). Some of these online worlds persist for weeks or even months at a time

❑ Mobile access to these games means that, when away from their desktop PC, someone can continue to participate in the game – albeit (usually) with a diminished user experience. Even though the experience is diminished, many people prefer to continue playing – it's like the fact that SMS has a poorer user experience than PC-based email, but that doesn't stop people using it.

Scenario 5 is the usage of a smartphone as an intelligent radio-cum-MP3 player. The OTA capabilities of a smartphone mean that users can retrieve and listen to specific music tracks whenever the idea occurs to them. The intelligence of a smart radio built into a smartphone means that it can learn user preferences, and can automatically jump between channels (in the same way that car radios sometimes automatically jump to channels with traffic information). The intelligence of the device also allows users to modify the music they hear (adding bass, changing the lyrics, skipping sections, repeating sections, etc.).

This scenario feeds back into messaging: users can mix new music of their own invention (modifications of existing tracks), and then send it to their friends. This is another example of how the richness of smartphones builds on top of itself: new applications swiftly take advantage of services provided by existing applications, in ways that can't happen anything like as quickly in feature phones.

4.4 Mobile knowledge access

Scenario 6 is when end-users can use their smartphones to look up all sorts of information. It's no surprise that many people have the home pages of their PC browsers set to Google. Google is a great starting place from which to find information of any kind.

Mobile versions of this are increasingly popular. Refinements to the UI will make it easier for people to find the information they are looking for – *any* information they are looking for. The kinds of questions asked to the AQA service, provided by IssueBits, gives some idea as to what mobile users want to know. With the larger screen display area of smartphones (compared to the information that can be put into a single SMS answer, as used by AQA) and rich UIs, there are great opportunities for meaningful knowledge transfer. Mobile users will have the accumulated knowledge of human society at their fingertips, wherever they go.

Scenario 7 is a specific example of mobile knowledge access: a mobile language translator. Smartphones with this service can take advantage of huge server-side databases and processing power. Translation modes include:

❏ The user types in some text

❏ The user takes a picture of some text (for example, on a street sign, or on a menu); this is particularly useful when the text is written in an unfamiliar alphabet

❏ The user holds the phone to someone, who speaks into it.

E-books ("electronic books") are another important special case of "mobile knowledge access", and comprise **Scenario 8**. People have spoken in the past about how electronic books will start to take over from physical books. This has been a long time coming, but the market is slowing expanding for E-books on PDAs. Better screen technology means that people are now more prepared to spend a longer time reading from their phones.

One advantage of having an E-book service built into a smartphone is that new books can be easily downloaded OTA – perhaps chapter by chapter on demand. Other advantages include ease of searching, bookmarks, cross-referencing, and simply the fact that users can access many more books via their smartphone than they could ever hope to pack into their holiday luggage. (So it's much easier to change your mind about what book to read next.)

Yet more possibilities arise when you replace books, in the above scenario, with videos, or combine videos and books...

4.5 Organizers and finance

Scenario 9 is usage of a smartphone as a personal organizer. Wherever I go in the world, people remark on the good use that I am able to make of my Psion Series 5mx (a PDA with a superb keyboard attached). "Where can you buy a device like that?" they often ask (especially in the USA and in Japan/Korea). The case for a good personal organizer remains.

Most phones today contain very rudimentary personal organizers – lists of contacts, simple access to agenda entries, and basic note-taking capabilities. Once people realize that the smartphone their friend has bought (and which they are thinking of buying for themselves too) also contains very useful (and easy-to-learn) PDA functionality, it will increase the attractiveness of these phones in their eyes. Mobile users will become better organized, better informed, and more effective. In short, mobile users will be smarter.

Scenario 10 is actually around 20 scenarios in one: usage of a smartphone as a corporate information organizer. Once smartphones are recognized as providing easy access to corporate information that helps users to carry out their work functions, they will increase in attractiveness – perhaps even to the point of addiction (as in the RIM BlackBerry "Crack-berry").

The most important information, for most workers, is their corporate email. After this comes the corporate scheduler, corporate databases including customer information, stock information, sales catalogs, process information, etc. All this can be accessed on smartphones, without the need for additional portable devices. More and more people will leave their laptops behind, with their smartphones becoming their primary mobile work device.

Scenario 11 is the usage of smartphones to trade stocks and shares, any time, any place. Personal investors often like to be able to take prompt action on hearing breaking news. Smartphone applications include the following features:

❏ Real-time quotes from markets worldwide
❏ News feeds from third-party content providers
❏ Alerts triggering the application on market events.

End-users can then use the application to buy or sell stock immediately.

4.6 Pocket consolidators

It has been said that, if you want to know the future of mobile phones, you should look at the contents of your pocket. Over time, more and more of the items we carry with us will be subsumed into just one – the phone. Thus phones are already subsuming people's watches, calculators, address books, diaries, cameras, mobile games terminals, and phrase books.

Scenario 12 is the usage of smartphones as tickets and vouchers. Smartphones can incorporate an electronic train ticket – a bit like the Oyster system used on the London Underground. That's one less thing for people to need to remember to carry around with them.

Another kind of "ticket" that can be conveniently stored inside a phone is a "discount voucher". These are already in significant use in Japan. Emails to phones contain vouchers allowing a discount when purchasing concert tickets, items of (youth) clothing, etc. Rather than needing to print out the voucher, or writing down the number of a discount code, the user takes the phone to the point-of-sale, and the voucher is read electronically.

Scenario 13 is the usage of smartphones as electronic wallets. Smartphones are on the point of taking over some of the functionality of credit cards. Again, it will allow people to carry fewer items with them. This will enable a phenomenon called "mCommerce", meaning "Mobile Commerce". Arguably "mCommerce" will be even bigger than "eCommerce" (electronic commerce, using PCs) since:

❏ People carry their mobile phones with them everywhere – whereas their desktop computers stay at desks

❏ Mobile payments rely on features that all mobile phones include (a processor, a screen, input mechanisms, wireless communications capabilities, and on-board software), with the result that mobile payment can be enabled in an invisible (non-obtrusive) way.

Scenario 14 is the usage of smartphones as keys and security badges. Hardware embedded into mobile phones can be programmed to emit suitable signals, to allow the degree of access appropriate to each end-user. Again, that's one less thing that people need to remember to carry around with them. It also enables some dramatic new usage models for keys and security badges.

I've called this section "pocket consolidators", but that's not quite adequate to describe what's happening. Because the functionality of different items is present in a single device that users always carry with them you can consider new user scenarios, involving cross-links between these different items of functionality. So it's not just *consolidation* of different pocket items; it's *synergy* between them, when the whole exceeds the sum of the parts. Think again about two examples from earlier:

- The synergy between music downloading, using the UI of the device to mix new tracks, and then using the messaging capabilities of the device to instantly send the result to a friend

- The synergy between using the camera to take a picture of a notice written in a foreign language, and then using the on-board intelligence and network connectivity to learn what that notice means.

These two examples are the tip of a huge set of creative possibilities. By my count, a smartphone consolidates at least 30 conventional items. In mathematical terms, there are over 4000 ways of picking three items from 30, to try to combine them in an innovative way. Even if only 1% of these combinations turn out to provide applications with consistent appeal to end-users, that still means there are around 40 new killer apps waiting to be discovered on forthcoming smartphones. I wish you happy hunting!

4.7 Social tools

Scenario 15 is the usage of smartphones as electronic photo albums. Advances in screen technology mean that photos can be displayed in stunning quality on mobile phones. An application that is of great interest to many users is the ability to access their entire photograph album while mobile. No longer do people have to dig out physical photo albums from physical storage space; they are now able to look at pictures of their nearest and dearest (and anyone and anything else) at any time of their choosing. The intelligence on a smartphone supports convenient searching and sorting. In time, people will increasingly also be able to access libraries of their personal videos.

    Scenario 16 is the involvement of smartphones in mobile blogging. Blogging is the name given to the creation of on-line diaries – collect-ions of thoughts on various topics, available for the world at large to read on the web. Mobile blogging tools allow people to make notes to themselves at any time on their smartphones, along with pictures and video, etc. These notes can be automatically backed up onto a network for them to read again at any convenient time (e.g. from a PC) and then selectively publish. In a way, mobile blogging subsumes the functionality for which some people previously used a paper-and-pencil journal. Blogging is part of the movement by which more and more people are becoming *creators* and *publishers* rather than just *consumers.*

Continuing the social theme, **Scenario 17** is the usage of smartphones to help people find dates (meaning in this case, human personal companions, rather than slots in a diary). People have made lots of jokes about the capabilities of mobile phones (equipped with Bluetooth) to allow users to define their own "personal profiles" and then leave it to wireless networks to identify suitable personal matches at venues such as night clubs and bars. It looks as though early implementations haven't always been successful, but it can only be a matter of time, as there is (apparently) great demand for such services.

This takes us to **Scenario 18** – the involvement of smartphones in so-called "adult entertainment". Historically, many new categories of device were driven forwards by the availability of new channels for sex-related purposes: cameras, video players, web-cams, PCs for home use, etc. It is the same for smartphones. The powerful graphics screens on new mobile phones, coupled with their "invisible portability", their built-in camera, their rich UIs, and their "always connected" status, means that there is (presumably) great opportunity for innovative applications in this category.

To illustrate this general point, here's an incident from the development of the software system for the Psion Series 3a. One demo application that gave this device a great boost of interest, even before it was launched, was a certain "Dancer.OPO" that caused sharp intakes of breath when first viewed (even though the lady dancer in question was animated in only four shades of gray). Two young Psion software engineers seemed to spend an inordinately long time in skunkworks activity to optimize the performance of parts of the OPL run-time (and underlying graphics sub-system) to ensure a good effect here. This effort to optimize the software system, however motivated, helped to benefit OPL for all kinds of other purposes.

4.8 Personal development

Scenario 19 is the usage of smartphones to boost personal health. Health overtook sex some time ago as the topic most searched for on the PC Internet. There is great potential for smartphones to provide applications that help to monitor users' health. This can involve local wireless communication from simple monitors, e.g. heart monitors. Applications can also prompt users to carry out simple medical tests at fixed times, and then store the result. In case of any abnormal trend of results, the phone can sound an alarm or notify the appropriate emergency services. Related usage involves mobile access to personal health records.

Finally, **Scenario 20** is the usage of smartphones as a kind of personal coach. The old mainframe program "Eliza" was surprisingly effective in providing users with a sense of therapy. It contained a fairly simple AI that carried on an apparently intelligent conversation with the user. "Tell me how you've been...?", "Why do you say that...?", etc. The abundant computing power on smartphones – backed up (if needed) by huge data resources stored on the network – means that phones can play a much larger role as a "personal coach". Users can type in some of their personal frustrations and issues to the phone, and get helpful advice in return. Looking further forwards in time, smartphones might give their users feedback on how they conducted an interview or handled themselves in an argument.

4.9 Phones win

Some of the user scenarios above don't, on the face of things, have much to do with phones. They could also be achieved (in part) using different kinds of portable electronic devices. However, Symbian's strong bet is that "the phone wins", and becomes the preferred portable computing device for the vast majority of users. These users won't think of their phone as a computer, but they'll use it to carry out many computer-like functions, and they won't need also to carry other mobile electronic devices.

The reason "the phone wins" is that the phone is the most compelling use case of all – allowing basic mobile communication with other users. Given that (nearly) everyone will be carrying a mobile phone with them, increasingly nearly everywhere they go, it's inevitable that these other functions will be absorbed into the phone.

Symbian's bet, further, is that the phone will remain the dominant function. In the eyes of most users, the device won't end up "half computer and half phone", but will be a phone that happens to support some extra features that are really useful. The name for the category, after all, isn't "computer-phone" (or "converged device" or whatever), but "smartphone".

Incidentally, I don't claim that the 20 scenarios listed above are anything like "the *best* 20 scenarios". No doubt others can think of better examples – perhaps involving the likes of location-based services, maps and navigation, presence (where the network knows which of your contacts are available to receive voice calls), voice over IP, or text-to-speech. But in either set of scenarios, it's clear that there is a wide range of compelling use-cases, which can drive the displacement of feature phones by smartphones.

4.10 Openness wins

While describing the user scenarios, I've tried not to talk much about the underlying technologies. However, behind each of the user scenarios lurks a huge amount of technology, including:

- Security (so that users will trust their phones with personal data, including credit card details)
- Multimedia
- Digital Rights Management
- Bluetooth – for "Personal Area Networking"
- Internet protocols
- High-bandwidth data communications
- Tools and developer services
- A UI that's simultaneously rich but straightforward
- Telephony itself
- Data storage and data synchronization.

New scenarios will require yet more technology. Feature phones are comfortable with a certain degree of technology, but their architecture dates back to a time when the technology needs of phones were very much less than what we now contemplate. As a result, feature phones are much more cumbersome to change. The in-house programming systems at the core of feature phones have come a long way from their original design inceptions, but will not be able to keep on coping with the oncoming rush of new functionality and technology.

Here's a recent real-life example (but I have to disguise the names, for confidentiality reasons):

- Phone manufacturer X announced that they were bringing a new Symbian OS smartphone to the market
- Phone manufacturer X showed this phone to major network operator Y
- Network operator Y liked what they saw...
- But asked manufacturer X to add a set of suggested apps, in order to achieve differentiation
- Seven applications were selected from those already written for Symbian OS for other phones
- The applications were added into the phone in just nine days – fully tested.

That's why I say, "Feature phones are dying". There is no rich collection of add-on applications available for new feature phones, since these phones are only restrictedly programmable. So there's limited customization capabilities for operators, and limited value for end-users. As time passes, the disparity between the value of feature phones and the value of smartphones will grow and grow.

Part 2

Thriving on scale

Part 2 (continued)

- ❑ Codeline strategy – single projects
- ❑ Codeline strategy – multiple projects
- ❑ Beyond codeline strategy

8 Managing integration

- ❑ Integration vs. creation
- ❑ Mainlines and development codelines
- ❑ Iterative development
- ❑ Gate-keeping and integration tests
- ❑ Dealing with build or test failures
- ❑ The weekly integration cycle
- ❑ Integration discipline

9 Managing interfaces

- ❑ Knowing when components belong together
- ❑ Limits of rebuilding source code
- ❑ Forms of compatibility
- ❑ The compatibility virtuous cycle
- ❑ System compatibility board
- ❑ Responsibilities with regard to compatibility
- ❑ Interface access and interface status
- ❑ Versioning
- ❑ Future-proofing interfaces

10 Managing testing

- ❑ Beyond complete testing
- ❑ Testing in context
- ❑ Functional tests
- ❑ Basic Acceptance Tests

Part 2 (continued)

- ❏ Specialist tests
- ❏ Friendly User Tests
- ❏ Mandatory tests
- ❏ Automated tests

11 Managing tools
- ❏ The need for a tools champion
- ❏ Debuggers
- ❏ Emulators
- ❏ Profilers and loggers
- ❏ Static code analysis
- ❏ Build system
- ❏ Distribution system
- ❏ Miscellaneous tools
- ❏ Dangers with tools

12 Managing plans and change
- ❏ Beyond complete planning
- ❏ Causes of change
- ❏ Handling change requests
- ❏ Variable task estimates
- ❏ Practical example of agile scheduling
- ❏ Accepting slack
- ❏ Aggressive vs. defensive scheduling
- ❏ Authentic vs. inauthentic scheduling
- ❏ Beyond meeting customer requests

13 Managing uncertainty
- ❏ The 80–20 rule for planning

Part 2 (continued)

- ❏ Identifying the project planning hot list
- ❏ Iterating the project plan
- ❏ Developing features outside the agreed core
- ❏ The 80–20 rule for task estimation
- ❏ Typical project trouble spots
- ❏ Pros and cons of milestone reviews
- ❏ Dealing with milestone delays
- ❏ Cut features not corners

14 Simplifying smartphone projects

- ❏ Beyond difficulty
- ❏ Reuse rather than reinvent
- ❏ The benefits of frequent releases
- ❏ Symbian's adoption of the frequent release model
- ❏ Use of reference designs
- ❏ Silver bullets vs. disruption

5
Managing large projects

5.1 Smartphone projects vs. feature phone projects

Symbian OS smartphone projects have the potential to be large – *very* large. A smartphone ROM contains upwards of 24MB of software, compiled from around 10 million lines of source code. Numerous third parties can be involved, with a combined team size of more than 100 software engineers. That's a great deal for the project leader to handle.

It's particularly a great deal when you compare it to the kinds of project that teams in phone manufacturers frequently conduct – projects to create feature phones (phones that are one level of sophistication down from smartphones). Feature phones are complex in their own way, but their complexity is an order of magnitude smaller than for smartphones. They have significantly less software – perhaps a quarter of the ROM size, and less than a tenth the number of lines of source code. Equally noteworthy, teams in phone manufacturers tend to have extensive prior experience in creating feature phones. Feature phones are demanding to create, but the phone manufacturer is used to these particular demands, and has accumulated special methods, over many years, to handle them.

In contrast, smartphones introduce disruptive aspects that undermine this prior knowledge base:

- The existence of open APIs, which are published in SDKs for third parties to access (and which the third parties rely on being present), causes complications

- The operating system is supplied by a third party, outside the direct control of the project team; likewise for many of the other components in the ROM

- Whereas the functionality of a feature phone is small enough that a single person can reasonably hope to understand all of it, the functionality of a smartphone is so extensive and open-ended that there is probably no person on the team who understands all of it

❑ Whereas the software architecture of a feature phone is small enough that a single software engineer can, with time, reasonably hope to understand all of it, the software architecture of a smartphone is so extensive and open-ended that there is probably no person on the team who understands all of it

❑ Whereas the phone manufacturer is deeply familiar with the operating systems used in feature phones, "warts and all" (that is, being well aware of their defects and shortcomings) and has developed practical workarounds over many years to these problems, Symbian OS comes with a huge new set of risks and issues, which remain largely unknown and unfathomed by the new project team.

5.2 Three approaches to large projects

Faced with the challenge of a project that is larger than any previously undertaken, a project team can adopt one of three approaches:

❑ *Denial*: imagine that basically the same approach as before will be sufficient (except that the team will be expected to work harder than ever)

❑ *Qualitative change*: recognize that the extent of the changes in project scope requires new working methods – the quantitative change in size needs to be answered by a qualitative change in approach

❑ *Reduction*: find ways to change the large project back into a series of smaller projects, for which the previous working methods remain well suited.

Denial is the least helpful approach of the three. Project teams can become stuck in denial because:

❑ They fail to appreciate the full extent of the differences in a smartphone project

❑ They are insufficiently aware of the new kinds of methods that can be applied

❑ They are aware of possible new methods, but they fear that these methods will be too heavyweight or bureaucratic, and will stifle the agility and speed of the project team.

It is my goal in this book to lead smartphone project teams out of denial – so that they can embrace a successful combination of the other two approaches.

5.3 How large projects differ from small projects

The key difference between large and small projects is that there needs to be more rigor and formality in the processes adopted in large projects. It is no longer possible to rely entirely upon informal processes. That's because there are many more people involved, and therefore *very* many more relationships involved. (If there are n people working on a project, the number of relationships is $\frac{1}{2}n(n-1)$.)

In large projects, project knowledge cannot be allowed just to remain in the heads of individuals. It needs to be captured into a format that is more permanent and more visible. Likewise, project skills cannot be allowed just to remain in the heads of individuals. They need to be documented, so that other team members are able to step in to replace the original personnel, yet still follow the same processes.

Areas where formal processes are required include:

- ❑ Project communications – email and beyond
- ❑ Defect management
- ❑ Source code management
- ❑ Integration management (including gate-keeping)
- ❑ Interface management
- ❑ Testing
- ❑ Tools
- ❑ Change requests
- ❑ Planning.

I cover the first of these topics in the remainder of this chapter; the others each have their own chapters.

Some readers may say that what's written in these chapters is simply good software engineering common sense. I don't deny that these principles are quite widely known within the industry. Sadly, it's also my experience that, at the same time, these principles are widely *unk*nown. But in any case it's not just a question of *knowing* the principles; it's a matter of *applying* them, speedily and effectively, in the heat of a complex project, when many other questions and issues are jostling for attention. At such times, there's a strong temptation to regress to simpler (less effective) practices.

The best defense against regression, in the midst of project turmoil, is to have deep internal commitment to sound software management processes. This commitment can be strengthened by regular review of these processes, so that they become second nature. It's especially helpful to review each process in the specific light of smartphone project issues and hotspots. You'll see that the special features of Symbian OS inject a distinctive flavor into the overall process melting pot.

5.4 Project groupware

In small project teams, everyone is familiar with what everyone else is doing. Informal discussions between team members are sufficient to keep people informed. Team meetings occur when needed, often without much advance warning (since it is easy to gather everyone together), often without a formal agenda, and often with no permanent record of what was covered. In small projects, there is little need for formal agendas or meeting minutes.

In small project teams, email is another essential communication mechanism, which exists alongside the set of face-to-face (F2F) discussions. Email creates a more permanent record of discussions, allowing reference back, after the event, to decisions and reasons. This introduces some support for archiving, searching, and sorting. Email also goes some way to reduce the effect of "Chinese whispers", whereby instructions become distorted through frequent retelling.

But for larger projects, more is needed. F2F and email are no longer sufficient. The project needs some kind of database system which is the repository for project communications. This is commonly called the "groupware" of the project. The project groupware consists of knowledgebases, online discussion forums, and so forth.

Groupware is a structured dynamic body of data that allows a group of people to collaborate in an effective way over extended time duration. Groupware permits:

- Easy access to the information by newcomers to the team (in a way that is difficult to achieve using email alone)
- Easy tracking, by management, of issues that have been raised (for example, technical questions awaiting answer)
- Easy reference, by all members of the team, to official documents and decisions.

Without groupware, it is easy for issues to become lost in sprawling email threads that lack clear owners. With groupware, there is greater visibility and shared understanding of project issues.

The mere existence of a formal database for project communication will not stop the flow of email within the project team (and nor should it). Email remains a highly useful communications method. However, all project members need to be ready to copy sanitized portions of email threads into the formal database, whenever they judge that an email exchange has interest to a wider group of people. In such cases, the alternative to copying the email thread into the project groupware is to extend the CC list of the email discussion. However, it seems to me that the CC list is never quite large enough – there are potentially lots more people who have a genuine stake in the discussion (and who might be able to supply the best answer). That's why the groupware storage mechanism is better.

Provided team members observe the discipline of moving important discussions out of email into groupware, it will often become apparent that certain questions keep recurring. (Sometimes, indeed, the same person will raise the same question several times, to different people, until an answer is given that satisfies the questioner.) When groupware is used, the questions can quickly be answered, by reference to previous times the questions were raised. But if the discussion sticks to email, there is a big risk of duplicated and suboptimal effort.

5.5 Confidentiality issues

In my view, it is better to err on the side of sharing too much information than sharing too little. If team members are able to read the explanations for various decisions, as well as other relevant background information, it will in general help them to carry out their jobs more intelligently.

But certain kinds of information may need to be stored in the groupware in a way that limits access to a smaller group of people. Examples include information about project finances, or about the performance of suppliers or partners. Therefore, you may decide to restrict access to some information stored within the groupware. During the project setup phase, project leaders should check that the groupware system they adopt is capable of different levels of access.

However, if you do write documents that speak about partner companies behind their backs, you'd better be double-sure that none of these remarks finds its way into the hands of these companies! Otherwise, the relationship may suffer irreparable damage. One useful safeguard here is to encrypt documents containing particularly sensitive information, using the encryption keys of only a small number of people.

5.6 Five central project documents

Here are five types of document that should be available in the project groupware:

- ❏ Documents detailing "who does what", so that it is easy for team members (including people in partner companies) to know who to contact about specific matters. Everyone's email address should be included, together, ideally, with a map of who sits where. The documents should also contain photographs of the team personnel, thereby forming an "illustrated organization chart", allowing team members to match the names and faces of their colleagues

- ❏ The project "release notes", which describe the changes between the different internal baseline versions of project software (for example, stating which defects have been fixed, and which versions of external software have been included)

- ❏ The latest "integration schedule", which gives the expected timetable for forthcoming new internal versions of the project software, along with the anticipated contents of these versions (evidently, the integration schedule gives the predicted contents for future release notes)

- ❏ The latest "risk list" for the project, where the project manager lists the most significant hurdles facing the project, along with the measures being taken to ward off these risks

- ❏ The latest "focus list" for the project, where the project manager states the matters requiring the highest level of attention in the project at the present time, thereby establishing priorities. (Sometimes this document is called the "issue list".)

These documents all need to be kept up to date on a regular basis. This may be viewed as a tedious chore, but for larger projects, the effort will be well repaid, through better dissemination of key project data. The project leaders will also find that the discipline to create and maintain these documents forces them to review different aspects of the overall progress of the project. They are likely to have important "aha!" realizations whilst working on these documents.

5.7 Auditing document readership

From time to time, project leaders should conduct an informal audit of who is reading the documents being produced. The purpose of this audit is to identify whether any documents have become mainly "write-only", in the sense that people write them but no-one reads them (or the readership is smaller than expected). If any such documents are discovered, the project leaders need to determine whether:

- ❏ The existence of these documents needs to be better publicized
- ❏ The content of the documents needs to be changed (to better meet the needs of the expected readership)
- ❏ The documents should be reduced in size, or eliminated altogether.

There is little point in putting in the effort to create documents that hardly anyone reads. However, the documents that I have specifically mentioned (organization chart, release notes, integration schedule, risk list, and focus list) are documents that I strongly believe are well worth both writing and reading. If the readership is poor in these cases, it is time to check whether the documents are being sufficiently well written:

- ❏ Are the documents repetitive? If so, they should be streamlined

- ❏ Are the documents over-wordy? If so, consider adding diagrams, charts, and tables

- ❏ Are the documents clear? If not, encourage the writers to put themselves more often into the shoes of their intended audience. Customer-focus is as important in writing documents as in writing software.

5.8 Processes and agility: education vs. processes

Please do not conclude that, because I talk a lot about the importance of processes in large projects, I am in favor of *heavyweight* processes. That would be a wrong conclusion. I am in favor of formal processes, but not heavyweight ones that consume large amounts of time. What I do favor, is the importance of project teams taking real care over the way that their work is carried out. In view of the multiple connections between all the different pieces of software in a smartphone project, software development on the project cannot be allowed to be entirely spontaneous. It needs to be carefully thought through in advance, and carefully reviewed afterwards. Furthermore, individuals on the project team cannot be allowed to take all their own decisions in isolation from one another; their actions need constant coordination with other team members.

These goals (that work is carried out with real care, that individual pieces of software development need to be planned and reviewed, and that there needs to be constant coordination of individual outputs) are entirely consistent with *lightweight* processes. There is no necessity for any one process to take a long time to carry out.

Instead of heavyweight processes, I champion heavyweight education, with the education covering the "why" as well as the "what". That is, all team members should understand:

❑ The reasons why it is important to review work carefully
❑ The reasons why certain review methods are believed to be the most effective ones
❑ The kinds of things that can go wrong when shortcuts are taken.

Instead of lots of time being consumed by people filling in lots of paperwork, the majority of time should be spent on the following activities:

❑ Planning and design
❑ Actual execution ("the real work")
❑ Peer review
❑ Discussion of lessons learned ("education").

Companies that impose heavyweight processes often do so out of a lack of trust and respect for their team members. In such companies, there is a strong belief that team members are likely to make mistakes, so processes are used as correctives. This kind of pessimistic belief system is unlikely to lead team members into high performance (and as such, it tends to become a self-fulfilling prophecy). Furthermore, heavyweight processes prevent a team from responding in an agile manner to change requests. In contrast, an education system that is oriented to spreading an understanding of underlying principles is likely to result in much better accomplishment.

So, team members should all be made aware of practical examples of problems arising in smartphone projects when insufficient care is taken on some aspects of the development work. Provided these examples are well understood, team members will appreciate, by themselves, the reasons why various kinds of spontaneous software development cannot be accepted as part of a large smartphone project. There will be no need for managers to spend a lot of time carefully double-checking the work of their team members. Team members will, autonomously, coordinate their work, and attain higher quality levels.

5.9 Problems when groupware is short-cut

Here are some examples of what goes wrong in large smartphone projects if shortcuts are taken with the project groupware:

❑ In the absence of a useful illustrated organization chart, team members often fail to realize who they should be talking to about various project issues. They may not know the right email addresses to use. And they may not recognize other team members, when passing each other in corridors, and thereby lose the chance for important impromptu F2F discussions

❑ In the absence of accurate release notes, team members won't realize that various defects have already been fixed (or are known to still be unfixed) in the latest internal software version. They also won't know how important it is for them to be using or testing a particular new software version

❑ In the absence of a useful integration schedule, team members will miss the opportunity to submit their changes in time for particular integration steps to take place, and will fail to realize what submissions are expected at which times in the days and weeks ahead

❑ In the absence of a carefully thought through risk list, nasty risks will creep up unnoticed on a project and may overwhelm it

❑ In the absence of a carefully thought through focus list, team members will devote too much of their time to issues of lesser overall importance to the project

❑ If the groupware as a whole is substandard, new team members will spend an excessive amount of time working out what they are meant to be doing on the project, and managers will fail to realize that various important issues lack clear owners.

In short, lack of time spent to create and maintain project groupware results in much greater overall loss of time as a result of poorly informed and poorly coordinated team members.

5.10 Symbian's use of groupware

The software team in Psion adopted Lotus Notes in late 1994. Since that time, many hundreds of customized Notes databases have been designed. Many have subsequently withered and expired, but some have flourished, and are still going strong, ten years later:

❏ The oldest posting in our in-house "Programming" database is one I made on 19th March 1995 (on the subject of the Rational Rose design tool). The "About" screen for this database reads as follows: *This database is for general discussion on programming – discussion potentially of interest to all software developers, regardless of their current project. This database is available to all Symbian personnel. Non-Symbian personnel have no access. You can use this database for passing on programming tips and hints, and for asking if anyone knows a way to do such and such a thing. You can argue about "in-house programming style" in here too. (For example, "In my previous job we did things in a far better way than the way Symbian forces me to use now.") In due course, ideas raised in this database may become adopted as official company policy, for one or more projects, and will transfer into other databases (e.g. the Symbian Standards database)*

❏ The oldest posting in our in-house "EPOC Software Design" database is one (coincidentally also made by myself) dated 3rd January 1995, on the subject of the design of FORM32 – the formatting and layout software component of Symbian OS.

Among many other purposes, we have also used Notes databases for defect tracking, for change control systems, for FAQs, for company-wide news, for storing standards, for release notes, for integration schedules, for booking training courses, for tracking meetings and actions, for organizing social events, and for our corporate directory. Customer-facing project teams typically also have databases dedicated to the workflow arising from these projects. Despite this heavy use (or perhaps in part *because* of this heavy use), Notes has had plenty of critics inside Symbian. In retrospect, it's clear that:

❏ We often under-invested in the design of specific databases, relying too quickly on simple modifications of general purpose databases instead of spending more time upfront customizing a database to our particular needs. The moral here is that it's easy to neglect investment in tools, but the team pays the price for this many times over

❏ In some cases, it really is better to adopt a different tool, tailor-made to its intended purpose. For example, for defect tracking we switched away from Notes during 2002, and adopted TeamTrack for this specific purpose. Also, we nowadays also have extensive extranets and intranets (including a TWiki), where teams publish and review information

❑ Regardless of the tools used, people need to invest the time, on a regular basis, on "librarian" activities, including data reclassification, archiving, and creating new top-level guides to the groupware.

For confidential data exchange with partners and customers, we specify the use of PGP encryption for sensitive material (in cases where there is no dedicated secure connection). PGP is a hassle to learn and a moderate inconvenience to use, but once people have come through the initial learning curve, it becomes virtually second nature. Symbian's insistence on treating our partners' confidential information with great care is another reason why our partners are able to trust us to such a high extent.

6
Managing defects

6.1 Introduction to smartphone defect management

One of the really central items of smartphone project groupware is the defects database – the database of all known or suspected defects in the product. At all stages of the project, team leaders should be spending a substantial amount of their time monitoring and reviewing the material in the defects database. By doing this, they can accelerate the following:

- Identifying and eliminating the most serious defects in the product
- Evaluating the quality level in the product
- Evaluating the quality of work from different teams in the project
- Determining when the product is likely to be ready for release to the market.

Optimal defect management consists of the following subprocesses:

- The initial raising of "incident reports"
- Analysis of these incident reports – to determine if there is an actual product defect
- Prioritization of product defects
- Evaluation of candidate fixes
- Testing of candidate fixes
- Overall review.

The defects database is formed from a large number of "incident reports", which are raised by testers and other team members. (In a healthy project, testing is carried out by a much wider set of people than just the designated full-time testers.) Incidents are raised when someone notices behavior in the product that they consider to be questionable or wrong. An incident report should include:

❑ A clear statement of the actual behavior observed, as well as what the expected behavior was

❑ A description of the hardware and software test environment (such as the hardware and software version numbers) including, if relevant, the telephony network in use, and the type of SIM used

❑ A description of the steps to take to produce the problematic behavior.

Once an incident report has been created, other team members can add extra information, which appears in the database as "responses" to the report.

It needs to be clear to all team members that not every incident report contains a defect. Just because an incident report has been raised does not mean that the software has a defect that needs to be fixed. Instead, on many occasions, the correct response to an incident report is "not a defect". For example, the team member who raised the incident may have misunderstood an aspect of the intended functionality of the product. Hopefully, once the intended functionality is explained, the originator of the incident report will be happy to close the incident (meaning that it does not need any further attention). In case the originator is still dissatisfied (thinking, for example, that the intended functionality has a bad UI), this fact should be noted, with the incident marked for the attention of product management:

❑ Members of the product management team should be regularly involved in reviewing specification-related issues arising from the defects database

❑ These matters should not be left solely in the hands of software engineers to resolve. The opinion of software engineers on these matters is valuable, but is insufficient to determine the decision. It is a different skill-set that is needed to arbitrate between competing conceptions of how end-users should experience the product

❑ In turn, this requires software engineers to recognize the limitations of their own expertise, and to know when to ask for help from other areas of the team.

Something else that needs to be clear to all team members is that, even once it has been agreed that an incident report identifies a defect, this does not mean that there is approval for this defect to be fixed. There are many potential drawbacks to every fix that is made:

❑ The code changes that fix a defect may have side-effects which are worse than the original defect

❑ For example, other parts of the software may be relying (intentionally or unintentionally) on the current notionally defective behavior; fixing this defect may therefore break another part of the software, sometimes with very significant consequences

❑ Even if there are no bad side-effects, it will still take time to apply the fix, and then to test that there are no bad side-effects; all this consumes time, and risks delaying the product launch

❑ Finally, even the best software engineers have limited energy, and need to focus on the truly critical defects.

For all these reasons, engineers need to discuss with their team leaders whether to try to fix particular defects. It may be better to live with a defect, rather than to fix it:

❑ On some occasions, the decision may be to *defer* the defect fix until a later date, after the next public release of the product. For example, there may be more time to fix the defect (and to check the fix) in between the initial public release and a follow-up maintenance release

❑ On other occasions, the decision may simply be "not going to fix", where there is no intention of revisiting the defect in the foreseeable future.

6.2 Living with defects

Many people are perturbed by the concept of releasing a product that is known to contain defects. There are three aspects to this:

❑ Some team members may believe that it is an intolerable indication of poor software that defects remain in the product. Out of a sense of pride, they want to fix all defects that are reported

❑ Other team members take the practical point of view that any defect is going to annoy at least some users, resulting in lost revenue, and damage to the good brand name of the company

❏ Yet other team members come from a background of shipping simpler phones (such as feature phones) for which the QA (Quality Assurance) team insist as a matter of process that all defects found during the QA period need to be fixed before the product is approved for release. They argue that, since smartphones are said to be improvements on feature phones, they should have even fewer defects than feature phones.

However, the reality is that, unless software leaders take a broad-minded approach to defects, the smartphone will *never* be ready to come to market. There will always be aspects of the software that cause difficulties or problems to some users. That's because of the vast open-ended nature of the software in smartphones. Typically a smartphone ROM has around four times as much software as a feature phone. Taking into account the numerous *interactions* between different aspects of the software, a smartphone can easily have at least ten times as many plausible "use cases" as a feature phone. So, other things being equal, it's not surprising that testers will eventually find many more defects in a smartphone than in a feature phone. That's no cause for panic. It's something to keep in perspective.

The decision on whether a product is ready to ship needs to take into account, not just the number of defects contained (that is, items which will cause problems to users), but also the number of positive use cases supported (that is, items that deliver value to users). Delaying the release of a product, because it still contains some defects, means that there is also a delay in users receiving all the value available in the positive use cases supported by the product. It's a tough decision.

6.3 Aside: an embarrassing moment with defects

The first million-selling product that I helped to build was the Psion Series 3a handheld computer. This was designed as a distinct evolutionary step-up from its predecessor, the original Series 3 (often called the "Series 3 classic" in retrospect). The screen size on the Series 3a was double that on the Series 3: 480×320 pixels instead of 240×160. One reason for the success of the 3a was the clear focus, in the project, on just a small number of specification improvements over the 3. The original specification document listed nearly one hundred potential significant upgrades. But the project team wisely chose to focus on just a few points:

❏ The larger screen (and the shades of gray that it supported)

❏ Support for print preview (to show off the extra graphics power of the device)
❏ A complete rewrite of the agenda application (sometimes also called "Calendar" or "Diary").

All other applications were restricted to minor upgrades, so that the lion's share of the team's creative effort could be applied to implement an agenda application that (in contrast to its Series 3 predecessor) would persuade users to abandon paper-and-pencil agendas for good. We had around seven people working more-or-less flat out on this application – an unprecedented number for Psion at that time.

At last the day came (several weeks late, as it happened) to ship the software to Japan, where it would be flashed into large numbers of chips ready to assemble into production Series 3a devices. It was ROM version 3.20. No sooner was it sent than panic set into the development team. Two of us had independently noticed a new defect in the agenda application. If a user set an alarm on a repeating entry, and then adjusted the time of this entry, in some circumstances the alarm would fail to ring. We reasoned that this was a really bad defect – after all, two of us had independently found it.

The engineer who had written the engine for the application – the part dealing with all data manipulation algorithms, including calculating alarm times – studied his code, and came up with a fix. We were hesitant, since it was complex code. So we performed a mass code review: lots of the best brains in the team talked through the details of the fix. After 24 hours, we decided the fix was good. So we recalled 3.20, and released 3.21 in its place. To our relief, no chips were lost in the process: the flashing had not yet started.

Following standard practice, we upgraded the prototype devices of everyone in the development team, to run 3.21. As we waited for the chips to return, we kept using our devices – continuing (in the jargon of the team) to "eat our own dog food". Strangely, there were a few new puzzling problems with alarms on entries. Actually, it soon became clear these problems were a lot *worse* than the problem that had just been fixed. As we diagnosed these new problems, a sinking feeling grew. Despite our intense care (but probably because of the intense pressure) we had failed to fully consider all the routes through the agenda engine code; the change made for 3.21 was actually a regression on previous behavior.

Once again, we made a phone call to Japan. This time, we were too late to prevent some tens of thousands of wasted chips. We put the agenda engine code back to its previous state, and decided that was good enough! (Because of some other minor changes, the shipping version number was incremented to 3.22.) We decided to live with one defect, in order not to hold up production any longer.

We were expecting to hear more news about this particular defect from the Psion technical support teams, but the call never came. This defect never featured on the list of defects reported by end-users. In retrospect, we had been misled by the fact that two of us had independently found this defect during the final test phase: this distorted our priority call. We eventually produced a proper fix several months later, but the press had already declared the Series 3a agenda application a stunning success.

Of course, the decision on whether a product is ready to ship needs to consider, not just the *number* of remaining defects, but also the *severity* of the remaining defects. This takes us to the topic of assigning defect priorities.

6.4 Defect priorities

Discussions of whether to try to fix particular defects are informed by the priorities assigned to the incident report. I recommend the following five-fold priority classification:

- ❏ *Immediate patch required* – meaning that the defect is holding up other important aspects of product development. For example, a defect may be such that it prevents whole other areas of function-ality from being tested

- ❏ *Showstopper* (sometimes instead called "critical", or abbreviated as "SS") – meaning that the product cannot launch until this defect is fixed. The defect is judged likely to result in a significant number of product returns (with dissatisfied users returning their phones to the shop for a refund) and/or adverse publicity

- ❏ *High* – meaning that the defect is probably a showstopper, but further investigation is needed. If it turns out to be too hard to fix the defect, it may be acceptable to launch the product with a small number of high priority defects still present

- ❏ *Medium* – this should be the default priority status for new incident reports. It essentially means that further investigation is required as to whether or not the defect needs to be fixed. If the fix is straightforward, it should probably go ahead (depending on other priorities), but otherwise it is up to a judgment call from the team leaders involved

- ❏ *Low* – meaning that there is probably no need to fix this defect, unless it is particularly simple to do so. An important reason for recording a low priority defect is to allow other people to carry out further investigation, in case it turns out that the same defect will have more serious consequences in other settings. Low and medium priority defects are also good material to review when determining the spec of future products.

Note that "showstopper" defects are *not* the most urgent to fix!

It takes a special kind of skill to know which kinds of defects are likely to cause real problems in the marketplace – a skill borne out of considerable experience. Software leaders need to nurture that skill in their team members, wherever they find it.

Some team members may want to assign virtually every defect to "high" priority (or higher). However, they need to beware the effects of "priority inflation". If too many defects are assigned to high priorities, it lessens the impact. This kind of abdication of proper prioritization means that resources are allocated on a suboptimal basis. In such cases, defects which are genuinely more serious may end up being overlooked.

6.5 The process of verifying a defect fix

Once a candidate fix has been found for a defect, there needs to be a further decision as to whether to actually apply that candidate fix into the product. This again involves peer review. There must be no presumption that all candidate fixes are automatically applied. Items to review, before approving the fix, are whether the candidate fix has the intended result, whether any side-effects can be noticed, whether the new source code meets generally agreed criteria, and whether an alternative fix might be preferable.

It is worth looking in more detail at the process of verifying that a fix has been successful:

❏ Before starting work on a fix, the engineer should check that it is possible to reproduce the defect. There is no point in taking the time and effort to make changes to some software, showing afterwards that the defect does not occur, if the defect could not be reproduced in the first place

❏ Learning how to reproduce the defect will often throw up additional useful information. This may involve further discussion with the originator of the defect

❏ So, ideally, the engineer reaches a situation where it is known that, in a particular context, a specified list of user operations reliably results in an agreed undesirable outcome

❑ Once the fix has been developed and applied, this same context and list of user operations should be repeated, several times over, without the undesirable outcome being observed. If so, then it can be agreed that the fix is successful

❑ The context and list of user operations should be documented, and added to the overall set of "test lore" for the project. This is a set of test cases that should be revisited on occasion, to check that the fix remains effective in later releases of the software

❑ It is important to ask the originator of the incident report to confirm, in due course (that means, once software containing the fix has been released), that they no longer see examples of the problem they originally reported. Sometimes a developer believes that a fix has been successful, whereas it only covers a small part of the problem as experienced by the original tester.

Even when a fix seems not to have worked, this does not mean the fix was wrong. Sometimes, there are layers of defects, all impacting phone behavior in some area. Fixing the first defect then causes focus to fall on the second defect in that area. Sometimes the second defect is much harder than the first. This is another reason why it is important to prioritize defects. Attention needs to be given, first, to the most urgent defects – not the defects which happen to be most interesting to the developer in question. It can end up taking a lot longer than expected to fix any given defect.

6.6 Advanced defect investigation

Unfortunately, some defects are hard to reproduce. Testers notice that, from time to time, something bad happens on the phone (for example, an application terminates without warning, or the whole phone becomes unresponsive) without being able to say what series of actions precipitates the defect. These defects form a category of "hard to reproduce". They pose special difficulties to smartphone projects.

Special skills need to be brought to bear to handle such defects. Different software engineers possess these skills in different measures. People who are particularly skilled at dealing with "hard to reproduce" defects should be highly valued by project leaders, even if they are only average in other aspects of software engineering. Here are the skills in question:

❑ The ability to notice unexpected correlations (therefore, great observation skills)

❑ The ability to try lots of different approaches, in attempts to make the defect reproducible

❑ The ability to scan other incident reports in the database, to highlight possible connections with the defect under investigation. (This is one reason to encourage team members to record low priority defects into the defects database, even when these defects don't, by themselves, require a fix. The information recorded in a low priority incident report may turn out to provide a defect investigator with the key intellectual breakthrough needed to solve a different defect.)

Investigation of "hard to reproduce" defects can go a lot faster if the investigators have a good overall understanding of the system software. More knowledge of the system makes it more likely that you know what's worth observing. Experience on previous smartphone projects helps a lot here. Skilled defect investigators will be able to call upon lots of memories of roughly similar defects from prior projects. This is a reason to ensure that a smartphone project team contains at least a sprinkling of Symbian OS veterans.

Investigation of "hard to reproduce" defects can also go faster if internal logging information can be collected from the software. In this way, internal diagnostics can be added to the externally visible information. This is an important example of how good tools make a big difference to the effectiveness of smartphone project teams.

Another big problem with "hard to reproduce" defects is that it is hard to tell whether they have been fixed. It is common to hear people say something like "... we haven't seen this defect for some time, and we suspect that it may have been fixed by the same fix as was introduced for defect N" (quoting the unique identifier for the second defect). What's needed in such cases is:

❑ A wide variety of willing testers, who employ different approaches in their use of the smartphone

❑ A system for communicating to these testers a list of possible defects to try to notice: the "critical test areas" at any given time in the project.

There is an argument for the whole team (from top to bottom) setting aside an hour, every week or so, to try to reproduce the most critical "hard to reproduce" defects.

6.7 Defect status values

Let's recap on some of the different status values that can be assigned to an incident report:

- ❏ *"Awaiting investigation"* – the default status of new incident reports

- ❏ *"Under investigation"* – someone has taken ownership of the incident and has started to analyze it

- ❏ *"Not a defect"* – the product is actually working as designed, despite what the tester may have thought when raising the incident

- ❏ *"Duplicate"* – the incident covers the same defect as another incident report. In that case, a link needs to be provided to the other report

- ❏ *"Deferred"* – the defect will not be fixed ahead of the next public release of the software, but should be reinvestigated at some later occasion

- ❏ *"Not going to fix"* – it is acknowledged that a defect exists, but there is no plan to fix it in the foreseeable future

- ❏ *"Hard to reproduce"* – further investigation is needed of the potential circumstances when the defect occurs

- ❏ *"Fix being evaluated"* – a candidate fix has been prepared, and the team is reviewing whether it should be accepted

- ❏ *"Awaiting verification"* – a candidate fix has been applied, and the team is waiting for the next internal release of the overall software system, to verify that the fix works in the context of the whole product

- ❏ *"Fix verified"* – the fix has been verified as correct.

The set of defect status values is orthogonal to the set of defect priority values.

The status values divide into two types: "open" and "closed". Incidents are "closed" if they have been assigned as "not a defect", "duplicate", "deferred", "not going to fix", or "fix verified". Otherwise, the incident is "open". The whole purpose of the defects management system is to move defects into one of the closed states in a way that is controlled, thoughtful, yet systematic. Any defect that spends a long time in one of the open states deserves management attention.

6.8 Defect database requirements

Here are some specific requirements on the way the defects database works:

- ❑ The database should be easily searchable, so that people who are investigating a possible defect can quickly notice other incident reports that may be relevant to this defect

- ❑ The database needs to be able to cope with up to tens of thousands of incident reports, and potentially with more than one hundred users accessing it simultaneously, without it becoming slow or unresponsive. Databases that work well on small projects may fail to scale to the greater demands of larger projects

- ❑ The database should avoid generating floods of automated emails. Automated email notifications and reminders may seem like a good idea in the context of small projects, but for larger projects, the result is that email inboxes quickly saturate with automated messages. Instead, team members need to acquire the discipline to search the database on a regular basis for matters relevant to them. In turn, this requires that it is clear (for example, by using "unread marks") where there have been recent additions to discussions on particular defects

- ❑ The database should support the on-demand generation of a variety of statistics and reports, for example by outputting summary information into an editable spreadsheet.

It is a good idea to publicize the key trends with the defect statistics, for example by printing out graphs and sticking them up on walls in team areas. However, be sure that people understand the contents of the graphs. All metrics are potentially dangerous, and defects metrics are no exception.

6.9 The role of the project leader in managing defects

By way of a summary, here is the responsibility of the project leader (or an assigned deputy) in managing defects:

- ❑ Teach team members the best practices of creating and handling incident reports

❑ Actively review and adjust defect priorities. Prevent defect priority inflation. Establish objective criteria for the higher defect priorities

❑ Prevent "defect ping-pong" between different teams

❑ Ensure that relevant experts from different teams work together well, to investigate defects which span more than one sub-team; this includes product management representatives when needed

❑ Assign suitably skilled people as defect investigators and coordinators, and be sure that they are given sufficient support

❑ Notice, from the defect statistics, when particular teams are running into difficulty (for example, with slow defect turnaround times), and take steps to deal with these difficulties

❑ By ensuring that sufficient attention is given to areas needing focus, drive down the number of open major defects.

7
Managing configurations

7.1 Introduction to configuration management

Configuration management (commonly abbreviated to "CM") is a discipline that allows software teams to keep track of multiple changes in the software being developed. CM becomes particularly important when several different people work on the same source code.

(Sometimes the term "SCM" is used instead – standing for Software Configuration Management.)

A configuration is a consistent set of files comprising:

- ❑ Source code
- ❑ Header files
- ❑ Static libraries (for example, *.LIB files)
- ❑ Dynamic libraries (for example, *.DLL files)
- ❑ Other run-time files (such as a complete test environment)
- ❑ Tools (batch files, compilers, etc.) required to build the software in this configuration
- ❑ Documentation associated with this software.

During a smartphone project, many of the above files will change, many times over. The goal of CM is to make it easy to:

- ❑ Identify a consistent set of changes. For example, a certain change made in a header file probably requires corresponding changes made in several of the other files in a configuration

- ❑ Identify the meaning of a set of changes, for example being able to tell which changes are associated with a particular defect fix

- ❑ Merge the outcomes of two or more sets of changes in source code – made by different team members, and/or by suppliers or partners

- ❑ Selectively decide whether to accept a set of changes

❑ If need be, reverse out a specific set of changes, whilst preserving other changes made at about the same time.

My core advice to smartphone project leaders, about CM, is the following:

❑ Invest in an industry-standard CM tool, for storage of source code

❑ Take the time to train all members of the team in your chosen CM tool

❑ Embrace the full possibilities of CM. Adopt the philosophy of CM, rather than just making occasional pragmatic usage of CM

❑ Place source code changes into configuration management often

❑ Place source code changes into configuration management separately (rather than as monolithic updates)

❑ Review all differences regularly – to guard against unintended changes

❑ Devise and execute a *codeline* strategy to complement your *configuration management* strategy

❑ Appreciate how configuration management and codeline management fit into various higher-level processes (discussed at the end of this chapter).

Note: despite its name, a CM tool does not store complete software configurations. It stores source code, along with information about that source code. It also provides the means for distributing versions of source code among the development team. However, you need separate tools to handle the storage and efficient distribution of the other files in a software configuration. Symbian uses a tool called "CBR" (Component Based Releases Tool) for this purpose. See Chapter 11 for more details.

7.2 Aside: learning about configuration management

When the software team at Psion started work in the late 1980s on EPOC16 (the 16-bit precursor of Symbian OS), there were only four layers in the software stack:

❑ The lowest level was the operating system itself, along with a PLIB access library (the "P" in PLIB stood for "Psion")

❏ On top of this came WSRV, the Window Server library that implemented low-level graphics (all our libraries were restricted to four-letter names, as a side-effect of a naming convention that layered over MS-DOS 8.3 filenames)

❏ Next came WIMP, our toolbox of widgets to implement a GUI: bordered windows, clickable icons, pull-down menus, and active mouse pointers

❏ Finally came the applications – such as the contacts database, a diary, a spreadsheet, and (the team where I worked) a word processor. (This over-simplifies things a bit: the applications were in turn split religiously into "engine" and "UI" parts, with the engine parts having no dependency on WSRV or WIMP. But let's leave that to one side for the moment.)

In retrospect, the way that new internal releases worked through this system was comical. (However, 15 years later, I confess that I still occasionally suffer déjà vu while studying practices on some novice smartphone projects.) New releases of PLIB were placed onto a floppy disk. The Window Server team added a matching new version of WSRV, and passed the disk on to the WIMP team. In turn, the WIMP team added their matching new version, and the disk started passing around the various apps teams. Because the floppy disk got lost several times, we resorted to tying a string to the floppy disk cover, so we could notice more easily where the disk had become held up.

Once, shortly after I installed a new set of libraries from the string floppy disk, the Word app I was writing failed to start up properly. After some investigation, I called over the gurus from the WSRV team. An hour or so later, the conclusion was that there was a bug in the copy of the WSRV libraries on my PC. I was given a patch, and development proceeded. A few days later, the disk came round again. This time, after the installation, the Word app failed again, but in a different way. Again, the WSRV gurus eventually tracked down the problem. Unfortunately, it was the same underlying problem as before: the WSRV library I had taken from the string floppy disk was *different* from the one the WSRV team had put onto it. It turned out that the hand-crafted batch file used by the WIMP team to copy the latest WIMP libraries onto the string floppy disk had the unintentional side-effect of also copying on an old version of the WSRV library, from an unused directory on the main PC in the WIMP team. In other words, it was not a software defect per se, but rather a process defect.

This was far from being an isolated incident. By the time we realized how much debugging and development time was being wasted by this kind of process defect, we collectively decided to learn about formal configuration management. We knew we needed something that was more reliable than hand-crafted batch files. After studying some of the options available from commercial suppliers, we adopted PVCS, which served us well for many years. Later (1999), for various reasons, we switched to Perforce.

7.3 Consequences of weak configuration management

The main consequences of a smartphone project making only weak use of CM (or, worse, not having any formal CM system) are as follows:

❑ Source code changes get lost. People investigating defects find that they have already fixed these defects, but the code changes to implement the fixes have somehow been discarded or over-written by subsequent changes in the software

❑ Team members cannot confidently reproduce a specified configuration. This means that defects being analyzed or debugged on one PC cannot reliably also be analyzed or debugged on other PCs. It also means that there can be little confidence that the results of testing carried out on one PC are applicable to the software configuration on another PC. In short, people cannot be sure if defects have actually been fixed

❑ Too much time needs to be spent on manual code manipulation, instead of benefiting from the automation and power of a modern CM system

❑ The team becomes unnecessarily fearful of changes. A good CM system allows changes from diverse sources to be evaluated and merged (or de-merged) in a straightforward fashion

❑ Because it is time-consuming to properly reverse out a set of changes, candidate defect fixes (as discussed in the previous chapter) tend to remain in the main code system, even when a more prudent outcome would be to cancel a proposed fix. Instead of returning to a known original state of the code, the team applies one candidate fix on top of the remnants of another. It is no wonder that the code can quickly become messy.

The larger the scale of the overall project, the more damage is caused by the above problems – hence the greater the need to adopt a good CM system.

7.4 Basic principles of configuration management

At any moment in a smartphone project, each of many software components will be in a state of flux, with one or more of the following taking place:

- New features are being added
- Defects are being fixed
- Performance is being optimized
- Design is being refactored
- Other experimental changes are being made.

In the midst of a large project, it is very unlikely that you can take the latest versions of all the components, and expect them to work together well. Instead, the development of individual components typically runs on in advance of the latest working overall configuration of the software system. For this reason, version labels need to be defined, on a regular basis, as progress markers for each component. An overall configuration of the smartphone software system is composed of a list of defined versions of each of the components. A key task of the project leaders, therefore, is to ensure that:

- Each component applies version labels to their files at suitable times
- Overall system configurations are correctly defined in terms of sets of version numbers of components
- Team members can reliably and efficiently collect, onto their PCs, all the files making up an overall configuration.

The source files are stored in a central CM database, sometimes called a "repository" or a "depot". In general, the CM database contains multiple different versions of these files. It is usual to access this database through a client–server interface. Given that several hundred PCs running CM client software may be accessing this database simultaneously, reading and writing different versions of files, the CM tool needs to be high quality. A poor choice of CM tool will lead to engineers being tempted to side-step the CM system, losing many of the benefits that CM should bring.

Basic features of a CM system include:

- Easy display of the source-code differences between any two versions of software. Among other things, this helps to highlight any unintentional changes – for example, experimental changes that

were incompletely undone, through the developer being interrupted part-way through, and then forgetting the train of thought

❑ Easy display of who has been editing a file, along with the changes
they have made. (Historically, development teams used in-source
comments to track this kind of thing. But such comments are
notoriously unreliable, and also obscure the main logic of the
source code. A CM tool calculates this kind of information automatically, and stores it as "meta-information" accompanying the
source code)

❑ Easy branching of a set of files to start a new chain of development.
The previous branch still exists, and can continue to be modified.
The new branch can also be modified independently. The CM
tool should then make it easy for selective changes made in either
branch to be applied into the other one (this process is known as
"branch integration"). A good CM tool speeds things up further,
making it easy for people working on one branch to review and
selectively apply just those changes made in another branch since
a previous branch integration point occurred

❑ Easy source code conflict resolution, for when two or more people
have been working on the same set of files at the same time; ideally,
the CM tool will show graphically all the different sets of changes,
and guide the engineer through the set of choices available.

Many of the features of the CM tool become more powerful once
the project team moves over to a working model of submitting
their changes into the CM system on a frequent basis. For example,
each individual defect fix should be submitted separately into the
CM system. The alternative is to wait longer between submissions,
resulting in a monolithic change. The problem with a model of
monolithic changes is that the CM system loses information about
which parts of the change can be acted on individually. In turn,
this makes it harder to automate actions on the individual smaller
changes – where these smaller changes could be selectively undone,
merged, or integrated to a different branch.

7.5 Codeline strategy – single projects

Choosing a CM tool is an important step, but it's only the start.
Project leaders also need to decide on a codeline strategy. A codeline
is a body of code *together with a set of policies and processes
governing how that code changes.* In a project to create a smartphone

there will usually be at least four primary codelines within the local CM database:

- One for Symbian OS
- One for the UI system (such as Series 60 or UIQ)
- One for the base port that is provided by the silicon supplier of the application processor
- One for the smartphone itself – known as the "mainline".

Here, the first three codelines are "import" codelines, holding source code from suppliers. The only changes occurring in these codelines are when the suppliers release new code.

To be clear, the same Symbian OS files will end up in two different codelines: the Symbian OS supplier codeline, and the smartphone mainline codeline. Likewise, the files provided by the other suppliers will also end up in two codelines. The reason for making two copies of the files is to be able to take advantage of the power of the CM tool. This works as follows:

- At the beginning of the project, a specific version of Symbian OS will be used as the starting point for a supplier codeline

- A copy of this code should also be included in the smartphone codeline

- Development takes place, during which time some of the project members may alter some of the Symbian OS files (in ways permitted by Symbian's standard licensing contract). These changes are placed into the smartphone codeline. Files in the import codeline are *not* touched

- After some time, a new release of Symbian OS will become available (new releases of Symbian OS are generally made once every two weeks). This new release cannot simply be copied into the smartphone codeline, since that would overwrite the changes made locally. Instead, it is placed into the import codeline

- The CM tool is then used to perform an integration of the two branches, with the result being placed into the smartphone codeline. During this process, the integration team can easily review the different sets of changes, and (in most cases) it is straightforward to decide how to proceed (see Figure 7.1).

This process continues round many more loops. Each time round the loop, the benefit of using the separate import codeline and the CM tool becomes stronger. Trying to do the same code merge manually becomes harder and harder.

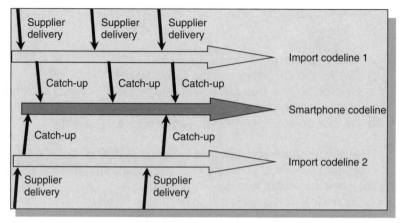

Figure 7.1   Import codelines

The basic rule for creating an import codeline is: create such a codeline if there is any prospect of the project team making independent changes to the supplier's code. If independent changes occur in supplier code outside of the CM system, there is a significant risk of these changes becoming lost.

In addition to the above codelines, a project will typically have a number of "development codelines" (sometimes called "team codelines"). These are owned by sub-teams within the project, such as multimedia, telephony, UI, and applications. As their name implies, development codelines are where the majority of actual development takes place. Code is published on a regular basis from the development codeline into the overall smartphone codeline.

That is not all. In many cases, individuals on a team will also have their own personal codelines, which they use for experimental development purposes. Once the experiment has been concluded, the resulting changes (if any) can be published from personal codelines to the local development codeline (see Figure 7.2).

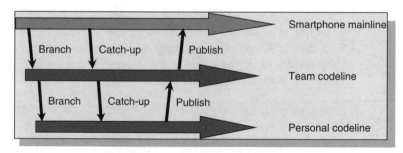

Figure 7.2   Team and personal codelines

7.6 Codeline strategy – multiple projects

To maximize its return on investment in developing smartphone technologies, a company needs to create, not just one product, but rather a whole series of products, including variant products, maintenance upgrades, and distinct new models in the same product family. Each new product reuses a great deal of the software from its predecessors. This introduces an extra twist of complexity into the codeline picture.

From this point of view, the "smartphone codeline" would arguably be better termed the "platform codeline", since it serves the needs of a platform of products rather than a single, specific, product.

The overall team then needs, from time to time, to create new codelines from the platform codeline. These are sometimes known as "release codelines", since they are the vehicles for the actual release of products. There will be one release codeline for each significantly different product created from the shared underlying software system. (Another common name for a release codeline is a "steady-state codeline", since the amount of change in such a codeline is expected to be reduced.) The release codelines evolve towards a reasonably fixed product specification, whereas the platform codeline continues to evolve to meet later product requirements.

For example, imagine that a company starts by producing product A, but it is also planning to release product B six months later, with significant additional features. In view of the long time period involved in development, the development of code for B will start before product A is released. To complicate things further, it is likely that, shortly after the initial release of A, one or more maintenance releases (A2, A3, say) will be needed, to fix defects reported by the first tranche of users. The code for A2 will be based very heavily on that in A, and will have very few (if any) of the changes that are in the process of being developed for B.

In codeline terms, one way this could be implemented is as follows:

❏ There is a project codeline entirely dedicated to the creation of product A

❏ When the time comes to start developing product B, a new codeline is formed for that product, branching from the first

❏ On a regular basis thereafter, catch-up integrations take place, in which code changes from the A codeline are integrated into the B codeline

❏ After A is released, its codeline continues to exist, and is used for A2, then A3, etc.

However, a better approach is as follows:

❑ The first codeline is initially dedicated to the creation of product A

❑ When the time of the release of product A grows close, a release branch is created, from the initial branch, and the development of product A then takes place in the release branch, followed in due course by the development of maintenance release A2

❑ The main codeline is used from this time on for the larger development changes needed to create product B

❑ As in the previous model, catch-up integrations take place on a regular basis

❑ In due course, a release branch is created for B as well, with ongoing platform development targeted at yet further products continuing in the main codeline.

In principle, there is little to differentiate these two approaches. However, some detailed aspects of the way the CM tool works may impose a preference. For complex sets of projects, the second approach has the advantage that the status (and hence the policy) of a codeline remains the same throughout its lifetime: it is either a "main" codeline (where significant development takes place) or a "release" codeline (with a greater degree of stability, and hence, tighter change control). This is the approach I recommend.

Finally, consider the case when a company is developing two products in parallel, sharing a lot of the same code. For example, one product may be a smartphone for the enterprise market, and the other might be targeted more at consumers. Or one might be 2.5G whilst the other is 3G. In such a case, the software that is shared between the two projects should be placed into a common codeline. Then individual branches are formed, to cater for the needs of the individual products.

Evidently, in general there can be more than one possible approach to codelines. The key point, however, is that project leaders need to devote time to planning their use of codelines, and then publishing the agreed policy (this usually involves a series of codeline diagrams), so that everyone in the project has a shared understanding of the decisions. You'll probably find that different parts of your overall organization have conflicting desires as regards codeline policies. Consider appointing an overall "CM authority" in your organization, to identify and handle these conflicting desires.

7.7 Beyond codeline strategy

The management of complex changing software configurations involves five levels of process:

❏ Adoption and use of a CM tool for storing and distributing source code
❏ Adoption and use of a codeline strategy
❏ Adoption and use of an integration management strategy
❏ Adoption and use of an interface management strategy
❏ Adoption and use of a component distribution strategy, for incrementally distributing binaries throughout an extended team.

The CM tool and the codeline strategy provide the basis for coping with complex changing systems. They make it possible to review and track individual changes in the midst of much larger system changes. For example, if someone decides to copy a fix from one product development to another, the CM tool will make it clear what parts of which files need to change (and can automate the required changes). However, an integration management strategy is required to coordinate the timing and approval of individual changes ranging across wide areas of software. This is the subject of the following chapter. Following on from that, I will look at a special subdiscipline of integration management known as interface management: the more precise study of changes which involve interfaces between different areas of software.

8
Managing integration

8.1 Integration vs. creation

Here is one model for developing software. According to this model, the most difficult part of the overall task is creating new software. That is where the best developers should be assigned. Less competent developers can be assigned to less critical tasks, such as build, integration, and test.

I mention this model in order to say that it is completely inappropriate for most smartphone development projects. If followed, it will result in project failure. Some pieces of software that are individually enchanting may be created in the process, but these pieces will not reach the market.

Instead, it is a cardinal principle of successful smartphone development that you assign some of the most experienced and skilled engineers to the tasks of build, integration, and test. These tasks cannot be thought of as somehow secondary, deserving only the ''B team''. You must think of these tasks as having primary importance, deserving staffing from the ''A team''.

Many developers prefer doing ''green field'' development of brand new pieces of software, to working with existing software that has been developed by other people. This is a natural psychological tendency. However, project leaders need to fight this tendency. The vast bulk of software used by any given smartphone project has already been written, by people in other teams or in other companies. You cannot seriously contemplate rewriting anything more than a small fraction of this software. Do not underestimate the extent of the effort that has already been expended. Instead, you need to take the time to figure out how to interface with this existing software, in order to take advantage of its power. In other words, you have to invest lots of energy in *integration*, rather than in *creation*.

The greater the amount of software in the product, the larger is the requirement for key people who understand and safeguard the entire system. The integration team are the people who perform this role.

Note also that "integration" is not the same as "build". Build is concerned with getting the software to compile and link. But just because something compiles, it doesn't mean that it works. Integration is concerned with getting things to work.

8.2 Mainlines and development codelines

Recall the basic principles of mainlines and development codelines:

❑ Development codelines are created from time to time from the project mainline, for use by groups of developers

❑ Code produced in a development codeline needs to find its way back into the mainline in due course, if it is to reach the market; products are released from the project mainline, not from development branches

❑ Once the development in a development codeline is stable, and once suitable tests have taken place (as discussed later in this chapter), the outcome is published back to the project mainline

❑ At this time, the development mainline is closed down, and a new one is created, seeded from the latest mainline, and the cycle continues.

Note in particular:

❑ At any given time, there are multiple different development codelines in existence, being used by different teams
❑ The mainline serves the needs of the whole project, not just the needs of individual teams.

The mainline is owned by the integration team. In a healthy project, the integration team are receiving submissions from development teams almost every day of the week (depending on the scale of the project). This means that the mainline goes through a great deal of flux, as the various submissions are reviewed, optimized, and (in some cases) rejected. However, on a regular basis, the mainline needs to reach a state of suitable quality to be adopted by the rest of the team. These points are known as "baseline" releases. In other words, the mainline periodically issues baseline releases, with steadily increasing quality level.

The reason for teams to have their own development codelines is to provide them with a stable environment while they are making their own changes. It is too disruptive to keep on having to adjust, day-by-day, to every change made in the mainline. However, it is an important rule that development codelines should, as far as possible, adopt the changes made in every *baseline* release of the mainline. This prevents the development codelines from drifting too far away from the contents of the mainline – something that would complicate the subsequent integration back into the mainline. Therefore, throughout the lifetime of any development codeline, catch-up integrations should be occurring on a regular basis, to propagate the changes from the latest project baseline into the development codelines.

In most cases, development branches should perform a catch-up with each baseline release, whenever it becomes available (see Figure 8.1). On occasion, if a development branch is in a great state of flux, the catch-up with a baseline can be temporarily delayed. However, the longer this delay, the harder the eventual integration becomes.

There is an underlying "integration contract" here: development teams can commit to regularly updating to the latest baselines provided the integration team in turn commits to ensuring:

❑ That baselines don't regress in quality
❑ That interface changes in baselines (as discussed in the next chapter) are carefully communicated in advance.

The final stage of this underlying contract is that the quality of the baselines in turn depends upon the quality of the submissions made by the development teams into the mainline.

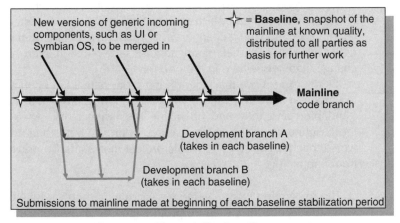

Figure 8.1   The mainline/baseline concept

When the conditions of this underlying contract are fulfilled, there is a powerful build rhythm in the project: good quality baselines make it easier for the development teams to produce good quality submissions, which in turn make it easier for the integration team to produce the next good quality baselines.

8.3 Iterative development

Integration proceeds as a series of iterations, with each iteration resulting in a baseline release.

It is important for project leaders to plan:

❑ The overall sequence of baselines: what changes are expected to be made in each baseline
❑ The process that applies *in between* any two baseline releases.

The first part covers the macro-evolution of the project, and is commonly called the "integration schedule". The second part covers the micro-steps that need to be taken, day-by-day (and even hour-by-hour) in order to keep to the overall integration schedule.

In both cases, it is important for the project team not to attempt too much at any one step. In both cases, the work should be spread throughout the available time.

To be successful in their roles, the integration team need to withstand some powerful pressures. These pressures are to try to do more, in a short time, than is practical. Naturally, project stakeholders want as much functionality to be present in the product, as early as possible. At any time, this leads to pressure for a great number of changes to be accepted into the next baseline. However, the more changes that are submitted, the greater the likelihood of the integration failing. Each individual change, whilst internally consistent in its own right, has the potential of an adverse side-reaction with another change made elsewhere in the system.

It's my experience that smartphone projects that fail often attempt too much in a given iteration. They want to move fast – that's understandable – and they end up taking too large a risk. As a result, the baseline regresses: some features improve, but others turn out worse than previously. The whole project then stalls. To prevent this from happening:

❑ The integration team need to have strong authority – fully backed by the leaders of the entire project (and by their senior management)

❑ If the integration team believes that certain submissions are too risky, at a given time, these submissions need to be rejected, even if the submissions receive powerful backing from project stakeholders.

Once the build rhythm of a project breaks, it can be hard to restart it. Development teams resist adopting the latest baseline, since it introduces new problems. That means the eventual integration of their code into the mainline at a later date becomes harder to carry out. That, in turn, delays the release of the next baseline, or (even worse) causes corners to be cut in releasing the next baseline. Either way, the next baseline turns out to be as unpopular as the previous one (refer to Figure 8.2). So once the build rhythm breaks, it needs to be fixed as soon as possible, to prevent the usual virtuous cycle of quality improvement becoming a vicious cycle of quality degradation.

To maintain a healthy build rhythm, the following principles should be followed:

❑ Integrate little and often (which is similar to the general software maxim, "iterate little and often")

❑ Publish the integration schedule in advance, and ensure that development teams follow it

❑ Define and follow effective "gate-keeping" principles, to prevent bad changes from being accepted into the mainline

❑ Define and follow effective "integration test" processes, as a further check of the goodness of a baseline, before it is released

❑ Ensure that the integration team has sufficient technical skills to quickly investigate and resolve problems that arise during submissions

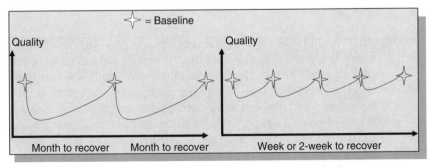

Figure 8.2   Frequent integrations keep quality higher

❑ Empower the integration team to have the absolute authority to reject submissions, regardless of the degree of influence possessed by the sponsors of these submissions

❑ If development teams persistently make bad submissions, deal with this failure at a management level.

8.4 Gate-keeping and integration tests

Before the integration team accepts a development team submission into the mainline, they need to check for evidence that:

❑ The change has been authorized and approved by the relevant team leader

❑ The change has been code-reviewed by a peer engineer: *all* code and changes should be peer-reviewed by at least one person other than the author

❑ The submission has been tested against the latest baseline release (not just against a special set-up on some developer's PC)

❑ Consideration has been given to dependencies (that is, what will be affected by this change)

❑ Consideration has been given to interface breaks (as covered in the following chapter), and that formal approval has been received for any changes.

If these conditions are all met, the code can be integrated into the mainline and included in the next build (which typically happens every working day). However, this does not yet mean that the code will be present in the next baseline. That depends on the results of further tests:

❑ After each build of the mainline, a so-called set of "smoke tests" is carried out, covering the very basic functionality of the phone – does it start, can it make and receive calls and text messages, can entries be saved into the contacts list, can photographs be taken, etc. (the name is derived from similar test systems for electronics systems, in which the tester checks for smoke, sparks, or other dramatic signs of system failure when power is applied)

❏ Towards the end of the integration cycle, a fuller set of tests is carried out, sometimes called the BAT ("Basic Acceptance Tests").

In either case, if tests fail, and investigation highlights problems with the code submitted by a development team, there is an option for the integration team to reverse out that set of changes:

❏ If the build fails its smoke test, it cannot be released, in any circumstances

❏ The BAT score for a baseline must be at least as good (overall) as the BAT score of the previous baseline: quality must improve continuously.

There is an argument to perform BAT on every daily build of the mainline. However, you have to weigh up the costs. Whereas a smoke test typically lasts about an hour, the BAT can last about half a day, and involves several people.

8.5 Dealing with build or test failures

To recap: just because a development submission passes the gate-keeper review, does not mean it will necessarily be included in the next baseline release. It could still be rejected, through causing build problems or test failures.

On the other hand, the fact that a submission causes a build problem or a test failure does not mean that it will necessarily be rejected. There may still be a chance for it to be fixed in time for the baseline release. But this requires agility, skill, and flexibility:

❏ It requires technical skill on the part of the integration team, to quickly diagnose the likely area of the problem

❏ It requires commitment from the development team personnel, to drop whatever else they are doing, to attend the needs of the integration team (at critical stages of the project, this may require team members to come back into office outside normal working hours)

❏ It requires nimble thinking on the part of all concerned.

If all this is done, it can avoid delaying the appearance of the functionality in question in the next baseline.

However, development teams cannot be allowed to fall into any kind of habit of making bad submissions. Every time a submission causes the mainline build to break, or causes a regression in tests, the following should occur:

❑ The development team involved need to appreciate the disruption caused to the project; they should desire not to repeat this kind of error

❑ The overall team should reflect on whether improved tests or processes would have detected this problem more quickly; if this is true, consider making these changes to the system

❑ Either way, consider giving wider publicity within the team to what went wrong, so that everyone can learn from it.

One other thing that is required is the discipline to resist "quick fixes" that store up more problems for later. This is a hard judgment call to make. The potential problem is that a quick fix, introduced under time pressure to allow a build to pass, will become enshrined in the software system, and will be difficult to alter later. In such cases, it is probably better to reject the submission, until such time as a proper fix can be put in place.

8.6 The weekly integration cycle

Yet another thing that allows the overall team some freedom to fix problems with submissions is if the development teams submit sufficiently early during the integration cycle. This brings us to the topic of the weekly integration cycle.

Depending on project scale, and the maturity of the overall team, the integration team may release baselines about once a week, or once every fortnight. In between releases, they are preparing for the next release. This involves:

❑ Integrating any releases made by suppliers, for example a new release of Symbian OS, or a release of the UI system (these releases are typically made available about once every fortnight)

❑ Selectively reviewing and accepting submissions from development teams

❑ Running the smoke test, usually once every working day

❑ Running the BAT, shortly ahead of the intended release

❑ Taking the time to address problems noticed.

Clearly, if submissions all happen towards the end of the weekly integration cycle the effectiveness of the integration team is severely constrained. They have too much to do at the end of the cycle.

For this reason, software leaders need to encourage teams to spread their submissions throughout the integration cycle. If teams persist in making submissions right at the end of the integration cycle, this should be raised at a management level.

One way to spread out submissions is for each team to make multiple submissions, throughout the week. This fits with the principle discussed in the previous chapter, of avoiding making monolithic changes into the CM tool. It's far better for teams to submit their changes to the integration team as soon as they are ready, split into separate submissions for each individual change (for example, one submission for each independent defect fix).

8.7 Integration discipline

To summarize, integration requires special skills and special discipline:

❑ To avoid regression of already working functionality

❑ To cope with new releases of incoming software (particularly when it has been modified locally)

❑ To change working code as little as possible – over-ruling people's temptation to tinker

❑ To diagnose and solve complex interaction problems

❑ To insist on changing the *right* part of a complex software system, not (always) the *easiest* part

❑ To be able to understand exactly what has changed between two versions of code

❑ To insist on strong usage of configuration management

❑ To ensure that all members of the distributed team are working on the same software configuration, as available in the latest baseline release.

Software leaders should cultivate a special attitude towards the baseline. It must always increase in stability and quality, and never fall back:

- ❏ From as early as possible in the project, the baseline should be at "always ready to ship" quality, even if functionally incomplete

- ❏ Do not tolerate poor quality software in the baseline to be fixed later – it's always harder to fix later

- ❏ Don't wait to the end of the project to fix stability or crash problems – it will be more rushed then, and a more complex system to debug

- ❏ Don't accept a culture where engineers ignore problems because they are not "theirs" – record all defects noticed, and make sure that all problems are assigned an owner.

In this way, software leaders drive up the quality level of the software, from baseline to baseline.

9
Managing interfaces

9.1 Knowing when components belong together

A surprising amount of time can be wasted on a smartphone project on account of different components in the overall software mix unexpectedly being inconsistent with each other. The art of preventing these inconsistencies is known as "interface management". Good interface management is a core skill of a successful smartphone development team.

Here's a typical experience. A product team is testing some functionality, and it doesn't work. Initial debugging finds no obvious problems, so more time is required. Eventually (perhaps after several days), the problem is traced to some far-away piece of code – often a place outside the direct experience of the project team. The problem is that far-away piece of code component C is calling far-away piece of code component D, but D misinterprets the call, with chaotic results.

For example, component C may think it is calling function 42 in component D, that takes three parameters, but function 42 in component D actually needs four parameters. So D processes a function call with a random fourth parameter. Or, component C may think that the first parameter to the function call has a particular data field at offset 20 (say) inside itself, but component D thinks that this data field is at offset 24 inside the parameter. So it accesses the wrong data. In both examples, C and D are inconsistent. Perhaps C has been built using version 126 of a shared header file, whereas D has been built using version 127 of that header file. Whatever, the interface provided by D has changed, but the version of C used hasn't changed to match. There's been a failure of interface management.

Other changes in interface are more subtle in meaning (but can have equally dramatic effects). For example, the parameters to a function call might stay the same, but the interpretation of possible values of some of the parameters might change. Or there may be a change in the meaning of one of the possible values returned from the function. (Sometimes these changes are called *semantic* breaks in compatibility, as compared to the earlier cases, which are *syntactic* breaks in compatibility.)

As you can imagine, this topic involves lots of technical details, concerning C++ virtual functions, function signatures, dynamic vs. static linking, class layout, DLL layout, the use of. DEF files to freeze interfaces, the mechanics of unfreezing and refreezing, and so on. But in this book, I want to concentrate, instead, upon the *managerial* aspects of changes in interface:

- The importance of educating all team members about interface management
- The importance of having processes governing changes in interface
- The importance of clear communications about any changes in interface
- The value of acquiring and using tools to help track changes in interface
- The importance of planning ahead to try to minimize future interface changes.

9.2 Limits of rebuilding source code

A smartphone product potentially contains (or interfaces with) hundreds of different software components, obtained from numerous different suppliers. In many cases, these components are supplied only in *binary* format, meaning they are ready to include straightaway into a smartphone product; the alternative to binary format is *source* format, which requires to be built (compiled and linked) into binary format before being placed onto a smartphone.

Because only a portion of the product is available in source code format, this rules out one idea for avoiding compatibility problems, which would be to rebuild every component every time a version of the product is prepared. In fact, there are two *more* reasons why "rebuild everything" is not a viable solution:

- In some cases, your product has to interface with smartphones that have already been released into the marketplace; there's no question of rebuilding the contents of the ROMs of these phones

before your application runs on them; you have to deal with these
phones as you find them

❑ In some cases, old source code will fail to build when compiled
against new header files; this is called a break of SC ("Source Compatibility") – as opposed to a break in BC ("Binary Compatibility")
when two components are incompatible at the binary level.

Even when source code *is* available, there is a powerful pragmatic argument to avoid unnecessary rebuilding of the entire source
tree. This argument is that it takes time – many hours – to rebuild
every component. A developer who is in the midst of an extended
test–debug–fix–compile–test cycle does not want to hold up the
cycle for several hours each time around the loop. The developer
needs to be able to reason as follows: "I've only changed such-and-
such in these modules of code; this doesn't alter any interfaces; so
nothing else needs rebuilding". (Or occasionally, and more risky,
"I've only altered these interfaces, which are only used by a fixed
number of components, so only the following modules need rebuilding".) That reasoning works, so long as the developer has a good
understanding of interfaces.

In practice, it's vital to interleave *partial* builds with *total* builds:

❑ A partial build is where developers, to save time, only rebuild the
components that they believe are liable to change
❑ A total build is where developers rebuild all the software they have.

The outputs of the two types of build should be compared, on a
regular basis. Symbian supplies tools such as "Evalid" to assist with
this: Evalid understands the format of Symbian OS binary files, and
knows to disregard changes that are irrelevant from the point of
view of software execution (aspects such as embedded date–time
stamps). Any remaining difference highlighted by the tool is a reason
for developers:

❑ To identify the interface linkage responsible for these unexpected
differences
❑ To increase their understanding of interface management as
a whole
❑ To modify their work practices (for example, changing the way
they carry out partial rebuilds).

9.3 Forms of compatibility

I've already mentioned BC and SC:

❏ BC, binary compatibility, is where the APIs of two platform versions are such that executable code built on one version will successfully run on the other without being rebuilt

❏ SC, source compatibility, is where the APIs of two platform versions are such that source code which compiles on one version will successfully compile on the other without modification.

Note that neither BC nor SC implies the other.

There are many variants and sub-cases. For example, there is *backwards* BC and *forwards* BC:

❏ Backwards compatibility is when code (for example, an application) written against a previous version of the platform works on current versions of the platform without modification; the platform has maintained backwards compatibility with older APIs as it evolves

❏ Forwards compatibility is when code written against the current platform works on previous versions of the platform (for example, on older smartphones) without modification; the relevant APIs in the older platform have turned out to be forwards compatible with future changes.

An example of backwards compatibility is when an application built with the SDK for Symbian OS v6.1 runs fine on smartphones built with Symbian OS v8.0a. An example of forwards compatibility is when an application built with the SDK for Symbian OS v8.0a runs fine on smartphones built with Symbian OS v6.1.

Developers also need to bear in mind the concept of "data compatibility", in which the data file formats of two versions are such that a data file created on one version can be read on the other.

The concept of "bug compatibility" is particularly interesting. Some components may be relying (knowingly or unknowingly) on bugs which exist in a platform (where we use the word "bug" because the behavior fails to match the explicit specification). Fixing a bug in the platform can therefore have the consequence of breaking functionality in other components.

Here are some other, less obvious, ways in which "improvements" to the platform can have undesirable side-effects:

❑ Extra functionality can cause increases in the size of a component, so that the software no longer fits within its target ROM size

❑ Extra functionality can put increased demands on memory usage, so that the software no longer conforms to its target RAM usage

❑ Improved functionality can alter the timing of various operations, invalidating any hard-wired assumptions in other code about the length of time required (any such assumptions are, of course, suspect software engineering, but they can be present in commercially important applications)

❑ Increasing security checks in a function (to guard against invalid input) can break calling code that expects greater tolerance.

9.4 The compatibility virtuous cycle

In an environment where new releases of smartphone software maintain compatibility:

❑ End-users can purchase add-on applications and services for their smartphone of choice

❑ Later, they can purchase upgrades to some of these applications, without losing any data or settings entered onto their smartphone with the previous versions

❑ Independently, they can upgrade their smartphone (perhaps choosing one from a different manufacturer), and the applications and services they have bought will still work, transferred onto the new phone

❑ Later again, they can purchase yet more applications, confident in the knowledge that they will run on both the new phone and the old phone (which by this time may be owned by another family member)

❑ In this way, both applications and smartphones have greater longevity – and hence greater value (since purchasers don't need to worry about having to assemble their portfolio from scratch again just a short time after making their previous purchase)

❑ Customer satisfaction fuels developer satisfaction, and vice versa.

The same principle applies, in a smaller (though more hectic) way, during the development lifecycle of a single smartphone product. Provided compatibility is maintained, it is easy to accept upgrades to all the different components in the product during the development phase. Where compatibility applies, it avoids long build chains, where component C has to be released before component D. It allows faster turnaround of bug fixes via patches. But if a supplier acquires a reputation for bad interface management, the project leader will be justified in rejecting functional upgrades from that supplier. Better in that case (reasons the project leader) to stick with the old functionality, than to accept new features which might have the side-effect of destabilizing the overall project.

Data compatibility can be another big issue during a project. If you get this wrong, you could end up wasting a lot of time. In the integration and productization phase, it's common for old configuration files or data files to exist on smartphones which are flashed with new baselines of the software. Do not rely on the phone storage being clean each time the software is upgraded. Friendly users like to keep their data. For example, they may restore their previous files onto a new smartphone setup from an old backup. It is therefore important that your software is robust and can run on a "dirty" device. Put some version information into your data files and configuration files, and change the version every time the file format changes. Otherwise, you risk encountering puzzling behavior during testing, occurring on only a small number of smartphones – namely those that happen to have old data on them.

9.5 System compatibility board

So far in this chapter, I've been emphasizing the potential drawbacks to changes in software. But of course, there are many positive aspects to changes – not least that the later versions can improve their performance, remove defects, and enable functionality being demanded by end-users. And there can be many positive aspects to *interface* changes too:

- ❑ A new interface can allow significantly greater efficiency
- ❑ A new interface can support greater functionality
- ❑ A new interface can remove problems in an old interface (for example, a security weakness or a maintenance nightmare)
- ❑ A new data format can support new kinds of information saved to file, or faster file searching, etc.

So there can be no cast iron prohibition on interface changes. Instead, there has to be a process for:

❑ Noticing when interface changes are about to be made (or are proposed to be made)

❑ Deciding whether or not the benefits of these changes outweigh their drawbacks

❑ If it is decided to go ahead with them, making sure that all stakeholders receive good warning of the changes, as well as good advice about how to cope with them.

In summary, the two keywords are *control* and *communicate*:

❑ Make sure that interface changes are controlled – only happening after careful review and decision

❑ Make sure that any interface changes are clearly communicated to the people who might otherwise waste a lot of their development time, as a result of not knowing about these changes.

Any large smartphone project team should consider having something akin to the "SCB" (System Compatibility Board) that meets regularly within Symbian, which formally reviews the "BRs" (Break Requests) that have been submitted to it. Part of the mission of the SCB is to ensure that all engineers at Symbian "think about compatibility issues with every line of code written – just as we think about avoiding defects with every line of code written". The SCB also seeks to suggest alternative ways in which engineers can meet the requirements for which they thought they needed to break compatibility. In difficult cases, the SCB will request that a detailed impact analysis is carried out, and may also double-check with representatives of customers for their opinion about the BR.

The SCB at Symbian also keeps statistics of "unintended breaks" – changes in interface that reached customers without advance warning. Thankfully, these are relatively few these days. However, each such occurrence is followed by its own investigation, to see what lessons can be learned.

9.6 Responsibilities with regard to compatibility

You may get the idea that responsibilities with regard to compatibility mainly rest with platform providers (such as Symbian, or a UI system provider). Platform providers deliver large numbers of APIs, and therefore have the greatest responsibility for care regarding interface breaks.

However, other companies also need to exercise care:

❏ Teams who modify code delivered by platform providers need to be aware that they might be interfering with the intended flow of interface management. For example, if you modify component D to insert some additional debugging code, and then stick with your own version of D when a new biweekly platform release is adopted, you may eventually find that component C in the platform code is incompatible with your version of component D

❏ Teams who receive biweekly platform releases need to take care to read the accompanying release notes, paying particular attention to the section on interface breaks. This information needs to be spread throughout the team, and to all affected sub-teams

❏ A team that starts off by developing the software for one smartphone may evolve into a team that is delivering shared libraries to be used by *several* smartphone projects. In other words, they have become a platform provider in their own right, in which case they need to elevate their consideration of interface management

❏ Any team that delivers add-on software (such as an application, or some enabling middleware) for use on multiple smartphones needs to pay special attention to the variations in interfaces on these different phones

❏ Any team that delivers add-on software should only use APIs with "Published All" access type and "Released" status (see the following section for more details).

In all cases, a team is advised to carry out regular explicit tests of binary compatibility. In a project to create an actual smartphone, this can be done by running a representative suite of third-party applications (for example, a set of applications that have passed the Symbian Signed accreditation) on that smartphone, and checking that they all behave as intended. Failures generally indicate that the smartphone code has inadvertently broken one or more of the interfaces used by a third-party application. That then raises the question of whether the third-party application was *entitled* to use that particular interface – which in turn brings us to the topic that not all interfaces are equal.

9.7 Interface access and interface status

In order to provide greater flexibility and understanding of interface management, each API in Symbian OS has both an "interface access type" and an "interface status".

The interface access type is one of the following:

❏ *Published All* – means that this is a public interface of Symbian OS, potentially with many clients

❏ *Published Partner* – this interface is exposed to a smaller set of partners (involved in smartphone creation), but is not included on public SDKs as used for the creation of add-on software

❏ *Published Internal* – this interface is only for use by components within Symbian OS (in fact there are several variants of Internal, but the differences are not relevant to the present discussion).

The interface status is one of the following:

❏ *Prototype* – the interface is experimental for the time being. It may be used in development kits and tools, and in prototype phones for development and evaluation purposes, but not in phones released to end-users

❏ *Interim* – the interface is not stabilized yet. It will be either Released or Removed shortly

❏ *Released* – the interface has been stabilized and released. It is available for use in real phones intended for release to end-users, and in development kits and tools which support such phones

❏ *Deprecated* – the interface is deprecated and is available for backward compatibility reasons only. The interface may be withdrawn in the future

❏ *Removed* – the interface is no longer supported

❏ *Unspecified* – the interface is not to be used.

As you can imagine, problems arise when software uses APIs in violation of the above rules. So long as third-party applications stick to the APIs published in SDKs, everything works well. However, when applications start relying on information *not* in SDKs (and which is not intended to be in SDKs), it means that, although these applications will probably run fine on a small number of phones, they will fail on others. For example, an application may stop working when a phone manufacturer makes a silent maintenance release (namely, when the software moves to a later version, but where no publicity is given to this occurrence).

Certification programs for add-on applications, such as Symbian Signed, seek to endorse only those applications which stick to the rules regarding the APIs they can use. However, API classification is an imperfect science and, from time to time, we find applications that are unintentionally relying on information that is not meant to be part of any public SDK. When such cases arise, the governing board for Symbian Signed takes a pragmatic decision on whether to:

❑ Retrospectively change the classification of an API
❑ Request the application to use a different programming method
❑ Accept the incompatibility, and to store this information about the applications concerned.

The BC testing for any new smartphone typically highlights a small number of new cases of complications in the use of APIs by third-party applications. Clearly, it's better to discover these complications some time ahead of the launch of the smartphone, to allow more time to decide how to respond.

9.8 Versioning

Versioning is an important technique that allows the same piece of software to work well with more than one interface. As such, versioning provides the means for software to have greater longevity, and to run on a wider number of platforms and phones.

The basic idea is to carry out run-time tests on the capabilities supported by the platform. For example:

❑ An application can check which type of compression software is supported in a given communication channel, and dynamically choose the type to use

❑ Software that reads data from a file can check which of several possible file formats is used in that file; it carries the code to interpret all different file formats.

Other checks can be carried out at install-time, or at download-time. For example:

❑ The installation procedure can check to see if the ROM contains a particular DLL. If not, the installation can download this onto the phone, so that the application can use it

❑ The installation procedure can check which UI system is used on the phone, and can download the appropriate UI layer of the application (such as UIQ or Series 60).

The advantage of a check at installation time is that it avoids the need for the ROM to contain unused code.

All the above tests rely on it being possible to detect the actual capabilities of the environment. In principle, there should be an official way to do this. In case there is no official API to report the required information about capabilities, we end up back in the same situation we started from: we may be able to use an *unofficial* method to determine the capabilities of the environment, but this method is liable not to work in future settings. So we need to proceed carefully.

One final extension of the concept of versioning is of interest to providers of add-on software. The idea is that, when a user purchases an application, they are actually purchasing, not the binary contents of the application itself, but the right to use the application on a range of different smartphones, throughout the life of the application. Provided the user retains some kind of token of proof of purchase, they should be able to download, onto a different phone, a new version of the application (that is, with the same functionality, but suited to work on the new phone). This relies on a mechanism to disable the use of the application on the original phone (for example, the application may need to connect OTA to a server every so often).

Various different commercial models are possible, including:

❑ Improved support for transferring relevant data and settings from one phone to the other

❑ Possible additional charges to allow wider usage (or to support additional features that have become available since the initial purchase).

9.9 Future-proofing interfaces

Software leaders should bear in mind the requirement for their software to evolve in the future. With the progress of time, their software will need to provide additional features. This often leads software architects to want to revise the interfaces of their classes. As we know, these changes can introduce all sorts of problems. However, with some careful forethought, the software architecture can accommodate certain kinds of expansion with minimal impact on compatibility (and without the need for clients to make specific checks on versions).

Here is an outline of some of the ideas involved:

❑ Follow standard principles of data hiding, encapsulation, and abstraction

❏ Consider placing "spare" data members and "reserved" virtual functions into class definitions, for future usage

❏ Follow suitable design patterns with names (given by the OO community) such as Façade, Adaptor, Handle/Body, and Extension.

The owner of an API set can extend that set by adding new functions at the end of the API set: these will be assigned new ordinal numbers, that don't correspond to any existing functions. But if you are *not* the owner of an API set, things become trickier. If you want to extend an API set that is provided by another company, you will store up future trouble if you add new functions at the end – since the provider of that API set may do the same thing in a future release (and there will be a clash in the ordinal numbers assigned to the various new functions).

In such a case, you should consider instead using a separate "extension DLL", where the new APIs are defined, in such a way that they in turn call through to a modified version of the platform DLL, using a private mechanism not included in the main (published) table of functions. If the platform provider subsequently adds new functions at the end of the original set, you need to reapply your own additions, and then rebuild both the resulting DLL and your extension DLL, so that the extension still calls the same functions as before (but they now have different ordinals). The key point is that the interface into the extension API remains unchanged, so the resulting system is compatible *both* with apps written to your own extensions, and with apps written to the extensions from the platform provider.

We see here an example of a general principle. With ingenuity, it is possible for you to make all kinds of modification in code that is provided by suppliers. However, in all such cases, modifying the original intent of the code should be a last resort. Instead, I strongly advise you to discuss your requirements with the owner of the platform code. Between the two of you, you may well find a better solution (such as an "extension DLL"). You may also avoid making the mistake of doing something that is very clever in the short term, but very constrictive in the medium and long term. Given that Symbian OS is going to be around for many generations of smartphones, you definitely want to avoid constrictive choices.

10
Managing testing

10.1 Beyond complete testing

For small enough projects, it's possible to make do without structured testing. An informal set of tests is sufficient to provide a good indication of whether the software meets its intended requirements.

For larger projects, such as feature phones, testing becomes much more formal. There are a large number of test cases, called "system tests", covering the full set of functionality of the phone. The phone can be exhaustively tested for defects. Many companies follow the rule that a feature phone cannot be released to the market, if even one of the system tests fails. The feature has to be fixed before the phone is released.

However, smartphone projects are yet larger again, with an open-ended functionality set. This means that a new approach to testing is needed. You can't adequately test a smartphone by just repeating the same methods used to test a feature phone. It's another case when simply "working harder" is insufficient. Any idea of "complete testing" isn't feasible for a smartphone project:

❑ There is an unbounded number of different combinations of applications that can be running at the same time (including add-on third-party applications that have not yet been written!)

❑ Each different combination of applications, in principle, throws up new potential interaction issues.

Not only is "complete testing" infeasible, trying to execute it is an inefficient (wasteful) policy:

❑ Many of the potential tests are essentially duplicates of each other

❑ In many cases, repeating a large batch of tests won't provide any additional real information, beyond what can be inferred from just a small number of these tests.

So what's needed is a testing system that:

❑ Focuses on the *quality* of test cases rather than their *quantity*

❑ Combines a pre-configured set of tests with the involvement of a large set of representative "real users" (often called "friendly users") who try out whatever comes to their minds

❑ Keeps reviewing the outcomes of tests, to check which tests are adding the greatest value

❑ Keeps evolving the formal set of tests, in the light of experience and feedback.

What's also needed is a high-caliber software leader who is assigned overall responsibility for testing.

To be clear, testing should not be conceived as being in any sense a secondary activity, with lower skills requirements. Any software leader who is assigned responsibility for testing should regard this as a great career opportunity, rather than a second-rate assignment. It's a role that requires deep thoughtfulness, agile execution, and far-sighted imagination, as well as dogged thoroughness.

10.2 Testing in context

The purpose of testing is to anticipate, as efficiently as possible, the full range of operations which end-users will carry out on a smartphone product, and to verify that the outcomes are broadly in line with reasonable expectations.

Note the following aspects of this definition:

❑ *". . . as efficiently as possible"* – so that the testing resources are applied in the most effective way, avoiding unnecessary repetitions

❑ *". . . full range of operations"* – there's no point in exhaustively showing that the smartphone works well in only a subset of typical use-cases, when it habitually fails in other common situations

❑ *". . . broadly in line"* – it's not practical to ensure that the outcomes are *completely* in line with expectations; you have to make a judgment call on which defects to fix, and which to live with

❑ *". . . reasonable expectations"* – this presupposes the question of what users are likely to expect; bearing in mind that user expectations can change quickly (in light of their own experience, and in light of market developments and competitive new products). This is a *particularly* hard judgment call to make.

So testing is both a science and an art.

It's also something that can be *extremely* expensive. By some estimates, around 60% of the cost of developing an advanced smartphone product is used up in the effort to test the software in that product. Testing, therefore, is an activity with huge potential for both gains and losses:

❑ Gains, if smarter ways can be found to test the overall system
❑ Losses, if mistakes in the testing process allow critical defects to impact product sales.

10.3 Functional tests

The documented set of "how the smartphone is expected to behave" is a vital piece of groupware for the project. This is commonly called the "functional test specification" (with the word "specification" often being shortened to "spec"): the description of the functionality that is built into the phone, and the set of test cases that will demonstrate if the functionality works. It's a sizable document, containing the accumulated output of several scores of person-years of writing effort. It consists of material from multiple sources:

❑ Parts of the test specification come from Symbian – covering the functionality of Symbian OS (for example, the test specs of the low-level E32 and F32 components)

❑ A large part of the test specification comes from the UI system provider, and covers the applications that are delivered along with the UI system

❑ Other third-party applications that are included in the product should also have their own test specifications, provided by the third parties

❑ New applications developed within the project itself also need their test specifications

❑ All of the above is embedded into a wider set of "test lore" (as described in Chapter 6).

The functional test specifications are full of individual test cases having the following general format:

- ❏ A test environment – a set of files in various directories, perhaps a given telephone network
- ❏ A set of operations to be taken
- ❏ The expected outcome
- ❏ Any special considerations.

Additionally, the functional test specifications should (despite their name) include what are sometimes known as "nonfunctional" specifications, covering aspects such as performance, responsiveness, start-up behavior, and memory (ROM and RAM) usage. If you omit to specify these nonfunctional aspects of your product behavior, don't be surprised if the development team delivers a product that fails to perform as highly as you expect.

The functional test spec is like a contract guiding the work of the development team. It lets everyone know whether the software has been developed and integrated as required. Without a good functional test spec, it's easy for a development team to overlook key product requirements. They will say, "I didn't know it was meant to do that", or perhaps, "we forgot about that particular test case".

The functional test spec is not a fixed document. Rather, it evolves as the project proceeds:

- ❏ It changes to reflect decisions taken about the actual functionality of the product (for example, if the behavior will be different from in a previous product, for stylistic reasons or otherwise)

- ❏ New test cases are added, when they are discovered to be useful, in the course of development and debugging.

The various components in the smartphone product should have their full functional tests run at least twice during the development process:

- ❏ Once, after the component has been integrated, and the integration is viewed as being stable
- ❏ Again, about a month before the intended launch date of the product.

The first test indicates whether the integration has been successful. The second test indicates whether the subsequent changes in the overall software and hardware mix have impacted any of the behavior of the component. In the case of a component that changes a lot, it is worth running the functional tests again.

10.4 Basic Acceptance Tests

The functional test spec describes the full extent of the expected behavior of the entire smartphone product, but it is far too lengthy to run through all its tests on a regular basis. For this reason, a successful smartphone development project team needs to create a much shorter set of representative tests, called the "Basic Acceptance Tests" (BAT). This set of tests should:

❑ Be capable of being run through, by the test team, in about half a day
❑ Be suitable to be carried out during each integration cycle (weekly or biweekly, depending on the project rhythm)
❑ Provide a good overall coverage of the basic functionality of the smartphone product.

BAT plays a central role in the integration process. Software leaders will carefully monitor two statistics, for the BAT results in each integration cycle:

❑ The proportion of the BAT tests that can be run (as opposed to needing to be skipped, since not enough of the overall integration has taken place yet)

❑ The proportion of the tests that pass (as opposed to giving the wrong result, or not being able to be run).

As the project proceeds, both statistics should rise steadily, towards 100%. Any deterioration in the results is cause for immediate management investigation.

The single allowed exception to the law of constantly improving BAT results is when the contents of the BAT are themselves changed. Test leaders should, from time to time, alter the contents of the BAT, in the light of project experience: adding some new tests, retiring others (as providing little extra value), and modifying yet others. Typically the BAT results will temporarily become lower as a result of such a change, as the new tests will generally be more challenging than the old ones.

10.5 Specialist tests

At regular intervals throughout the project – for example, around once a month – the test team should put a special effort into stress testing. Stress tests focus on operations that can throw up issues with performance and reliability:

❑ Operations which start and stop a lot of phone calls (including multi-person conference calls)
❑ Operations which use a lot of memory
❑ Operations in which there are large numbers of contacts, agenda entries, or other data
❑ Operations with a lot of data traffic
❑ Operations with multiple events happening in parallel
❑ Operations (interruptions) while the phone is still starting (from being switched off)
❑ Operations (interruptions) while other applications are starting
❑ Operations while memory cards are being inserted or removed.

Stress tests should be an integral part of the functional test specification. However, there is good reason to give them their own focus on a regular basis:

❑ Stress tests can highlight issues that only become apparent as integration proceeds
❑ Stress test failures often highlight system architectural problems; the sooner these are uncovered, the better.

Another set of specialist tests that should also be carried out around once a month, with its own focus, is compatibility tests of the smartphone product against existing third-party solutions. A wide range of popular add-on applications should be tested against the smartphone product:

❑ Do the applications install as expected?
❑ Do the applications function as expected?
❑ Do the applications coexist as expected with the software suite on the new smartphone?
❑ Do the applications uninstall as expected?

For advice on a suitable set of applications to test, discuss with the provider of the UI system framework. Also take a look at the catalog of "Symbian Signed" applications (as described in Chapter 3).

When defects are found with any third-party application, running on the new smartphone, the smartphone software team needs to reach a decision:

❑ Is it acceptable for this application to fail? Perhaps the application is superfluous on this new smartphone, because the smartphone itself contains the same functionality in a different way

❑ Is it desirable to work together with the provider of the third-party application to seek a new solution or agreed workaround?

❑ Is the defect attributable to an unintentional break in binary compatibility? See Chapter 9 for more information.

A final set of specialist tests that deserves careful attention is IOT: tests of the inter-operability of the smartphone product with other devices that are in circulation:

❑ How does the product cope with various Bluetooth headsets and other peripherals?

❑ Can the product exchange data (using Bluetooth, infrared, USB, and so on) with various common products (PDAs, laptops, and other phones)?

❑ Can the product exchange various *types* of data with these other products, such as calendar entries, contacts entries, etc.?

IOT faces the difficulty (which also applies in the case of compatibility tests with third-party Symbian OS applications) that standards are often defined *de facto* rather than *de jure*: it's not just a case of how the other products are *supposed* to work, it's a case of how these other products *actually* work. For example, it's no good telling an irate user that the reason a particular popular Bluetooth headset fails to work with your smartphone product is because the headset deviates from the usual spec. If possible, you have to find out about this inter-operability problem ahead of your own product reaching market. To catch this kind of problem, you need to be committed to open-ended testing.

10.6 Friendly User Tests

"Friendly User Testing" (FUT) is the name of an important method of open-ended testing that is used by companies that successfully ship Symbian OS smartphone products.

"Friendly users" are employees from the companies that are involved in the development project. These users commit to using the smartphone in question as their main phone, and providing regular feedback about it. They are "friendly" in the sense that they take the time to provide constructive feedback.

The advantages of a program of FUT are as follows:

❑ Friendly users often find important defects before they are found by formal verification or system testing programs. This allows these defects to be analyzed and fixed (or worked around) earlier

❑ Because of their different ways of using phones, friendly users often find important defects that formal verification and system testing completely miss

❑ Friendly users highlight usability and performance issues that formal testing programs often miss

❑ Management can monitor the statistics from friendly user feedback, and can use this information to help decide when the product is ready to ship.

Typically there are 50–100 participants in an FUT program. The participants can usefully include people from Sales, Marketing, Consulting, Operations, Engineering, and senior management.

Friendly users make the following commitment:

❑ To use these phones as their "real phones", in place of any other phones they own

❑ To use these phones for social purposes as well as business ones – in other words, to use them around the clock

❑ To avoid specific information about these new phones leaking to the outside world

❑ To regularly update the software on the phones to the latest baseline release

❑ To install selected third-party add-on software (if available) to see how the phone copes

❑ To report all defects experienced, in a helpful manner

❑ To give general feedback on their perception of the phones – stability, usability, performance, good and bad features, etc. – and whether the phone is ready for release to the market.

Friendly users are asked to fill out a feedback form (for example, a spreadsheet) on a regular basis – typically once a week. This feedback form includes open questions as well as tick-boxes.

Friendly users gain the following personal benefits from their involvement in the program:

❑ Early access to the newest phones and technologies
❑ Opportunity to influence product development
❑ Opportunity to help drive up product quality
❑ Deeper understanding of the product and its capabilities and potential
❑ Experience of being at the leading edge of product development.

An FUT program needs an administrator to make it work. The role of the FUT administrator is as follows:

❑ To keep track of the people who are participating in the program

❑ To keep track of all the phones that are being used in the program, along with other equipment (flashing stations, power chargers, memory cards, etc.)

❑ To assist participants to provide regular feedback (for example, by emailing them reminders)

❑ To assist participants to upgrade their phones to the latest releases, when available

❑ To amalgamate the overall feedback statistics and present this in a suitable summary format

❑ To notice and draw attention to trends in the feedback results

❑ To notice unusual feedback that may have particular importance (for example, new defects)

❑ To ensure that all important defects are recorded in the main defects database for the project

❑ To suggest areas of functionality that various participants should spend time testing

❑ To notice when participants are failing to provide proper feedback, and (in case of poor participation) to remove them from the program, giving their phones to someone else instead.

10.7 Mandatory tests

In parallel with all the tests described above, there are some formal tests that need to be carried out by external bodies, before the phone (or parts of its software) is allowed to reach the market:

❑ *Bluetooth qualification* – tests using kits available from BQBs (Bluetooth Qualification Bodies) as authorized by the Bluetooth SIG (Special Interest Group).

❑ *FTA* – Full Type Approval, a set of tests mandated by the GSM/ CDMA authorities

❑ *Java TCK* – tests using one or more "Technology Compatibility Kits" available from the JCP (Java Community Process)

Members of smartphone project teams are often already familiar with these three processes. My advice for the special context of Symbian smartphone projects is as follows:

❑ Because of the large amount of Java and Bluetooth technology that Symbian OS smartphones generally incorporate, the formal Java and Bluetooth qualification tests can last several weeks (sometimes more than a month) – considerably longer than the corresponding tests for feature phones

❑ These tests can be accelerated by use of third parties with particular experience in this area, and by use of specially designed tools

❑ Adequate time for these tests needs to be set aside in the over-all project plan, with named individuals having responsibility to ensure that good progress takes place.

10.8 Automated tests

Software leaders should always be on the lookout for ways to auto-mate key parts of the test processes for their smartphone products. As in other areas of software, tools can play a large role here:

❑ Removal of drudgery of tests that involve human operation
❑ Easier recording and reviewing of test results
❑ Handling of much larger numbers of test cases.

Also as in other areas of software, it takes time to develop automated test systems. That's why it makes sense to take advantage of some of the systems for automated testing that have been developed by third parties:

- ❑ Tests dedicated to the telephony features of a smartphone
- ❑ Tests for specific areas of functionality
- ❑ Tests that automatically compare the display on the screen with a record of what is expected
- ❑ Tests that simulate all kinds of different user input
- ❑ Tests that simulate key features of telephone network performance
- ❑ Tests that simulate failures (such as shortage of memory, or poor network connectivity).

See *www.symbian.com/partners* for some pointers to providers of such tools.

11
Managing tools

11.1 The need for a tools champion

Every software development project uses tools, ranging from batch files and Perl scripts, through ad hoc utility applications created in-house by team members, to commercial offerings purchased from third parties (including compilers and IDEs). For smaller projects, teams can get by with an informal approach to tools: tools issues can be handled in "quiet times" by individual developers. However, for larger projects, you need to take a more systematic approach to tools.

For smartphone projects, my recommendation is that your team should have a "tools champion" – a dedicated senior engineer whose full-time job is the following:

❑ Understand all the software tools used by the project team
❑ Ensure that team members receive suitable training on how to get the best out of the tools available
❑ Understand and prioritize all the *potential* software tools that could be used by the project
❑ Evaluate the tools offerings available from third-party vendors
❑ Foresee possible problems with tools as the project proceeds, and plan ahead to forestall these problems
❑ Ensure that the need for good tools is kept in mind throughout the project, despite all the other pressures for mind-share
❑ Consider special subprojects to "productize" tools that have been developed internally, making them fit for wider use.

In short, the tools champion ensures that optimal use is made of tools throughout the project.

Tools often come under stress as a project proceeds:

❑ Extra code bulk, or heavier use of memory, can stop some tools from working

❑ Some tools can break when there are larger numbers of defect reports to be analyzed, or larger numbers of source code modules to be analyzed; these tools are insufficiently scalable

❑ Some tools can break because of interface changes in the software components they rely on

❑ When more people start using a tool, its intended usage can no longer be adequately communicated by word-of-mouth; more formal documentation is required

❑ In the increasing helter-skelter of project management activities, tools can become seen as expendable "nice to have" items, rather than the essential pieces of work equipment that they often are

❑ Tools tend to be excluded from the smoke test or BAT; therefore problems with tools typically take longer to notice. What makes this worse is that the defects database often has no provision to report defects about tools – so these problems don't appear in the official defect statistics

❑ Resources are reallocated away from tasks improving tools, onto other project tasks seen as having a higher priority.

Tools that work well in smaller settings often fail to work well in larger, more complex settings, such as those pertaining during smartphone project integration. Different tools can conflict with each other's intended usage, sowing confusion, and preventing each other from working. Another problem is that tools provided by third parties can have as many integration issues of their own as any other kind of new software component: they may work well in carefully specified test or demo environments, but fail to operate in the actual mix of software forming your smartphone project.

Tools take time to develop, time to deploy, time to learn, time to productize, and yet more time to maintain. You need to decide which tools can make the biggest difference between the success and failure of your project, and how much effort to invest in the above tasks. Please do not underestimate either the potential benefit from good tools, or the effort to carry out tools improvements.

In the remainder of this chapter, I review some of the tools that have particular significance for smartphone projects.

11.2 Debuggers

My own particular background as a software engineer leads me to nominate the debugger as perhaps the single most important development tool. I spent countless hours, time and again over many years, using various debuggers to deepen my understanding of how complex code systems were intended to work, and how they were actually working. With a good debugger, you can do the following (among much more):

❑ Step through code execution, following program flow into and out of subroutines
❑ Put breakpoints on given lines of code, to find out how they are being reached
❑ Look up and down the entire call stack, to understand the execution context
❑ Inspect the values of variables, to see how they are changing
❑ Put breakpoints on elements of data changing, to see how and why they actually change
❑ Change data dynamically, inside the debugger, to simulate hard-to-reach situations
❑ Examine the state of other threads and processes, in addition to the one currently being executed.

Software engineers should practice using the debugger of their choice until all the above operations are completely second nature – their fingers should know all the relevant shortcuts and hot-keys, without any conscious thought being required. This frees the conscious mind to attend fully to what is actually happening in the software being debugged.

Skilled use of a debugger can cut straight through what would otherwise take hours or even days of conjecture and analysis – identifying which lines of software are responsible for some observed problem. Almost at once, you can notice that (for example) there is a mismatch between the intended and actual meanings of parameters for a given function call somewhere in the call stack. Or you may notice a flawed assumption in the source code – such as that a given pointer could never be NULL, or that various events will always happen in a fixed order. With a good debugger, defects can often be diagnosed within minutes. Without a good debugger, these same defects can sometimes resist solution for weeks.

However, what makes things complicated is that various prerequisites are necessary before effective debugging can take place:

❑ Source code must be available (with some suppliers, this is not always possible – which is a reason to hesitate before using these suppliers)
❑ It must be possible to reproduce the problem in question

❑ It must be possible to debug the problem in question, without the act of debugging interfering with the problem to the extent of preventing it from recurring.

So the design of your product should include aspects of "designing for debugging". For example, you may need to include an extra comms port, for the debugger to use to monitor progress.

Some problems are very hard to reproduce under laboratory test conditions, and tend to occur only outside of a formal debugging session. To cope with these problems, you can take advantage of additional "crash debugging" capability in your smartphone (this requires some kernel-side programming). This is the ability of the smartphone:

❑ To enter a special debugging mode when certain critical events occur (for example, the death of a system thread)

❑ To enter this mode, as well, when a certain combination of keys is pressed simultaneously; this is very helpful when a "lock up" occurs (that is, no system threads have died, but the system has stopped responding to normal user input – this is often a sign of thread "deadlock")

❑ In this mode, to record information about the state of execution, and to support interrogation via commands piped down a serial port.

You then need to train your testers to notice when phones enter into this mode, and to bring these phones to the development team for further analysis. For example, the system software can put up a special display on the screen on commencing this crash debugging mode. For phones that will be in the hands of end-users, you probably want to change the behavior, so as *not* to put up any special screen display; instead, when production phones encounter a system thread failure, they should record some minimal information internally, and then quietly reboot. The crash information can be retrieved at a later date during servicing or diagnostic checks.

Analysis of crash debugger information relies on you having access to the "symbol" files corresponding to the smartphone ROM under investigation. These files contain the names of all functions in the ROM, along with their start address in memory. Symbol files are created as a byproduct of the ROM-build process. Look after them carefully. You can waste a lot of time if you have the wrong symbol files.

11.3 Emulators

Perhaps the second most important tool, during smartphone development, is a PC emulator of your smartphone product. This emulator should duplicate, as faithfully as possible, as many features as possible from your product.

Symbian OS is delivered as an emulator, as well as a set of header files, documentation, tools, and ARM binaries. Sample programs are delivered with "make files" that allow the software to be built in emulator (PC) mode as well as in ARM mode.

The benefits of the emulator include:

❑ Your team can develop software, on the emulator, even before the hardware is available

❑ Even when hardware is available, it is often available only in small quantities to start with – there may not be enough to give one smartphone to each person in the development team

❑ Carrying out tests on the emulator removes the delay of copying new versions of the software into the ROM of the smartphone

❑ The PC is, in many ways, an easier debugging environment than actual smartphone hardware – it avoids the problems of additional serial comms and remote debugging.

On the other hand, it takes effort to maintain the emulator. When you add new features into your product, it may take you extra time to add the corresponding features into the emulator version. For this reason, smartphone development projects often end up in the situation where the emulator is poor – because it has not been properly maintained. Unfortunately, this removes a very useful tool from the hands of your development team.

Your team also needs to appreciate the limitations of any PC emulator:

❑ Speed of execution is often quite different from real hardware – this can mislead your team as to the quality of performance of their software

❑ Pixel sizes and color shades may differ between the PC and real hardware – so a view that looks great on a PC may be less striking on real hardware (and vice versa)

❑ Aspects of the memory protection, memory alignment constraints, process isolation, and so on, are often different between the PC emulator and real hardware. This means that some software will cause a fault on real hardware, even though it runs fine on the emulator

❑ There may be differences in the lower-level drivers – including camera, networking, sound, and telephony.

For all these reasons, successful passing of tests on the PC emulator is no guarantee that the tests will pass on real hardware.

Despite these drawbacks, I recommend that your team members make thorough use of the emulator, and learn about the many helpful features it supports:

❑ Special keypress combinations enable or disable various logging modes

❑ Other keypresses trigger various checks of graphics, memory usage, and other resource usage; important internal integrity checks also take place whenever an application exits

❑ An "epoc.ini" file allows easy variation of numerous parameters, including amount of free memory, screen size, and types of peripheral drives emulated.

In summary, if you maintain a PC emulator as your project proceeds, you'll find that it repays your efforts handsomely.

11.4 Profilers and loggers

The role of a profiling tool is to assist the optimization of performance. It does this by identifying the parts of code where execution spends most time. From the output of a profiler, you can see:

❑ Times where there is no execution at all (the system is waiting for the next event)
❑ The threads that are executing, over various periods of time
❑ The functions that are being executed, over various periods of time.

Symbian's preferred profile analyzer (developed in-house) supports numerous configuration options, and displays results graphically. By looking at its output you may see that threads are executing in different proportions of time from what you expected. The output also highlights the functions that are most in need of optimization – the functions which are acting as the bottleneck to overall system performance.

A profiler is a special case of a logger – an onboard tool that records information for subsequent analysis. Logging can include information about protocol negotiations, locations where files were found, numbers of retries needed, run-time conditions that are unexpected but not fatal, and all kinds of progress reports.

In its default state, a smartphone has no logging enabled, since that consumes CPU, disk space (to hold the log output), and program space (to store the text strings from which the log output is composed). Several steps are involved in enabling logging:

❏ Versions of the software components that contain conditional logging code need to be used; generally this means using "debug" versions of the software instead of "release" versions

❏ The conditional logging code needs to be selectively enabled: this can happen via compile-time flags and/or run-time checks.

For example, many Symbian OS components create log output only if certain directories, that will receive the log output, already exist on the smartphone.

Depending on the component, log output is recorded to a file, and/or emitted down a serial port. (In this latter case, it is often called "trace" output rather than log output.)

As I said, logging is something you will want to be selective about. If you enable all possible kinds of logging, you will be swamped by the resulting output. What's more, the time taken to generate all this log information is likely to upset internal timing checks – such as the so-called "watchdog timer", that deliberately crashes a thread if it is unresponsive for too long a time.

The main role for logging is to generate additional information that can shed light on why a particular defect is occurring. A common response you'll see in the defect database to a defect report is a request for such-and-such logs to be generated and attached. Logging complements debugging as a way for developers to understand what's happening inside the software. In this way, they can quickly and accurately identify the causes of any problems observed.

11.5 Static code analysis

Something that's even better than a tool to track down a defect is a tool that prevents the insertion of the defect in the first place. Tools that perform static code analysis have a big role to play here. These tools encapsulate knowledge about potentially dangerous source code – fragments of source code that should be queried in any code review (for example, code with a single equals sign instead of a double equals sign inside an "if" statement, or code that has a semi-colon at the end of a line containing an "if" statement). The idea of the tool is to automate the application of this type of knowledge. Rather than relying on humans to review the code manually to spot this kind of problem, the tool can perform these checks automatically – allowing human code reviewers to concentrate on more subtle coding issues.

Software engineers have traditionally used a tool called "lint" for this purpose. Lint has, by itself, no particular knowledge of coding constructs that are specialized to Symbian OS. Hence the need for more specialized static code analysis tools.

Examples of potential defects that a Symbian-tailored code analysis tool can identify include (don't worry about the technical details):

- Classes that have names starting with "C" but which fail to derive from Symbian's CBase class
- Classes that have names starting with "T" or "M" but which have destructors
- Faulty use of the Cleanup classes
- Violation of Symbian's rules on naming of functions that can "Leave" (functions that should have names ending in "L")
- Places where there are no checks on the return values of functions which could fail
- Use of constructions known to have more efficient equivalents
- Destructors accessing the contents of pointers without checking for NULL.

Incidentally, Symbian has long operated a policy of "zero compiler warnings". Compilers emit warnings when they notice potentially faulty code. Symbian's internal processes state that when there is a compiler warning:

- The developer should rewrite the code (without losing any efficiency or readability) to avoid the warning
- Or, on rare occasions, this particular warning can be temporarily disabled (by use of #pragma instructions to the compiler).

The reason for not tolerating any compiler warnings is that developers can easily get into the habit of saying to themselves, "This module always has seven compiler warnings". Then they fail to check the list of warnings carefully each time, and fail to notice a new warning that turns out to be important.

Note that static code analysis tools do *not* remove the need for all code to be peer reviewed on a regular basis. Peer review continues to have valuable consequences:

❏ It's a good way for both reviewers and developers to learn new programming methods

❏ Reviewers can recommend different APIs that can be called

❏ Reviewers can ask good questions about design, and about alternative solutions, that will cause developers to think through their solution more carefully

❏ Reviewers can find defects that the static code analysis tools miss.

Each time a new defect is found, it's worth asking the question if it could have been found earlier, or by automated methods. As a result of these questions, tools and processes will both improve.

11.6 Build system

You may think that there's nothing much to say about the build system – the system that transforms source code into binary code that runs on a smartphone. However, there are quite a few issues that need care and attention.

First, there are many different build configurations:

❏ You can build in either "debug" or "release" mode. A debug version contains more logging code, and more internal checks (known as "asserts")

❏ You can build either for the PC emulator or for real hardware (typically, you will want to do both, though not always at the same time)

❏ There are several choices of ARM mode, depending on the precise ARM instruction set to be used.

Next, you have to consider different language variants (this is a process known as "localization"), or other variants (such as variants for specific network operators). You want to create new variants by altering as few of your source files as possible, and by rebuilding as few files as possible. Ideally, you should restrict these changes to files known as "resource files" that contain language-specific text, along with data files such as icons, wallpapers, and ringtones.

Finally, you have to consider the all-important trade-off between speed and safety:

❏ A full build of all the software in a smartphone can take the best part of a day

❑ However, if you build only a few files, you have the risk of ending up with an inconsistent set of binaries.

The way to balance the needs of speed and safety is:

❑ To minimize the number of changes you make to system files (or to files delivered to you by a supplier), thereby reducing the need to rebuild them

❑ To develop your understanding of the dependencies between different modules

❑ To seek, most of the time, to rebuild only a small number of files (based on your understanding of the dependencies): this is called an "incremental" build

❑ To check your understanding, by doing a fuller rebuild on a regular basis, and comparing the results (using the Symbian tool Evalid) with those from the incremental build.

There is a definite case for investing in a top-of-the-range PC to carry out the builds. The task of building the software can in fact be split across several PCs, working together in a so-called "build farm" (or "grid"). In such a case, it turns out to be important to put the files on a local file server with high-performance access.

Symbian supplies a build system that handles all the above requirements. Not surprisingly, it is a fairly complex system. My advice to you is to take the time to learn how to use this system well.

A critical part of the overall software build system for a smartphone project is the set of files that configure the ROM. This consists of text files with the extension .OBY and .IBY. Different software components (or groups of components) contribute their own IBY files, which are in turn "included" (hence the "I" of "IBY") by the overall OBY file. Between them, these files encapsulate the intelligence of dependencies between the software components that make up the ROM – which versions of which components work well together.

This may sound a relatively simple undertaking, but experience shows that it is quite common for the ROM configuration to become broken. Unfortunately, once the configuration is broken, it can take a significant effort to fix it again – especially when new software components are involved.

The following advice should guard against these problems:

❑ Treat the ROM configuration as a deliverable in its own right, which is owned by the integration team, and which is rigorously maintained for each baseline

❑ Ensure that the software system runs on representative phone hardware as soon as possible, even if there is limited functionality. Once real hardware is available, avoid the situation where the software only runs on a PC emulator

❑ Insist that all engineers test their software on phone hardware, rather than just on a PC emulator

❑ Keep the OBY and IBY files sacred; one false move here could mean that the phone won't boot – which is not a healthy situation when the project is under tight schedule pressure!

11.7 Distribution system

The essential factors that complicate the build system are:

❑ The fact that builds have to take place frequently (in the interest of good software discipline – see Chapter 8)
❑ The large amount of software that, potentially, needs rebuilding each time
❑ The range of different build configurations that need to be supported.

The same three factors also complicate the distribution system – the system whereby the latest baseline software is distributed on a regular basis among the team members (including to people on different sites and in different companies):

❑ Baseline releases need to be distributed throughout the extended team, either biweekly or weekly, depending on the build rhythm of the project

❑ A complete baseline release consists of several gigabytes of data – including binaries, libraries, header files, debug information files, map files, ROM symbol files, tools, and documentation – with much of this existing in several different build variants.

Just as there are significant gains in efficiency by adopting an incremental build system, there are also significant gains in efficiency from an incremental distribution system. For this reason, Symbian supplies tools known as Component Based Release (CBR) tools. These tools work as follows:

❑ The overall software system that needs distribution is split into a large number of different "components"

❑ Each component has its own version number

❑ Data transfer between sites and within sites is minimized, as only updated components need to be transferred.

As with incremental builds, incremental distribution comes at the cost of additional complexity (both syntactic complexity and conceptual complexity): the CBR tools support a range of options, which take some time to learn. However, once your team fully understands CBR, it will be easier to ensure that everyone is working with the right software distribution at all times. In the absence of CBR, what often happens is that different members of the team avoid the pain of upgrading the software files on their PCs, and they end up working with an out-of-date configuration. In that case, code that works on their PCs will often fail to work when integrated into the mainline.

11.8 Miscellaneous tools

The job of your tools champion is never finished – there are always new ideas for tools that could increase the productivity and effectiveness of your team members. Let me briefly mention a miscellaneous set of additional tools:

❑ See Chapter 10 for some ideas on automated test tools

❑ Third-party tools can simplify (or even automate) the porting of Symbian OS applications from one UI system to another (e.g. from Series 60 to UIQ)

❑ As a special case of incremental software distribution, consider the case of incrementally updating the software in the ROM of a smartphone. For example, if a developer has made a small change to one module, and wants to check the effect of that change, it should not be necessary to flash all of the 30MB+ ROM software afresh. Various tools exist to allow incremental ROM updates, thereby speeding up the test–debug–modify–test cycle. These tools generally depend upon the ROM being split into several different sections. Another option that some smartphones support is that some files in the ROM can be superseded (during development phase, if not in release phase) by more recent versions of these files found on additional disk drives

❑ One static code analysis tool deserves special mention: Symbian's "Code Data Base" (CDB) tool. This is designed to measure backwards compatibility between two releases of Symbian OS software. It checks many aspects of the public APIs, such as class layout, function ordinals and v-table organization. As such, it can avoid your team making mistakes with interface management

❑ The DepModel tool contains models of dependencies between different classes and components; among the views it supports are hierarchical views and a dependency graph

❑ Modern IDEs typically include sophisticated code browsing and code navigation features. For example, click on an `enum`, and the IDE will show you the value of the `enum`; click on a class name, and the IDE will show you where that class is defined, its inheritance tree, and so on. Add-on tools sometimes improve on the browsing capabilities of the IDE, thereby speeding up developers and making them more productive

❑ Some companies provide "simulators" that combine some of the best features of PC emulators and ARM hardware: they allow the execution and monitoring, on a PC, of a system that faithfully simulates the execution of ARM binaries – thereby potentially reducing the need to build and test PC emulation binaries of the software

❑ Inside Symbian, one of the tools that is used most heavily is the "x-ref" source-code cross-reference tool; this provides access to a database (rebuilt overnight, every night) of all supported versions of the entire Symbian OS source code, allowing developers to see exactly where various functions are used.

Interestingly, the x-ref tool was developed (using ***http://sourceforge. net/projects/lxr***) as a spare-time skunkworks project, pioneered by a single individual working in Symbian's consulting unit. The x-ref database was maintained on the first Linux servers inside Symbian, making the project "unauthorized" in a second way. Subsequently, as wider numbers of software engineers inside many groups at Symbian recognized the value of this new tool, it was adopted by the System Management Group, and the server is nowadays maintained by Symbian's IS department. I mention this to underscore the principle that ideas for good tools often arise at the periphery of an organization, and that a project team needs to be nimble in order to take best advantage of all these ideas.

11.9 Dangers with tools

Successful tools can develop their own momentum. A group of enthusiasts will evangelize their use, and formal processes may dictate their adoption. Momentum builds a tradition and, before long, people say, "But we always do things like that". However, tools are just tools.

Tools are not the ultimate goal of your software organization. Tools exist, not as an end in themselves, but to assist the timely delivery of substantial value to multiple customers. You need to keep monitoring the way tools are used in your team, watching for warning signs:

❑ Perhaps changing project circumstances mean that a tool is no longer as useful or as critical

❑ Perhaps the people supporting a specific tool lose sight of the overall business purpose of your team, and put inappropriate amounts of effort into maintaining it and developing it further

❑ Perhaps developers start overly relying on the power of a tool, and stop applying their own critical intelligence to find quicker (or better) solutions.

For example, sometimes developers will keep pressing "Step, step, step" in a debugger, mindlessly following through program execution, instead of thinking ahead about the likely outcome. (This is especially true if developers get too tired.) And I have already mentioned the potential drawbacks (as well as the benefits) of the PC emulators of Symbian OS. Over-reliance on a PC emulator can lead to:

❑ A distorted view of the performance bottlenecks in a software system
❑ A lack of awareness of specific hardware or telephony problems
❑ A lack of sensitivity to ARM instruction set issues
❑ Limited appreciation of power management questions
❑ Delays in testing on real ARM hardware
❑ Poor familiarity with the debugging tools available on real ARM hardware.

In summary, tools can have a tremendous impact on the success of your project. Chosen wisely, used wisely, and reviewed wisely (on a regular basis), they can provide you with significant competitive advantage. So assign one of the key managers in your team as your tools champion – someone who is comfortable with the technical details of tools, but who keeps in mind the overall goal of your organization.

12
Managing plans and change

12.1 Beyond complete planning

Here's one high-level method for software development:

❏ Agree a high-level plan for the project – this is known as "the planning phase"

❏ Agree what features need to be implemented – this is known as "the specification phase"

❏ Agree the technology to be used to implement these features – this is "the design phase"

❏ Then carry out the implementation – this is known as "the development phase"

❏ As the implementation proceeds, carry out tests to verify that the implementation meets the specification – this is known as "the testing phase".

In this methodology, the project starts by creating three inter-related documents – the project plan, the product spec, and the product design – and then ensures that the subsequent software development faithfully executes the intent of the original documents. The role of the project plan is:

❏ To identify the overall timetable for the project
❏ To allocate resources to specific tasks
❏ To establish "milestone" review points.

So far, so good. Any sizable smartphone project needs a project plan to guide it to completion. I fully agree with the adage that "if you fail to plan, you plan to fail". Planning is an absolutely essential activity in any successful smartphone project. However, here are some much harder questions:

- ❏ What level of detail should be in the plan?
- ❏ How should the plan cope with unexpected developments – such as new requirements introduced once the project is underway and other "change requests"?

One answer to these questions is to say, "The plan is king". According to this answer,

- ❏ The plan establishes what will be in the product
- ❏ The plan establishes how this can be delivered
- ❏ The plan represents a clear commitment to the customer (such as network operators)
- ❏ Customers depend utterly upon the project meeting its commitments: "predictable delivery" is key
- ❏ Any change to the plan invalidates the commitments, and opens the way to chaos
- ❏ Replanning is expensive, and consumes valuable resources to little good purpose
- ❏ Changes should be resisted vigorously.

As I'll explain in this chapter, such a view is a recipe for grief in any complex smartphone project:

- ❏ The project is so complex that it's neither possible nor necessary to plan it in full detail

- ❏ Any would-be complete plan is obsolete even before it's finished

- ❏ Rather than aiming at completeness, the plan needs to concentrate on the "critical chains" of development: the plan should identify these and analyze them carefully, but can leave many other aspects of the project in a relatively unplanned state

- ❏ Change is an inevitable aspect of a smartphone project

- ❏ The plan needs to be able to accommodate change; the watchword is "design for change"

- ❏ Rather than the plan being king, it is customer satisfaction that should be king

- ❏ The real point of the project is to deliver significant value to the customer, rather than to fulfill the commitments recorded in the previous version of the plan

- It's by no means a disaster if a milestone target is missed (although any such occurrence is a matter to investigate further)
- Like other aspects of project groupware, the plan is a living entity, which evolves and changes as the project proceeds.

12.2 Causes of change

It's worth listing some of the factors that will cause a smartphone project to deviate from its detailed plan:

- Individual tasks in the plan end up taking longer (or shorter) than estimated
- Individuals are unable to work on the project at the required times, due perhaps to illness, or to task interference from other responsibilities
- Defects are found that require a considerable amount of time to investigate and fix
- Problems are found with some aspects of the design of the product, necessitating a change in design
- Customers request new features, citing a change in market conditions, new competitive pressures, or breakthrough new ideas
- Senior executives request new features, citing any of the same kinds of reason
- It becomes clear that parts of the specification are inconsistent, unclear, or otherwise in need of clarification – resulting in project rework
- Hardware fails to function as expected, and needs a new iteration
- Suppliers deliver later than planned, or unexpectedly drop some of the anticipated features
- Senior managers are not available to approve project milestone transitions at the expected time.

Note that these are fundamental aspects of projects, which are likely to occur in virtually every smartphone project with significant duration. They are not "accidental" features which a project leader can realistically "hope" to avoid.

Best practice in project management theory makes the following recommendations:

- People should be alerted (reminded) ahead of time, on several occasions, of activities scheduled for them – to lessen the chance of them unexpectedly not being ready to attend to project duties

❑ The project manager should check, ahead of time, that people working on the project fully understand the tasks assigned to them. This lessens the chance that people carry out their tasks with a different output from that expected

❑ Although some degree of change is inevitable, there needs to be a bias against accepting change – everyone should be regularly reminded of the negative consequences to existing plans if changes are permitted

❑ Where there are risks to aspects of the project plan, alternative plans should be investigated and prepared in advance, as possible measures ready to be adopted

❑ Rather than always working with "best case" estimates, the plan must include some element of contingency

❑ In addition to contingency (which is allowance for task over-run), the plan should include some element of reserve – real people assigned to tasks that are currently unknown

❑ As the project progresses, the plan needs to be updated on a regular basis

❑ Progress needs to be monitored against pre-agreed review points, known as "milestones"

❑ Both actual and potential changes to the plan need to be communicated to the project stakeholders (including customers and senior managers), in a way that allows a collaborative review of options and joint decision-making.

In the remainder of this chapter, and in the one that follows, I'll look more closely at five crucial aspects:

❑ How to process change requests in an optimal way
❑ How to allocate both contingency and reserve into the plan
❑ How to strike the right balance between a schedule that is aggressive and one that is defensive
❑ How to define and monitor project milestone review points
❑ How to identify the tasks in the project that deserve the greatest planning attention.

12.3 Handling change requests

In earlier chapters, I've already highlighted two specific aspects of change control:

❑ See Chapter 6 for the importance of reviewing and controlling which defect fixes are attempted and/or adopted into the software

❑ See Chapter 9 for the importance of reviewing and controlling changes in interfaces in the software – the process for handling so-called BRs ("Break Requests").

In both these cases, the team needs to appreciate the benefits of a disciplined approach: changes which happen without careful review can destabilize the project, sometimes with disastrous consequences. But the discipline incorporates flexibility. Without acceptance of at least some changes, the software quality will be unacceptably poor.

It's the same with so-called "Change Requests" (CRs): requests for modifications to the previously agreed specification set. As for the previous cases, CRs need a disciplined approach that incorporates both rigor and flexibility.

Inside Symbian, the following processes govern CRs submitted against Symbian OS (you should consider how to copy or adapt these processes for your own smartphone project):

❑ There is an online database of all CRs submitted

❑ CRs need to submitted into this database using a carefully designed form

❑ CRs are reviewed in the first instance by the Technical Authority (TA) for the relevant part of Symbian OS

❑ Other interested parties are able to add online comments to the CRs; this often includes comments from the Requirements Analyst (RA) assigned to this part of Symbian OS

❑ For cases when the requirement is clear-cut and the amount of work involved is small, TAs can make their own decision about whether to accept the CR; ideally this decision can take place within a few working hours of the CR being submitted

❑ In larger cases – and also in cases where there is disagreement with the assessment of the TA – the decision is handled by the Change Control Board (CCB).

The CCB is a team of around a dozen senior engineers and customer project representatives which meets once a week to review outstanding CRs. It is a challenging task to sit on the CCB:

❑ Members of the CCB need to review CRs in advance of meetings

❑ Between them, they need to have a good understanding of the entire software system

❑ They sometimes have to weigh up strong conflicting pressures – one pressure to improve the quality of the software, versus another pressure to avoid delaying the project end-date.

The general process of deciding whether to accept a CR is as follows:

❑ Evaluate the business case for the change – the extra revenues that will potentially be realized if the change is made to the product

❑ Check the requirements analysis: whether the CR presupposes one particular *solution* to the real underlying *requirement*, whereas the underlying requirement could in fact be satisfied just as well through an alternative solution that would be easier to implement

❑ Evaluate the technical difficulty of the change – the effort the change will require

❑ Evaluate the risks involved – the possible knock-on effects on other aspects of the software system

❑ Evaluate alternative solutions – possible smaller changes, or other ways to realize the required end-result.

The process often splits into two:

❑ Start by deciding whether there is a strong enough business case to warrant taking the time to carry out a longer investigation (called an "impact analysis") into the technical feasibility of the change

❑ If the business case is strong enough, then carry out the impact analysis, and bring the results back to a later meeting of the CCB.

About 10% of the time, stakeholders end up in serious disagreement with the decision of the CCB. For this reason, there also exists an "escalation change control board", consisting of yet more senior engineers and customer project representatives. It's like a court of appeal.

Sometimes a debate arises as to whether a submitted CR ought instead to be regarded as a defect report:

❑ A defect report is when the software fails to function as specified
❑ A change request is when the specification itself is found to be at fault.

There's room for ambiguity because the specification is often unclear. One person can argue, for example, that a performance target was *implicit* in the specification (in which case it's a defect if the performance is actually worse than this), whereas someone else can say that there's no defect, because there's nothing written down about what performance is acceptable. In such cases, it's important not to get bogged down in bureaucracy or ideology. The process for reviewing defect reports should form a continuum with the process for reviewing CRs.

One of the key tasks of a software leader is to prevent items from languishing too long as either an unresolved CR or an unresolved (open) defect report. The software leader also needs to ensure that CRs and defect reports receive a fair hearing. Don't be tempted to steam-roller all of them into a "rejected" status too quickly. Individual CRs and defect reports sometimes indicate fundamental problems with the product conception or design. You can try to avoid considering these problems, but that won't make the problems go away. They can return with a horrible vengeance later in the project – perhaps when it's too late to deal with them (in which case, it could be curtains for the whole project).

In order to be able to approve CRs from time to time, the project plan needs to incorporate elements of both contingency and reserve. This brings us on to the fascinating topic of how to allocate contingency and reserve.

12.4 Variable task estimates

A smartphone project plan is made up from a large number of estimates for how long it will take to complete individual tasks. If the task involves novel work, or novel circumstances, or a novel integration environment, you can have a wide range of estimates for the length of time required.

It's similar to estimating how long you will take to complete an unfamiliar journey in a busy city with potentially unreliable transport infrastructure. Let's say that, if you are lucky, you might complete the journey in just 20 minutes. Perhaps 30 minutes is the most likely time duration. But in view of potential traffic hold-ups or train delays, you could take as long as one hour, or (in case of underground train derailments) even two hours or longer. So there's a range of estimates, with the distribution curve having a long tail on the right-hand side: there's a non-negligible probability that the task will take at least twice as long as the individual most likely outcome. It's often the same with estimating the length of time for a task within a project plan (see Figure 12.1).

Now imagine that the company culture puts a strong emphasis on fulfilling commitments, and never missing deadlines. If developers are asked to state a length of time in which they have (say) 95%

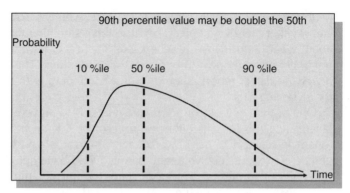

Figure 12.1   Varying estimates of task duration

confidence they will finish the task, they are likely to give an answer that is at least twice as long as the individual most likely outcome. They do so because:

❑ Customers may make large financial decisions dependent on the estimate – on the assumption that it will be met

❑ Bonus payments to developers may depend on hitting the target

❑ The developers have to plan on unforeseen task interference (and other changes)

❑ Any estimate the developers provide may get squashed down by aggressive senior managers (so they'd better pad their estimate in advance, making it even longer).

Ironically, even though such estimates are designed to be fulfilled around 95% of the time, they typically end up being fulfilled only around 50% of the time. This fact deserves some careful reflection. Even though the estimates were generous, it seems (at first sight) that they were not generous enough. In fact, here's what happens:

❑ In fulfillment of "Parkinson's Law", tasks expand to fill the available time. Developers can always find ways to improve and optimize their solutions – adding extra test cases, considering alternative algorithms and generalizations, and so forth

❑ Because there's a perception (in at least the beginning of the time period) of there being ample time, developers often put off becoming fully involved in their tasks. This is sometimes called "the student syndrome", from the observation that most students do most of the preparation for an exam in the time

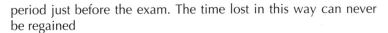
period just before the exam. The time lost in this way can never be regained

❑ Because there's a perception of there being ample time, developers can become involved in other activities at the same time. However, these other activities often last longer than intended. So the developer ends up multitasking between two (or more) activities. But multitasking involves significant task setup time – time to become deeply involved in each different task (time to enter "flow mode" for the task). So yet more time is wasted

❑ Critically, even when a task is ready to finish earlier than expected, the project plan can rarely take advantage of this fact. The people who were scheduled for the next task probably aren't ready to start it earlier than anticipated. So an early finish by one task rarely translates into an early start by the next task. On the other hand, a late finish by one task inevitably means a late start for the next start. This task asymmetry drives the whole schedule later.

In conclusion, in a company whose culture puts a strong emphasis upon fulfilling commitments and never missing deadlines, the agreed schedules are built from estimations up to twice as long as the individually most likely outcome, *and even so*, they often miss even these extended deadlines.

Once you see things in this light, the response is straightforward:

❑ Ask developers to provide estimates that they are 50% likely to achieve

❑ Build the entire plan around these shorter estimates, but include contingency at critical sections

❑ *Don't* put contingency time after each separate task; instead, put it before the end of the project, and also ahead of major integration steps

❑ Expect developers to work single-mindedly on individual tasks, when the time comes, and avoid multitasking among several tasks (with all the consequent risks of task interference and delays)

❑ Ensure that all team members have a flexible approach to when they are able to start on project tasks; provide them with regular updates on when they are actually likely to start individual tasks

❑ Don't penalize project teams just because they miss their estimates (around 50% of the time); make it clear that this is the expected outcome, and that the whole project benefits from such an attitude.

With this kind of culture (often known as an "agile culture") in place, the overall estimates for the project are shorter, and the projects meet their estimates more often. Moreover, the culture embraces the notion of change, allowing the product to more closely satisfy customers' evolving requirements.

12.5 Practical example of agile scheduling

Here's a simplified example to illustrate the reasoning of the previous section. Suppose that a project consists of 16 tasks in series:

❏ Each task is estimated as 50% likely to complete in two weeks
❏ And each is 90% likely to complete in three weeks.

A defensive schedule would allow three weeks for each task, resulting in a total schedule of 48 weeks (16 times three weeks). Given Parkinson's Law and the other effects mentioned, the overall project will tend to last at least 48 weeks.

Agile scheduling instead aggregates all the task variances to the end of the project. The resulting total contingency is one week times the square root of 16, namely four weeks. (The square root follows from some simple mathematical statistics. If you are interested to delve into this more fully, recall that it is the variances of statistical distributions that add, rather than their standard deviations. But if statistics is not your forte, don't panic. Just notice that individual deviations in the different task durations are likely to partially cancel each other out, so the overall deviation is less than the raw sum of the individual deviations.) So agile scheduling gives a total duration of 16 times two weeks, plus four weeks contingency, namely 36 weeks.

As you can see, in this case agile scheduling trims 25% off the schedule. That's by no means unusual.

The outcome is encouraging, but it relies on a particular culture to enable it to happen – with flexible team members and sophisticated team managers.

12.6 Accepting slack

My fervent advice to software leaders is to ensure that their project plans contain adequate amounts of slack. The slack meets three primary purposes:

❏ Slack arises when someone is ready to start a task earlier than the initially expected date; so if task 13 (say) finishes one week ahead of schedule, task 14 can start one week ahead of schedule

- Slack also arises when contingencies for aggregate tasks over-run and delays are placed at critical parts of the project plan – ahead of the final delivery, and ahead of each major integration point
- Finally, slack arises when a plan specifies that developers need to be ready to work on additional tasks, which are not known at the time the plan is created; these tasks will be defined by new CRs that are accepted by the CCB for the project.

Here's a simple recipe to calculate the amount of slack required:

- Start with a plan in which all the individual tasks complete in the amount of time that experienced developers say they have a 50% chance of meeting; put tasks in parallel when possible, and otherwise in series
- Add on an extra 50% of this total time, for contingency
- Distribute this 50% at selected points throughout the project plan, as mentioned earlier
- Ensure that an extra 20% of resources are ready to be allocated, beyond those in the original plan; these are the reserve resources to work on additional tasks arising from CRs (note that reserve is additional to contingency – they are two different concepts)
- Have highly experienced consultants review the plan, looking specifically for bottlenecks, critical resource chains, and other areas where extra resources may be needed.

As the project proceeds, the contingency and the reserve will gradually be released: the outcome becomes clearer to anticipate.

To some managers, the idea of slack is an abomination – an unacceptable waste of resources. These managers are used to pushing every member of their team to a perceived maximum performance. However, that's a point of view that only makes sense in a localized way. It's true that, with agile scheduling, individual resources often end up not being fully utilized working flat out on the project. So, some resources will use some of their time on activities that, from the point of view of the project, are far from critical. However, this allows the project as a whole to complete more quickly, and to deliver greater value to the customer.

The idea that slack is an abomination only makes sense when you try to optimize all the subtasks in a project, thinking that optimizing subtasks inevitably leads to optimizing the overall project. This is a mistaken viewpoint. What needs to be optimized is the project as a whole, not each subtask. Attempts to optimize each subtask are, rightly, often characterized as "suboptimal".

Slack has the important additional bonus that it provides staff with opportunities for research, training, rest, peer review, process innovation, and product innovation. They can undertake such activities while waiting to start the next task in the project – while waiting for the previous task in the project to finish. These activities make the developers stronger and smarter. It means that the developers are better prepared for their next development sprint.

12.7 Aggressive vs. defensive scheduling

If you follow my advice from the previous section, you will calculate your project end-date "bottom up", that is, by starting with estimates for the key individual tasks in the project. But of course, in the real world, project end-dates are often established by a very different process – a "top down" process where a senior manager declares the target end-date, by reference to market conditions and competitive pressures.

For example, you may be told in no uncertain terms, "you absolutely have to ship this product in time for the Christmas market". Or perhaps, "you need to have a product good enough to demo at next year's 3GSM conference".

This raises three questions:

❑ What options are there for truly quick projects (for example, creating a smartphone in six months or less)?

❑ What options are there to ensure that the agreed schedule is maintained – in other words, so that the project can proceed reliably to the target end-date?

❑ What is the particular role of aggression in ensuring timely project delivery – should timescales deliberately be set that are significantly quicker than developers estimate as being possible?

I return to the first of these three questions in Chapter 14. As for the second question, that is (of course) the subject of this entire book. That leaves the third question – the question of aggressive vs. defensive scheduling. To what extent should software leaders set project targets that are more ambitious than those arising from the project team's own estimates?

Here are the arguments in favor of aggressive scheduling:

❑ If people remain within their "comfort zone" without being stretched, they will be less effective

❑ If there is an aggressive schedule, it causes people to find creative new solutions, to finish the required tasks more quickly: aggression leads to "working smarter" as well as "working harder"

❑ Attack is the best method of defense!

❑ Even if the new schedule can't actually be fulfilled, and the project slips a few months, that's a better outcome than agreeing to the original schedule, and seeing that slip out a few months too; the point is that schedule slippage seems to be a fact of life, so it's better to slip from a short schedule than from a long schedule.

I have a lot of sympathy with these arguments. It is important that people enter a "flow mode" in which they are both highly creative and highly productive. If the team remains in comfort mode, the outcome is unlikely to be world class. On the other hand, there are significant drawbacks to a schedule that is overly aggressive:

❑ Everyone knows that the schedule is impossible (even if no-one dares to say so publicly), so the schedule falls into disrepute (people whisper to each other about "stupid bogus deadlines")

❑ Many creative solutions can emerge only after a process of calm reflection and review; in other words, you have to slow down in order to travel fast (another way of saying this is expressed in the proverb, "more haste, less speed").

Here are some practical real-life examples of cases when an over-aggressive schedule has led a project into deep problems:

❑ A project needed a significant number of consultants to travel to another country, for the final phase of the project. Visas were needed for these consultants. Because of an overly aggressive schedule, the consultants traveled to the country too early. Unfortunately, their visas expired before the project was finished, throwing the project into chaos

❑ Product management wanted to add feature X into a product. The timescale for this was estimated as five months. However, senior management said that the product absolutely had to reach the market in just three months. So there would be no time to add in the feature. As it happens, the product never had any real chance of reaching the market in six months, let alone three months. So with a realistic schedule, there *would* have been time to add in the feature. But the over-aggressive schedule had no time for the feature, so it was left out. Seven months later, the project was cancelled, even though it was now ready for release. Reason:

customers said that the product was unacceptable, on account of lacking feature X.

Happily, there is a third way, which achieves the targets of aggressive scheduling whilst avoiding its drawbacks. This third way is the method of "agile scheduling" covered earlier in this chapter. Another way of describing "agile scheduling" is as "authentic scheduling".

12.8 Authentic vs. inauthentic scheduling

If the estimates provided by developers are disregarded (or *appear* to be disregarded), it leaves the developers feeling disempowered, lacking motivation. If developers know in advance that their estimates are likely to be squashed by senior management, they are likely to increase them before submitting them (so that, when they are squashed, they come back to a figure the developer can support). This can lead to a very unhealthy "schedule arms race", with developers being in a kind of battle with their managers. The outcome is *inauthentic scheduling* – the schedule is made up of estimates that have been heavily altered from those originally submitted. A *far* better approach is agile scheduling:

❑ Estimates given by experienced developers, for being 50% confident of meeting the date, are used as the basis of the schedule

❑ These estimates are *not* altered by intervening layers of line managers and project managers

❑ Developers need to be ready to start work on tasks on a range of dates (depending on when exactly the previous tasks complete)

❑ When developers start work on a task, they are expected to work flat out on it

❑ Developers are expected to complete their work to an agreed quality level, rather than endlessly seeking further improvements

❑ There is contingency at the end of the project

❑ As a software leader, you communicate the full range of possible dates to interested stakeholders; you have to educate them in turn as to the benefits of agile scheduling.

I call the outcome "authentic scheduling" since everyone in the project team feels responsible to the plan and committed to the plan. In turn, the plan is recognized as being a hugely important tool, but not an end in itself. The plan serves the higher goal of delivering substantial value to customers through the completed product. The plan is an essential guide to the expected course of the project, but it's fully recognized that it will be subject to change, in numerous aspects. And when the project deviates from the agreed plan, there's no inherent cause for alarm. Instead, it's cause for:

❑ Simple modifications to the plan

❑ Clear communication to the project stakeholders about what has happened

❑ Reflection on whether the deviation was within the normal course of variation, or whether it indicates some specific aspect of sub-performance (in which case, other corrective action may be required).

12.9 Beyond meeting customer requests

Earlier, I said it was a mistake to treat the plan as king. Equally, however, it is a mistake to treat the customer as king. To be clear, what I said is, "rather than the plan being king, it is *customer satisfaction* that should be king". You have to give customers what they actually want, not what they say that they want. What's more, you have to satisfy the needs of your overall customer set, rather than just the needs of the most vocal of your customers.

Here are some reasons for not always providing customers with what they say that they want:

❑ Sometimes the person from the customer organization that talks to you may have no authority in that organization to actually convey product requirements; note in particular that just because someone is a senior manager does not mean they have the authority (or expertise) to speak on specific project matters

❑ Sometimes the customer representative may say something, in only a tentative way (even though it might not sound tentative); if you deliver the feature requested, you may later hear that "we didn't expect you to actually implement that feature"

❑ Sometimes the customer representative may ask for a feature, that would satisfy an unstated underlying requirement, but in fact there are other (easier) ways that the underlying requirement could be satisfied

❑ Sometimes the customer representative is confused or mistaken about the importance of a feature in the marketplace

❑ Sometimes a customer representative may ask for a feature which large numbers of other customers (including potential customers as well as actual customers) do *not* want.

In summary, you need to target your product at the market, rather than at an individual customer representative. If you implement every customer request, your project will suffer far too many changes, and your product will end up as inconsistent, flawed, and very late to market. To stop this from happening, you need to ensure that your team has access to in-house experts from the field known as "product management" – people who have:

❑ Their own well-grounded views of the likely pros and cons of possible product features

❑ The ability to listen carefully (and with an open mind) to requests from customers

❑ Skills in requirements analysis – for example, the ability to distinguish the underlying requirements from a proposed solution to these requirements.

On the other hand, it's very dangerous for any company to think that it systematically knows more than its customers. Even though customer requests are far from infallible, they remain the single best guide to market requirements. The more successful the customer, the higher the credence you should put on their requests. Bear in mind that, in a high-caliber customer organization, a great deal of process will be followed before a formal change request is made to you. The customer will check beforehand that:

❑ The request has a high priority, compared to others they have also been considering

❑ The request is founded on an important underlying requirement (even though the customer may, for confidentiality reasons, avoid spelling out this underlying requirement).

You may need to invest time with your customers to improve the quality of the change requests they raise:

❑ Give them feedback about issues you notice with the change requests they give you

❑ Act in a way that encourages your customers to share more of their thinking with you – treating you more like a partner than as a supplier. Once you understand their underlying thinking, you will be better placed to decide quickly on the suitability of specific CRs.

In other words, you need to couple excellent product management skills (mentioned above) with excellent account management skills. This way, you will gain the greatest benefit from customer requests.

13
Managing uncertainty

13.1 The 80–20 rule for planning

One of the most useful rules in successful projects – as in life generally – is the 80–20 rule: 80% of the possible value of an activity can be obtained by careful application of 20% of the possible effort. Conversely, 80% of the problems can arise from just 20% of the causes. For example,

- 20% of customers can account for about 80% of sales revenue
- 20% of the add-on applications can account for 80% of the sales of add-on applications
- 20% of the software engineers can cause 80% of the defects
- 80% of what you achieve in your job can come from 20% of the time spent
- 80% of the time on a smartphone is spent executing around 20% of its operating code
- 80% of the heartache in a smartphone project will be caused by 20% of the project tasks.

Of course, the numbers 80 and 20 aren't exact. In a given field of enterprise, it might be a 75–30 rule, or a 60–15 rule, or a 95–25 rule, instead of 80–20. But the point is that it's not 50–50. In other words, not all effort is equal. It's a very ineffective approach to try to refine and improve all aspects of a project plan at once. Instead, you have to identify the parts of the project that will have the biggest impact on the overall schedule. These are the parts that you need to plan in most detail.

Even before that decision, you have to identify the parts of the new functionality of the product that are the most important. These are the features that absolutely must be in the product – the ''mandatory'' features – whereas the other features are just "highly desirable" (and/or "nice to have"). So here's how you start to create your plan:

☐ List the product features that you understand to be mandatory

☐ Obtain a first set of estimates of the level of effort likely to be required for each of these features; for each feature, estimate both the 50% likely duration and the 90% likely duration (meaning the amounts of time that you are 50% and 90% sure the task will be finished within)

☐ In this process be sure to include, not only the headline new features – such as new applications and new technologies – but also productization elements such as integration, optimization, testing, certification, and operator acceptance. These elements are just as mandatory as any headline features

☐ Construct the first draft of the plan based only on these features, taking the 50% likely dates. Put as many elements of the plan in parallel as the anticipated resource availability is likely to allow (taking into account the skills profile of the people on the team). Whatever the total amount of time is, add on and distribute another 50% for contingency, as discussed in the previous chapter.

13.2 Identifying the project planning hot list

Now mark the following items as deserving high priority further attention:

☐ The 20% of items with the longest individual durations

☐ The 20% of items for which the 90% likely duration exceeds the 50% likely duration by the highest margin (e.g. 3 times or 2.5 times) – these are the items with the greatest risk

☐ The 20% of items which have the greatest potential for critical resource contention – meaning that they require skills to carry them out which (so far as you are aware) only a few members of the team possess; these are the items which are most likely to slip from their schedule because of lack of suitable resources to work on them

☐ The 20% of the "highly desirable" items which senior management are most likely (in your view) to insist on elevating into the "mandatory" category.

Collectively, this forms your draft "project planning hot list".

Before going further, cross-check your draft hot list against the set of typical smartphone project trouble spots listed later in this chapter (or against any evolved version of that list of trouble spots which your company maintains). If items are missing from your own hot list, consider adding them in. At this stage, your draft hot list is probably becoming rather long. So it's time to prioritize it further. I recommend that you chop it in half, and set a target to cover each of the items in the first half of the list in greater detail over the course of one more week of analysis.

This next round of analysis seeks to obtain, for each item, a greater understanding of:

❑ How likely it is that the item must be included in the product (that is, whether it is truly mandatory)
❑ The steps involved in implementing this part of the project
❑ The skill sets required for this part of the project
❑ The people likely to be assigned to this task
❑ 50% and 90% estimates for the task duration
❑ The risks involved in this part of the project – and how these risks can be alleviated.

13.3 Iterating the project plan

The project plan is dynamic. It keeps changing, in the light of events, and in the light of the increased understanding you gain from additional rounds of investigation.

Your project planning hot list is also dynamic. This is the list of items that urgently need further investigation, to remove uncertainty about them. Items can *leave* the hot list because:

❑ They have actually been completed
❑ The key risks involved have been passed, without things going wrong
❑ Your confidence grows that you have a sufficiently good understanding of these items
❑ You no longer think that these items will take a long time to complete.

Other items will remain on the hot list, but in a suspended state, because you don't think you can usefully increase your understanding of them at this time. You need to wait until further events happen before you analyze these items further (or you may be waiting for the arrival on the project of consultants with specific skills who can review the plans for these tasks in more detail). This is a dangerous situation to be in, but sometimes you can decide to accept it on a temporary basis. The reason for accepting it is, of course, that you wish instead to investigate other items at this time.

As items leave the hot list (or are temporarily suspended from it), you should add in others in their place. These are the items that have now become the highest priority to investigate further. These may be items from the previous draft hot list that you didn't have time, earlier, to investigate properly. Or they may be items that now satisfy any of the conditions noted above, regarding length of time, risk factor, critical resource contention, or likelihood (for new potential tasks) for insertion into the project.

So both the project plan and the project planning hot list change, typically on a weekly basis. Each iteration of the project plan gives rise to a new iteration of the hot list. In turn, the investigation of the items on the hot list gives rise to an improved project plan (refer to Figure 13.1).

Yet another activity happens in parallel: you add in more items to the full plan – items which were not on the original mandatory list, but which you believe will be included in the actual product. Some of these items can cause significant alterations to the plan. In such a case, if you can't re-jig the plan to avoid this disruption, you need to check with senior management whether it is permissible to omit them – leaving them (for example) to be included in a later version of the product.

Some people are uncomfortable with this kind of iterative planning. They prefer an approach in which the entire specification of the product is locked down at an early phase of planning. They seek to remove all uncertainty before proceeding. They argue that customers require complete knowledge, early, of what is going to be delivered to

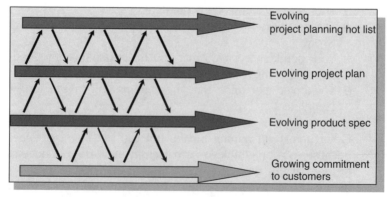

Figure 13.1   Iterating the plan

them. The argument is that customers cannot make their own plans, if they are uncertain about what is going to be delivered to them. For example, if a customer cannot be sure of taking delivery of some functionality from you, they will have to make alternative plans (such as implementing that functionality themselves).

In response, I agree that you have to be able to give reliable commitments regarding the mandatory features of the product. However, not every feature is mandatory. You have to decide what the core features of your product delivery are. Don't deceive yourself that every feature of your product is equally core. Your aim is to give a clear commitment, early, to deliver these features at an agreed time and with an agreed quality level. But if you want to be able to give a clear commitment to delivering a much wider set of features, that will take you much longer to plan. If you go down this route, don't be surprised if, by the time you have completed that longer planning exercise:

❑ Passage of time has made the plan irrelevant before it is ready
❑ Your customer has lost interest, and has made alternative plans (involving other suppliers).

So you have to live with uncertainty. And the customer has to live with uncertainty. But as in so many aspects of the relationship with the customer, for a smartphone project, the keywords are honesty, openness, communication, and trust:

❑ Let your customers know what you are highly confident you can deliver

❑ Also let your customers know the features that you are currently in the process of analyzing further: items that you would like to deliver, but which you can't yet guarantee

❑ Keep your customers regularly updated.

13.4 Developing features outside the agreed core

I often hear it said that every single item in a smartphone product specification is mandatory. This means that at least one important customer has made a very strong request that the item be included (and your product management personnel have confirmed that they agree with this customer's opinion). If that's really true, then you have no room for maneuver, no discretion, and a near-impossible planning and execution task ahead of you.

However, don't neglect the dimension of time. Despite what customers may say, it's usually unnecessary to deliver every feature at the same time. You should plan to deliver some features in version 1 of your smartphone product, and others at a later time (in version 2, say). For example, you should regard some features as mandatory for version 2, and as highly desirable for version 1. Start work on these items as soon as resourcing allows, and monitor the situation regularly. Defer until later the decision as to which of these features are actually included in version 1, and which are delayed until version 2. Be ready to switch resources on or off these tasks, but don't forget to keep your customers informed about what's happening.

I call these features "eventually mandatory" features. They are mandatory for eventual delivery, but it is optional whether they are included in the forthcoming release. In the meantime, you have to accept a degree of uncertainty about which version of the product will contain them.

Of course, the situation repeats itself when you start planning version 2 in greater detail. At that time, you should again designate some items as eventually mandatory: it is mandatory that they will be delivered in some release soon, but it is optional whether they are delivered in version 2 itself.

Here are reasons why a feature may be designated as eventually mandatory:

❑ It will take an unknown length of time for various associated technologies to become prevalent in the marketplace – for example, new network services, or relevant smartphone peripherals. In other words, market conditions for this feature may not be ready until a later date

❑ Despite your best efforts, it is likely to take too long to complete the features (and to integrate them fully) in time for the release date of the next version

❑ Despite the express wishes of your customers, you simply have too many other features already designated as mandatory for the forthcoming version.

The fact that a feature may be omitted from the forthcoming release is, however, no reason to automatically delay the start of its implementation (or the start of its planning):

❑ Especially if the task will take a long time to complete, you have to commence its implementation early – such items are called "long lead time items" (or "front end items")

❑ Especially if the task is conceptually unclear (in terms of requirements, design, and/or necessary skill-set to implement it), you have
to commence its planning early.

In this way, your team will need to dedicate some time to items
that are outside the agreed core of the forthcoming product. Doing
this means that the subsequent versions will have a flying start. It
also means that you will from time to time be able to delight your
customers by delivering some functionality ahead of the expected
schedule.

13.5 The 80–20 rule for task estimation

The 80–20 rule applies to the project plan as a whole: each week,
you should update the project planning hot list, and give priority
planning attention just to the items that are on that list.

Importantly, the 80–20 rule also applies to the process of estimating
an individual task. You can get around 80% of the accuracy in an
estimate by skillfully investing just 20% of the time required to get an
estimate that would have near 100% accuracy. In other words, if the
team takes three times as long to carry out an estimate of the work
required, the result will not be three times as accurate; it's likely to
be only around (say) 30% more accurate.

As a software leader, you need to coach your team members to
be able to provide good first-order estimates of task durations quickly
and effectively:

❑ They have to let go of any over-engineering or perfectionist attitude
to estimates

❑ They have to be confident that they will not be penalized for
occasionally getting estimates significantly wrong – so long as
they have not been negligent, and so long as they are ready to
learn from any mistakes

❑ They have to give regular updates, as they find more information,
as to their latest expectations on the range of likely durations for
the task.

In order to be able to estimate the length of a task, you need to be
able to see how the task is likely to compare with previous tasks
that have been completed in the past. If the task is totally new, you
can only make a wild guess as to how long it will take. If the task
is totally new *to you*, you need to ask for advice from people who

have done something similar before. This emphasizes how important it is:

❑ To involve in your planning people (such as consultants) who have worked on similar smartphone projects in the past

❑ To seek to retain key individuals from one smartphone project to the next, in order to keep their knowledge and experience in the team

❑ To seed new teams with people who have worked on previous smartphone projects.

You may be tempted to compare a task in a smartphone project with a task from a different kind of project:

❑ A feature phone project
❑ A desktop PC project.

That's OK, so long as you have taken to heart the various lessons in this book. But please don't underestimate the differences between smartphones and each of the feature phones and desktop PCs. If you are at all unsure, be sure to check with experienced advisors or consultants.

13.6 Typical project trouble spots

One of the first pieces of advice you will receive from any experienced smartphone developers is a set of typical smartphone project trouble spots – tasks that can (if mismanaged) end up consuming much more resource than initially expected. These tasks deserve close attention from the project management team throughout the project. They form the core of your project planning hot list. Here are some important examples:

❑ Any use of untried or breakthrough technology in your product – any technology said to be on the "bleeding edge"

❑ Power management – ensuring that software doesn't burn CPU cycles unnecessarily, therefore draining batteries too quickly

❑ Optimization of system start-up and application start-up

❑ Optimization of graphics – avoiding visible flicker or slow screen updates

❑ High performance data throughput and efficient flow control

- ❑ The development of special fast-booting start-up modes for use during the manufacturing process (this can include "test modes" to allow quick verification, during factory assembly, that aspects of the smartphone hardware are functioning correctly)

- ❑ Management of RAM and ROM – to avoid the software requiring more expensive hardware

- ❑ Performance of the system under stress

- ❑ Scalable use of tools and processes involved in integration, build, test, distribution, defect management, and configuration management

- ❑ Connectivity solutions between the smartphone and desktop PCs

- ❑ Putting all necessary legal contracts in place with third-party suppliers

- ❑ Integration of new software plug-ins for multimedia, security, telephony, and hardware peripherals

- ❑ Gaining formal certification for specific pieces of software (such as Java and Bluetooth)

- ❑ Gaining operator approval

- ❑ Integration of new third-party applications and services specified by individual operators.

13.7 Pros and cons of milestone reviews

A sure recipe for smartphone project failure is to allow yourself to become deceived about the extent of your progress. You need to be sure about the progress you have made: which tasks have been finished, and which still need more work.

For example, suppose that your project plan lists 300 tasks (at a certain level of detail), and has a duration of 40 weeks in total. Suppose (to simplify the discussion) that the plan states that after four weeks, 30 of these tasks should be finished. But when the four weeks have passed, how will you know how many of these tasks have actually been finished? Someone in your team may tell you that, for example, "the configuration management system has been rolled out to the team", so you will be tempted to tick that item as completed. But it's possible that the configuration management system has only been rolled out to part of the team, that it's only a trial version, or that a part of this system is still missing. In other words, it's possible that the task is only partially complete.

Here's another example. An item in the project plan may say "make the first phone call". But that could mean many different things. Someone could report that the task is finished, on account of seeing low-level software call the relevant telephony functions. But the real intent of that item in the plan could be something more substantial.

So we can see one way that projects end up running late: management is led to believe, in early portions of the project, that progress is faster than is actually the case. This follows from fuzziness in task definitions, and/or fuzziness in task monitoring. Because management fails to see the true situation in the project, they are unable to take early corrective action. As the adage states, "a stitch in time saves nine". Because corrective action does not happen in time, the project runs into greater difficulties.

It is for this reason that best practice in project management emphasizes the importance of clear task definition and clear project milestones. A milestone is an identifiable point of definite progress. For example, a good milestone definition is when all the following can happen:

❏ One user can pick up the smartphone and use its UI system to initiate a voice call to another smartphone

❏ Another user can use the UI system on the second smartphone to answer the call, and then sustain a conversation with the first smartphone for at least one minute, before terminating the call

❏ Both smartphones continue to function after the completion of the call.

Another example of a good milestone is when 50% of the tests in the BAT (Basic Acceptance Tests) pass.

In short, the purpose of milestones in smartphone projects is to:

❏ Define identifiable points of progress, with preset target dates

❏ Remove uncertainty about the state of the project

❏ Help spur on development tasks

❏ Allow the team to monitor progress, with a view (if necessary) to making changes to resource allocation or to other aspects of the plan.

Some milestone reviews can be linked to "go/no go" decisions for the next phase of a project; additional resources are allocated to the project only once a certain milestone is passed. (The word "tollgate" is sometimes used, instead of "milestone", for a progress review that determines whether or not to proceed to the next phase of the project.)

Done well, milestones provide a very useful intermediate level in between individual tasks and the entire project. If there are 300 tasks in the entire project plan, there might be something like 10 major milestones in the project. You can assess progress against 10 milestones more easily than you can track progress against each of 300 lower-level tasks.

However, milestones can cause problems of their own:

❑ In case a milestone review is delayed (because it requires senior managers to meet, and this takes time to organize), there is a risk of project work being held up in the meantime

❑ If important decisions (not to mention possible cash bonus payouts) are tied to the outcomes of milestone reviews, there is a risk of distorted thinking; for example, a milestone may be allowed to pass "with exceptions", meaning that some of the required conditions need to be completed later; in itself, this is OK, but the risk is that the project stakeholders fail to recognize the full implications of the exceptions – and become deceived about the true amount of progress made

❑ If metrics forming part of a milestone definition are given dis-proportionate emphasis, so that the project puts great effort into ensuring that these metrics reach the desired values, there is a risk of neglecting other tasks that actually should have a higher priority.

Earlier, I spoke about the problems in companies where "the plan is king". In such companies, milestones are often also given distorted prominence. Like the plan itself, milestones are only a tool to a higher purpose, namely the satisfaction of customer requirements. If you lose sight of this fact, don't be surprised if you experience milestone-induced problems.

13.8 Dealing with milestone delays

Suppose that the first milestone in a smartphone development project is due for completion after four weeks, out of the total project duration of 40 weeks. Suppose that, in fact, it takes six weeks to complete this first milestone. Here are three possible reactions that a team can have:

❑ They resolve to work especially hard, to make amends for the two-week delay, so that the project sticks to its original schedule of 40 weeks

❑ They accept that slippage has occurred, but resolve not to let any other slippage occur, so that the project is now expected to take 42 weeks in total

❑ They note that the project is taking 50% longer than expected, and therefore now predict that the total duration will be 60 weeks.

Actually, none of these responses, by themselves, is satisfactory. We need more information:

❑ Was the delay within the originally estimated contingency for that task? If so, the delay need not, by itself, lead to a change in the predicted end-date for the project

❑ Was the delay due to one-off factors, or to factors which still exist (and which are therefore likely to cause further schedule slippages)?

❑ How about other project tasks that have been proceeding in parallel – are they also delayed, or have they been finished in time?

In other words, the progress of the project plan cannot be determined by the milestones alone (even though the milestones are important). Smartphone projects are too complex to be reduced to individual milestone events. It's important to have clear milestone definitions, but it's even more important to have high caliber individuals continually monitoring the whole progress of the project. Your project management team continually refine the project plan, the associated project planning hot list, and the set of actions that need to be taken to maximize the likelihood of satisfying customer requirements. This is a full-time job.

13.9 Cut features not corners

Here's another big risk with milestone reviews. A team may be told that a certain milestone needs to be reached by a given date, or else the project is in jeopardy (senior management might cancel it). This has the advantage of spurring on additional effort by the team. But it can cause all kinds of ill-advised shortcuts to be taken, in the rush to meet the milestone deadline.

For example, a team may feel particular pressure to include one new feature ahead of the milestone review, or to fix one specific defect. This may lead them to disregard the architecture or the design of the product. They may, for example:

- ❑ Change a source file that is provided by a supplier and intended never to be changed
- ❑ Break the encapsulation or modularity of class design
- ❑ Add extra layers of complexity
- ❑ Slow down performance elsewhere in the system
- ❑ End up with a large amount of duplicated code
- ❑ Utilize an excessive amount of ROM, RAM, or CPU cycles
- ❑ Break interfaces (and potentially break the build)
- ❑ Make it harder to maintain the code.

In short, they may store up problems for the future – for development happening after the milestone. So the milestone review would have an unintended effect:

- ❑ Management perceives that the milestone has been met, since all the features they're looking for are in the product by this time
- ❑ So management perceives that the project is on schedule, and starts to relax
- ❑ However, aspects of the internals of the product are now in a bad state
- ❑ So in reality, the project is likely to take much longer than expected in its next phase
- ❑ Afterwards, management is extremely surprised at the eventual delays.

Sadly, this is a pattern I have seen on too many occasions.

My strong advice is: cut features, not corners. Resist pressures to short-cut processes. It's better to deliver 80% of the expected feature count, at 100% quality, than to deliver 100% of the expected feature count, at 80% quality. It's much easier to add in new features later, than to undo faulty software internals.

For this reason, I have never liked the concept of a "release that's functionally complete". In this concept, first you write all the software, and then you remove all the defects. Instead, I recommend that you address defects *as soon as you are aware of them*. Don't keep on writing new features on top of software which is known to have defects. You must put the foundations in good order first.

However, this won't remove the pressure for you to create special demo releases from time to time:

- ❑ Perhaps you need to show your product at a trade show, such as 3GSM or CTIA
- ❑ Perhaps you need to demonstrate the features of your product to potential customers

❑ Perhaps you need to receive early market feedback on some intended features or usage patterns.

To address these needs, here's what you need to do:

❑ Use prototyping systems to receive feedback on the intended features or usage patterns

❑ Use the branching features of your CM (Configuration Management) system in order to create a special "demo branch" ahead of a trade show; keep the demo branch separate from the mainline; use the features of your CM system to selectively propagate code between the two branches

❑ Keep a clear distinction between the demo codeline and the true codeline.

This allows you to have the best of both worlds. You'll have to work smarter – and rely on good tools to work hard on your behalf. But you'll end up with good features *and* good quality.

14
Simplifying smartphone projects

14.1 Beyond difficulty

If you've read carefully through the preceding chapters, you may have formed the view that it is really difficult to complete a Symbian OS smartphone project. There's so much to think about – such a lot of scope for things to go wrong.

To an extent, I will be satisfied if you reach that conclusion. A very common reason for smartphone projects to go wrong is if the project management team is over-confident. You need more than positive thinking to successfully complete a smartphone development project. If you think that you can go sailing through this kind of project, you are unlikely to succeed. You will be tripped up by one or more of the pitfalls described in the preceding pages. Your skills in (for example) feature phone software development or desktop PC software development will fail to transfer into the significantly different world of smartphone software development. So I want you to "look before you leap".

On the other hand, I don't want to over-state the difficulty of running a successful smartphone project. The skills involved are new (in part), but they are not impossible. In a way, the difficulty in running a successful smartphone project can be compared to the difficulty of driving a car in an unfamiliar busy city, or playing golf in a professional tournament and surviving the cut. In all three cases, there's a lot to think about: you need to do many things right, all at the same time. In all three cases, it will take you a number of years to become a real expert. But that doesn't rule out the possibility of success. It just means that it will take you time.

Another comparison is with learning the technical aspects of advanced software engineering. To be good at advanced software engineering, you need to master something like 20 significant individual skills, each of which takes time and considerable practice. It's the same with becoming good at the management side of leading a smartphone development project. Again, there is a set of something like 20 significant individual skills which you need to learn – as covered in various chapters in this book. That's a lot of different skills, but you may notice that this book is a lot slimmer than some of the classic primers on the technical aspects of advanced software engineering. So take heart.

However, you may still be thinking to yourself, "Isn't there an easier way?" Is it really necessary to master all the skills listed in all the chapters of this book, before you can successfully create a smartphone product? Isn't there some kind of short-cut to smartphone project success? And isn't there a quicker way to *finish* a smartphone development project?

In this chapter, I answer these questions, offering some suggestions for shortcuts to smartphone project success. But I'll say in advance that you can't get something from nothing. The suggestions in this chapter will help you to progress more quickly, but they all depend on work done by someone else (such as a reference design provider). If you want to secure yourself a sustainable competitive advantage over the other people who will also adopt the same shortcuts, you will need to develop, over time, a broader understanding of the smartphone development process. Perhaps you won't need to become world-class yourself in (to take one example) the skill of interface management, but you will need to become familiar with the basic concepts of that skill.

Anyone who offers you a "guaranteed get rich quick" system for smartphone development projects is doing you a disservice. There are plenty of tools, tips, and techniques that will speed your progress, but none of these can guarantee you sustained profits. There's no substitute for real knowledge and real experience. Welcome to the real world. Smartphone projects are hard, but the first step in dealing with hard projects is to recognize that projects are hard. Then you can start to deal with the difficulties, instead of seeking to bypass them.

14.2 Reuse rather than reinvent

The most important short-cut to smartphone project success is to follow the principle, "Reuse rather than reinvent". Instead of using lots of your own resources to invent a solution, you should take advantage of work that someone else has already done. If that previous work has already been fully integrated, fully optimized, and fully tested, so much the better.

Any smartphone project typically reuses work from at least four different providers:

- ❑ The smartphone operating system, supplied by Symbian
- ❑ A UI system (together with applications), supplied from an organization such as Series 60 or UIQ
- ❑ A base port of Symbian OS onto an application processor, supplied by a semiconductor vendor
- ❑ A wireless signaling stack, running on a baseband processor (for more details, see Chapter 2).

That's a very powerful start. However, you should look to be reusing a whole lot more than that. The very best kind of reuse, from the point of view of your company, is when you reuse technology that your own company has already developed. In particular, the quickest way for you to complete a smartphone project is if that project is the second version of a previous project.

So here's the answer to the question, "What's the quickest way to create a smartphone product?" The answer is, "Don't start from scratch". If you want to bring a smartphone to market in as little time as four months, your only hope for success is if that product is a variant or extension of a smartphone you have already brought to market. A v2 product can reach the market much quicker than a v1 product, provided that you:

- ❑ Keep large parts of the project team in place
- ❑ Keep most of the design of the product intact
- ❑ Use most of the same suppliers
- ❑ Avoid the "second system effect" of trying to rewrite everything completely the second time around.

If you break these rules, you can expect to take a lot longer for the second project – perhaps even as long as you took for the first project.

14.3 The benefits of frequent releases

A company that has brought a v1 smartphone product to market should be well positioned to bring a v2 product to market relatively quickly – and then a v3, a v4, and so on. This is what I have seen with the most successful of Symbian's partners. The first smartphone project can be rather traumatic, but follow-on projects proceed a lot more smoothly.

This is no accident. It reflects a fundamental principle of complex software development – the principle of regular iteration, which says that you should "iterate little and often". This applies both inside an individual project, and for a series of projects that collectively build on each other over time. Inside a project, you should be producing a baseline release once every one or two weeks, with the quality of that baseline release steadily increasing (see Chapter 8 for more details). You should be controlling how much functionality is added in each integration cycle – otherwise the integration will become too difficult (with the project becoming delayed). Stepping the discussion up a level, it's the same for the amount of functionality that you put into any one product.

Here are two different approaches for bringing a series of smartphone products to market:

❑ Each time, include a huge amount of new functionality in the product, resulting in a series of relatively major projects
❑ Each time, include only a modest amount of new functionality in the product, resulting in a series of relatively minor projects.

The first approach involves a smaller amount of large projects, whereas the second approach involves a larger amount of small projects. I strongly recommend the latter of these approaches – following the principle of "iterate little and often":

❑ For the first project, aim to deliver "the 20% that provides 80% of the immediate customer value" – or perhaps more realistically, the 40% (say) that delivers 60% of the value

❑ Be ruthless about rejecting, from the committed spec of the first version, functionality that could instead be supplied at a slightly later date

❑ Plan from the start to follow the first version with a series of later versions

❑ Maintain a product roadmap – listing the expected future versions, together with your current best guess on the likely features in these versions.

The advantages of the frequent release model are as follows:

❑ Because the projects are shorter, you have less chance of being surprised by market developments ahead of the release of the product

❑ Because the projects have less new functionality, the integration task is easier each time. Bear in mind that the effort involved in integrating new functionality increases at a rate something like the square of the number of new items of functionality

- ❏ Because products reach the market earlier, you receive all-important market feedback earlier

- ❏ You will reach financial payback earlier, and your development team will be self-financing earlier

- ❏ The discipline of shorter releases means that you are forced to take tougher decisions, early, about which functionality to exclude from the scope of the product; this is a healthy discipline

- ❏ Because the projects are shorter, there is less danger of spending a long time in "analysis paralysis" (a series of seemingly endless research workshops and review taskforces).

14.4 Symbian's adoption of the frequent release model

Symbian's own release model has evolved over the years. For a time, we were in the situation of taking around a year between releases of Symbian OS. This had the following drawbacks:

- ❏ Because releases were few and far between, customers were extremely interested in ensuring that functionality of potential interest to them was included in the specification of the next release

- ❏ Any functionality omitted from one release would have to wait around one year for inclusion in a subsequent release – this led customers to campaign hard for extra functionality to be included in the earlier release

- ❏ The releases ended up with large specifications, and therefore took a long time to integrate

- ❏ When a release did finally reach customers, the advance of time often meant that some items delivered were no longer so important to them; in other words, the releases ended up containing items of lesser value (along, of course, with huge amounts of material of high value).

In recognition of these drawbacks, in 2003–4 we switched to a system of frequent releases – with new versions of Symbian OS reaching customers about once every three or four months. The internal project to improve our release system was code-named "Mercury", in recognition of the rapid cycling around the sun made by this innermost planet. This system of rapid Symbian OS releases required an improved discipline in product engineering, but the effect has been well worth it:

❑ Each individual release has smaller content

❑ Each individual release is a more manageable project

❑ If an item cannot be included in a given release, there is only around four months to wait for the next release vehicle

❑ In general, items reach customers sooner – there is a shorter time between customers requesting an item, and that item being delivered in a release

❑ We receive earlier market feedback about the contents of items delivered in releases

❑ We receive earlier revenues from the contents of new releases.

As I say, this kind of working requires improved discipline (the benefits do not come "for free"):

❑ Our configuration management system needs to cope with several releases being developed at the same time

❑ Improved interface management is required, so that customers can start project work on one release, and then move up smoothly, midway through the project, to the next version of Symbian OS

❑ We need to identify and start work early on "long lead time items" for future releases

❑ We need to maintain and evolve a product roadmap, covering around six releases in total (reaching the market over a period of around two years)

❑ We need to cope with items moving from one release to another (either moving backwards or moving forwards), depending on their progress.

In smartphone development projects, you can't get something from nothing. With a frequent release model, you get the releases quicker, but you need greater software development discipline in order to achieve this.

14.5 Use of reference designs

If you can't reuse your own software (from an earlier version), the next best option is for you to reuse software which is part of an integrated reference design. *This is a particularly good option for companies that are relatively new to Symbian OS smartphones.* A reference design minimally delivers a working integrated combination of the following:

- A version of Symbian OS
- A matching version of a UI system
- An application processor and a baseband processor
- A wireless stack, running on the baseband processor
- A base port of Symbian OS onto the application processor
- A communications bridge between Symbian OS and the wireless stack
- A rudimentary phone application.

The reference design also includes everything else that is needed for the rudimentary phone application to work – including a phone application model (sometimes called a "phone engine"), a call log, a contacts database, and an audio system.

A reference design can be described as "something like 80% of the way to a complete phone". This is a big step up from the usual starting point, which is a base port of Symbian OS onto the application processor chip that is intended to be included in the phone. Other things being equal, it is approximately twice as easy to create a phone from a reference design, as from a raw base port.

A successful phone reference design removes a great deal of the risk and uncertainty from the integration of the technology set into a phone. You can put more of your own efforts into providing extra innovation and design on top of the reference design, rather than working at the integration ("plumbing") level. On the other hand, here are some points you need to consider:

- If a reference design is available to you, it is probably also available to your competitors

- Following a release of a new version of Symbian OS (or a new version of the UI system), it takes some time for a matching reference design to become available.

The best situation for you therefore may be to:

- Develop a close relationship with a supplier of a reference design

❑ Ensure that your own forward planning, for future products, dove-tails with the roadmap for future reference designs
❑ Receive early deliveries of the reference design, whilst it is still in the process of being integrated.

In this way, you become a so-called "lead customer" for the reference design. You have the benefits of early access, but the corresponding drawbacks of having to work with a system that is still under development. You may have the best of both worlds, but you'll need great skill to remain in that situation.

14.6 Silver bullets vs. disruption

From time to time, you will hear claims that such-and-such a tool can significantly reduce your time to market (TTM), or otherwise dramatically simplify your smartphone development project. As you saw in Chapter 11, I'm a big fan of tools. There's no doubt that good tools can make aspects of your development go much faster.

However, the development of a smartphone product that sells well in the market almost invariably involves *very many* different processes and phases. If one of these goes faster, there's a risk that you will relax prematurely, thinking that you've already succeeded, without realizing that you've only improved a small part of the overall methodology. So take care. You may have found a silver bullet that simplifies one of the hard tasks in creating a smartphone product. But that doesn't mean that all the difficulties yield.

Another dangerous kind of "silver bullet" is the idea that you can stick with a more familiar operating system, rather than making the jump into the challenging world of Symbian OS. Interestingly, you probably *can* complete an individual project faster, by sticking with an operating system you already know intimately. But the case for switching to Symbian OS doesn't hinge on the pros and cons of any one phone development project. You need to consider the effort taken to create a whole series of smartphone products going forwards. Once you've properly climbed the learning curve into the Symbian OS world, you'll find that you can create whole families of striking products, with much less effort than before. So the return on investment becomes higher and higher with each new Symbian OS project you undertake.

As someone who studied mathematics for four years at university, I like to compare entering the Symbian OS world with entering the world of formal algebra. Perhaps you can remember your first exposure to formal algebra. It might have gone like this. "I'm thinking of a number. Now I'm adding on 3 to that number. The answer is 7. What was the number I first had in mind?'' You want to shout out the answer, ''It's 4, of course''. But the teacher makes you write down some equation like $x + 3 = 7$, and then go through the rigmarole of subtracting 3 from each side. The point is that the formalism of algebra is overkill for such a simple problem, but you need it to solve harder problems. When you are faced with simultaneous equations in several unknowns, you can no longer solve the problems by simply shouting out the answer. You need to follow a more complex process. Then the rigmarole becomes your ally.

It's the same with Symbian OS. If all you want to create is a modest increment on your current product, you can probably carry that out most easily by sticking with your current software system. But if you want to create whole families of new generations of smartphone products, you need to switch.

Business analysts talk about ''disruptive technologies'': technologies that initially seem to take you backwards, but which have the capability to deliver much more in the long term than your existing technologies (see Figure 14.1). Interestingly, if you're looking for silver bullets, you'll miss the more sustained opportunities that come from disruptive technologies. Because they can take you backwards to start with, disruptive technologies are often hard to spot. For the first few years of Symbian's existence, Symbian OS was in that situation. Nowadays, happily, the capabilities of Symbian OS are undeniable, thanks to the rich variety of stunningly successful products being brought to the market by pioneering customers and partners. The position of Symbian OS as a breakthrough disruptive technology is now clear. But that doesn't take away the potential pain of the learning curve.

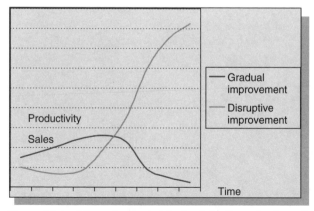

Figure 14.1   Disruptive technologies initially go backwards

In the next few chapters, I'll talk more about design and philosophy than about management and process. I'll share some of the thinking that guided the formation of Symbian OS. If your teams understand that thinking, it will help them to ride more quickly along the Symbian OS learning curve. Instead of fighting parts of the system, you'll be able to go with the flow. You'll complete successful smartphone projects more quickly and more reliably.

Part 3

Symbian's design philosophy

Part 3 (continued)

18 Designing for usability
- "The operation was a success, but the patient died"
- Enchantment
- Designing the user interface
- Multimedia performance
- Understanding the real competition
- Customer orientation for developers
- Designing panics

19 Designing for longevity
- Preparing for variants
- Be ready to fail fast
- Prepare your own SDK
- The value of codevelopment
- Basic principles for reusable solutions
- The value of architecture
- The value of ignorance

20 Designing for smartphones
- The licensing question
- Focus on strategy
- Smartphone heritage
- Active objects
- Power management
- Beware stray signals
- Final comments on asynchronous events

15
Design goals for Symbian OS

15.1 The birth of EPOC32

The first internal release of E32 took place in the software department at Psion on 10th December 1994. The release notes for this release state simply:

```
Version 0.01.001
================
(Made by Colly, 10 Dec 1994)
1) First release.
```

This contained the results of several months of prodigious labor by Colly Myers (who, three and a half years later, was to become Symbian's first CEO). E32 is the lowest level of what we now call Symbian OS, but which was at the time known as EPOC32 (see the annotated glossary of abbreviations, in the appendix, for some more details).

Although many months of activity had preceded the first release of E32, it was only a tiny fraction of the work that was to follow. Driven by the needs of an ever-larger team of software developers who were creating higher-level software components, new internal releases of E32 came thick and fast. Version 0.01.002 was released on 13 December, 0.01.003 on 14 December, and so on. There were no fewer than nine releases before the end of the year. 42 more releases followed at a somewhat more leisurely pace throughout 1995. 1996 saw another 31 internal releases of E32, and 28 more followed, up to release 1.01.110 made on 5th June 1997 – the release that was included in the ROM of the first shipping Psion Series 5 PDA. The release notes for E32 alone over this period fill nearly 10,000 lines of text, and credit more than 30 different people with providing code to E32 at various times.

E32 provides the core elements of the operating system. Meanwhile, on top of E32, a rapidly growing list of components started to be developed, including (in rough chronological order of their first appearance):

- F32, the file server and file systems
- G32 (later split into GDI and BITGDI), containing low-level graphics functionality
- WSERV, the window server, and FBSERV, a server handling fonts and bitmaps
- C32, the comms server, and ESOCK, the sockets server
- HCIL, the first UI library for EPOC32 (implementing the HCI – the Human Computer Interface)
- STOR, implementing robust stream storage, and DBMS, with database management services
- ETEXT, for manipulating rich editable text, and FORM, for text layout and formatting
- EALWL, a server for handling alarms and accessing data about world cities and countries
- BAFL, the so-called Basic Application Framework Library
- APPARC, defining application architecture – how the system associates data with applications
- IRDA, for infrared connectivity, and PLP, for PC connectivity
- TCPIP and many other networking libraries
- DIAL and ETEL, for access to telephony functionality
- Numerous application engines, application views, and application UIs.

HCIL later underwent a massive transformation to become EIKON, the UI library that shipped on the Psion Series 5 PDA. Along the way, a small UI-independent library called CONE was spun out, providing the so-called "Control Environment" – the environment supporting UI controls.

The Series 5 was publicly launched at One Whitehall Place, London, on 16th June 1997, and was available for sale in shops a couple of weeks later. The software had taken nearly three years to write, funded by revenues from continuing strong sales throughout this period from Psion PDAs (such as the Series 3c and the Siena) running SIBO, the 16-bit forerunner of Symbian OS.

15.2 Defining the EPOC RISC architecture

At the start of 1995, my business card announced my job title as "Software architect". In addition to being the primary author of first

HCIL and then BAFL, CONE, and EIKON, I had the responsibility to ensure that all the upper levels of EPOC32 software fitted together optimally. I saw this as having cultural aspects in addition to purely technological ones. Inspired by a chapter in Bjarne Stroustrup's "The design and evolution of C++", I took the time to write and publish a document on Psion's internal "EPOC Software Design" database, entitled "Goals for ERA software development". The database was just a few days old at the time – this document was only the eighth document posted to it. (The last time I checked, there were close to 8000 documents in this database. Even this figure is dwarfed by the nearly 24,000 articles contained in another long-lived internal database, "Programming".)

In the next section, I reproduce verbatim the entirety of the text from the document "Goals for ERA software development". The philosophy expressed in that document has influenced more than 10 years of EPOC32 development, and still makes good sense today. However, some of the codenames included in the document deserve some words of explanation:

❑ "Protea" was the codename for the Psion Series 5 PDA

❑ "ERA" stood for EPOC RISC Architecture; this term fell later into disuse, being replaced first by EPOC32, then by EPOC, and finally by Symbian OS

❑ "Eiger" was the codename for the Cirrus Logic CL-PS7111 – the custom hardware (an ARM core together with peripheral drivers) used inside Protea. (The lead designer for Eiger was Mark Gretton of Psion, who went on to be one of the founder directors of Psion Software.)

15.3 Software goals from 1995

Reproduced verbatim from the EPOC Software Design database:

Document title: "Goals for ERA software development".

This document lists, as a kind of "Credo", the general goals that people should keep in mind whilst developing ERA software. These are over-reaching goals rather than specifics (such as "develop a 3-D model of windows with shadows"), and concern general programming practice rather than any details of, eg, C++.

(Document last revised: 27th January 1995)

1. Generality
The ERA software system does not just exist to support what can be explicitly identified as the requirements of Protea applications. ERA

will support other products, in addition to Protea. In any case, it is wrong to try just to anticipate the specific requirements of Protea (it is impossibly difficult to see that far ahead clearly enough). ERA should provide generally useful services, which Protea (and other products) may or may not choose to utilize.

2. Modularity
The ERA software system should consist of elements that are coupled together loosely – not too tightly. Knowledge of the insides of any one class should not be allowed to be shared too far afield. That would make later changes too difficult to make safely.

3. Portability
The vast bulk of the ERA system software must be capable of running on any 32 bit hardware, not just on Eiger. All platform-dependent parts of ERA must be clearly identified and minimized. This will make ERA more readily transportable to new platforms.

4. Internationality
Another aspect of portability concerns assumptions about the locale or language of the end-user. These assumptions must also be clearly identified and minimized – making it easy to produce eg Japanese or Arabic versions of ERA.

5. Testability
All elements of ERA must be written so as to be independently testable, in all aspects. If these elements are thoroughly tested in their own right, it will greatly add to the reliability and the robustness of the overall system. Remember the concept of test points when designing modules. The test suite for a module should be designed at the same time as the module itself is designed. A module is not finished until its test code is also finished, and the test code must be maintained as the module evolves.

6. Clarity of interface
It must be clear exactly what a programmer can legally do with any of the elements in ERA. The limits of legal input must be sharply defined, with ERA guaranteeing that, so long as these limits are observed, the system software will behave properly. (And any input outside these limits should be immediately rejected.)

7. Simplicity of interface
To prevent the programming interface becoming too large and unwieldy, it shouldn't offer programmers too many equivalent ways of achieving the same end. The interface should be "complete" but not "more than complete". There's no need to hand-hold the programmer, who can be assumed to be already proficient in all aspects of C++.

(It's not part of the purpose of ERA to make it easy for programmers to learn C++.)

8. Cleanliness of interface
Although the code should make allowance for being tested, specialized test functions shouldn't appear in the public interface, not even under a `#ifdef DEBUG` flag – this is to prevent the interface becoming unnecessarily large or over-bearing. (A few standard test macros are specially defined as exceptions to this rule.)

9. Clarity of documentation
All ERA software intended for use by programmers must be clearly documented – explaining its scope, purpose, relationship to other modules, limitations, and any broader considerations. A module is not finished until its documentation is also finished, and the documentation must be maintained as the module evolves.

10. Clarity of design
The written documentation for ERA software should be accompanied by diagrams showing the key inter-relationships and mechanisms of each element. If these diagrams cannot be produced, it strongly suggests that the design is poor.

11. Speed
Excess reliance on intensive low-level operations (such as heap allocation and floating point arithmetic) must be avoided. Any software that loops repeatedly should be checked to see that the main section of the loop is as quick as possible.

12. Memory efficiency
Memory should be used sparingly, especially in data structures which will have multiple instances. Variable data storage mechanisms are generally preferable to fixed-length storage mechanisms.

13. Codesize
Due thought must always be given to codesize. Avoid coding practices which will lead to the generation of large amounts of code (even from small amounts of source code).

14. Performance
Application programmers should never feel the need to write their own version of ERA system code, just because the performance of the system code is unacceptably poor, or because the system code entails too great an overhead.

15. Accuracy
It goes without saying that the software should be bug-free. It is worth emphasizing in particular that bugs, once found, should be fixed as soon as possible, rather than being left to later (when memory of them may have faded).

16. Maintainability
The ERA system code should be written in such a way that its ownership can easily pass from one programmer to another. Personal

idiosyncrasies of style should be avoided, and transparency of intention is important. It should be possible to pass ownership of a module to another programmer with minimum verbal explanation, and it should not be necessary to say anything that is not in the documentation! Otherwise, the code will be all the harder to develop and to maintain.

15.4 Separating the engine

Most of the ideas summarized in the 1995 document "Goals for ERA software development" go back many years earlier. Take the case of "generality" and "modularity". A far-reaching example of these principles is the idea of "separating the engine". The first programming task that was assigned to me, on joining the software development team at Psion in June 1988, was to create the UI portion of a word processor application for SIBO. I learned that all the source files I worked on would go into a "SLAP" sub-directory of a folder called "WP" on our VAX VMS minicomputer. "WP" stood for Word Processor, and "SLAP" was a shortened form of "SIBO laptop". I was working under the guidance of Richard Harrison, whose own source files were in an "ENG" sub-directory of "WP". The "ENG" sub-directory was to contain the "engine" files of the Word Processor application.

This principle of separation of engine and UI is of fundamental importance in writing complex applications. The engine holds the parts of application logic that govern tasks such as:

❏ Data manipulation
❏ Searching and sorting
❏ Data storage and retrieval.

Just as the engine of a car provides the energy that propels it forward, the engine of an application contains its core strength. A given car engine is compatible with a large range of different dashboards – different arrangements of the indicator screens and controls used by the driver of the car. Likewise, a given application engine is compatible with a large range of different UIs. While I was working on files in WP\SLAP, another directory called WP\SHAN existed, ready to receive source files implementing the UI of the word processor application on an eventual SIBO handheld computer. The same WP\ENG files would serve the needs of both WP\SLAP and WP\SHAN. (The MC400 and MC200 laptop computers reached the market in late 1989. The Series 3 handheld PDA followed in September 1991. Large amounts of engine code were indeed shared between the word processor applications on these two computers.)

Separating the engine of an application allows reuse of that code in new contexts. For the 32-bit version of Symbian OS, we took the principle one stage further, and recommended that complex applications should be split into at least *three* components:

❑ The engine of the application, which had no knowledge of any graphics or UI features

❑ The views of the application, which contained code for the main displays of the application data, but had no knowledge of the specific UI on the device

❑ The UI for the application.

The operating system files as a whole were also split up in the same way. Some libraries provided services for application engines; others provided services for application views, and yet others provided the UI on the device. Examples of complex views that were developed for application reuse included grids (as used in spreadsheets), charts, clocks, calendars, scrolling list views, snaking list views, hierarchical list views, and rich text views.

Software developers who wish their software to be quickly portable between different Symbian OS smartphones should follow this same principle of separation into components. As much as possible of their software should be independent of the UI on any one smartphone. Done well, around 80% of the software will work on all Symbian OS phones, without any change. Only around 20% will benefit from optimizing to the particular UI family of a smartphone.

15.5 Nine passions

I haven't counted, but my guess is that my personal electronic archive of PowerPoint presentations contains at least 20 versions of a talk variously called "Symbian fundamentals" or "Symbian core". For example, I used to give versions of this presentation to new recruits to Symbian, at the Induction Day sessions held roughly once every three months. As explained in the opening slide of the presentation:

❑ The presentation was *not* about change – things to be done differently

❑ Instead, it was about items that should remain constant – passions guiding all EPOC development

❑ I saw these passions as being responsible for the past successes of the software development team, and as being required for our future success

❑ I used the term "passion" deliberately, to indicate deep-seated concerns (not just intellectual interest) that motivated great effort.

The presentation evolved over the years, but there were always nine passions – three groups, each with three passions (refer to Figure 15.1):

❑ Symbian's most visible passions concern *product* qualities
❑ These are sustained by passions concerning *processes* to follow
❑ In turn, these are sustained by passions concerning *people*.

The remainder of this book is essentially an elaboration of aspects of these nine passions – bringing these ideas up-to-date in the light of my subsequent experience, and also identifying new areas of learning and opportunity. The present group of chapters deal mainly with the first six passions (regarding product and processes), whereas the final chapters in the book revisit the people themes.

Passion 1 is for product **robustness** (reliability): the product should never let down end-users. No "user reset" should be necessary: individual misbehaving applications should have their effects isolated, to prevent loss of user data – regardless of any issues with shortage of memory, low batteries, breaks in communications channels, or unexpected user input. As a special case, memory should be used very carefully, avoiding "memory leaks" – allowing system processes to run literally for years between resets. For more details, see Chapter 17.

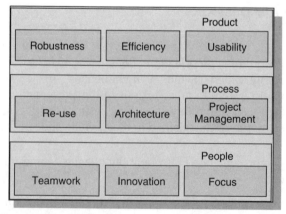

Figure 15.1   Nine core passions of Symbian development

Passion 2 is for product **efficiency** (performance): the product should meet users' expectations for speed and responsiveness, despite having hardware with capabilities that are limited in comparison to desktop PCs. Symbian software developers live and breathe "lean and mean", with a deep understanding of how to get maximum performance from hardware that has low cost (and hence the potential for mass-market adoption). For more details, see Chapter 16.

Passion 3 is for product **usability**. There's no point in a product being laden with technology, if real end-users are unable to use it. This leads to a constant emphasis on ease of use. Bear in mind that the real competition to the applications on a smartphone comes from pen, paper, and other low-tech tools – not the set of applications on some other smartphone (or other mobile computer). Being the best application of its type on any smartphone isn't good enough – you need to be better than low-tech alternatives, *and* you need to be satisfying real user needs. Otherwise end-users won't buy your application. So this passion is all about maintaining a strong customer focus. For more details, see Chapter 18.

Passion 4 is for software **reuse**. If you put a lot of effort into solving a problem, look for ways to have that solution reused in other situations. Take the time to separate the general principles of what you have done, from the accidental specifics of the actual circumstances. If you do this right, the same general principles can be applied in many other circumstances, specialized in new ways. For example, if you answer someone's question in an email, consider taking the extra time to create a FAQ from that interchange, so that others can benefit from it too. That's helpful for general reuse of ideas, but reuse of software inside complex systems tends to be much more difficult, and needs special skills. See Chapter 19 for more details.

Passion 5 is for software **architecture**. Good architecture is one of the main prerequisites for being able to reuse complex software, so that is also covered in Chapter 19. Done well, architecture provides important high-level simplifications, such as the idea mentioned earlier of splitting the software of an application into engine, view, and UI. Done badly, architecture leads to designs that cripple future development. Architecture involves drawing diagrams, but the key skill involves knowing which diagrams to draw.

Passion 6 is for **project management**. Good project management is what separates teams in which people merely work hard (even heroically hard), from teams that have a clear direction and process to their work. Good project management imposes the right level of control over systems for managing defects, build systems, testing, changes, risks, and schedules – all the topics covered in the preceding group of chapters.

Passion 7 is for **teamwork**. Software leaders need always to keep in mind three sets of priorities – the well-being of their project, the well-being of the individuals in their care, and the well-being of the team. These priorities have strong long-term links, but sometimes diverge in the short-term. When a great team spirit prevails, the individuals in the team become, collectively, more energized and more capable than they are as individuals. This benefits the project too. Individual differences and tensions are blended by mutual respect and appreciation. As I'll review in the final group of chapters in this book, teamwork has special dimensions in a smartphone development project.

Passion 8 is for **innovation** – the passion to be a leader, not just a follower. It's the passion to anticipate market requirements, and to work out, ahead of time, how to fulfill them. The root of innovation is to be proactive, avoiding any "blame culture". It's also a matter of being able to apply more time and resources to issues that are truly important, instead of those that are merely urgent. In turn, this leads us on to the final passion.

Passion 9 is for **focus** – deciding what's truly important, and what's just a "nice to have". If you don't focus, you spread yourself too thinly. Without focus, Symbian would drown in customer requirements. Collectively, our partners and customers ask us to insert enormous numbers of new features into forthcoming Symbian OS releases – at a rate about five times as fast as is possible. We need market wisdom in order to choose what goes into the operating system, and what should lie outside it. We have to try to pick the 20% of possible requirements that will deliver 80% (say) of the possible business benefit.

Focus means "doing less, in order to do more". Focus is about choosing between competing customer requirements, but it's more than that. In Symbian's history, this also led us to adopt a simple, focused business model, and a very small number of hardware platforms (namely, just ARM). And in the most important example of all, in our history, it led us to focus on the smartphone market to start with. That's discussed further in Chapter 20.

16
Designing for efficiency

16.1 The original electronic organizers

The first Psion organizer went on sale in 1984. Psion marketed it as "the world's first practical pocket computer". For 1984, it had an impressive feature list:

- 8KB "Datapak" (solid-state disk) for permanent storage of information
- A flat file "data" application for storage of all sorts of information
- A powerful calculator
- 24-hour clock and calendar
- A sliding case to protect the keyboard
- 4KB XIP (execute-in-place) ROM, 2KB RAM as standard
- Battery life of six months on a single 9V PP3 battery
- Optional additional program packs and Datapaks. (The optional program packs included a finance program, whose first version was written by David Potter, Psion's chairman.)

This feature list compared favorably with the micro computers of the time, such as the Commodore VIC 20 or Sinclair Spectrum.

A ROM budget of 4KB and a RAM budget of 2KB concentrate the mind wonderfully.

Of course, later Psion devices contained more memory. But the requirement for the software development team to write lean-and-mean code persisted. All through my time at Psion, limitations of memory size were regularly in mind.

Psion's first SIBO (16-bit operating system) computer, the MC400 laptop computer, was intended to have 256KB ROM and 256KB RAM. It had four slots for solid-state disks for additional programs or storage. In view of the amount of code written, it was eventually decided to use up one of these slots by shipping an extra 128KB disk with every computer, containing system software that would not fit in the ROM. So the ROM budget grew to 384KB. Later SIBO computers had ROM sizes of 512KB and even 1MB (accommodating large data sets for a spell-checker). During this period, there were several intense exercises to shrink the overall codesize:

❑ Software originally written in the C programming language was converted into hand-crafted assembler; before this, the entire development team went on a crash week-long course in Intel x86 assembler. Module after module was carefully converted, until the required target size was reached

❑ At another stage, Charles Davies (then Psion's Software Director, and nowadays Symbian's CTO) implemented a Huffman compression and decompression algorithm for the resource files containing language-specific text strings; the ROM ended up carrying a few hundred extra bytes of code (a highly efficient implementation of the decompression algorithm) and many thousands of bytes less data

❑ Another specialized compression system applied for the database of information about world cities and countries (a feature of Psion organizers since very early days); Colly Myers repeatedly optimized this specific algorithm, allowing more data to be accommodated in even fewer bytes in the ROM, whilst reducing the bytes of code used to implement the look-up algorithms.

Psion's first EPOC (32-bit operating system) computer, the Psion Series 5 PDA, shipped with 6MB of XIP ROM; options for RAM were 4MB and 8MB. That was another big step up from the memory budget of SIBO computers. But at the same time, the functionality supported in EPOC was significantly greater than that in SIBO – so efficiency considerations remained paramount. These considerations have their legacy in the fundamental design decisions of Symbian OS.

16.2 Limits of Moore's Law thinking

There is an argument that software efficiency considerations are an anachronism. This argument refers to the way in which Moore's Law has steadily decreased the cost of computing resources. The amount of computing power that can be purchased at a given cost roughly doubles once every 18 months. Extending this law over five years gives three and a third generations of 18 months, and therefore an increase in computing power of just over 10 times. Extending this law over *10* years gives a hundred-fold increase in computing power – literally two orders of magnitude in a decade. So, for the same cost to end-users, today's handheld computers have roughly one hundred times the ROM and RAM as those from 10 years ago. In this line of argument, even if it made sense 10 years ago to care about individual bits and bytes, any such constraints are a complete irrelevance nowadays.

However, there are many problems with this kind of thinking. First, Moore's Law only holds for certain kinds of computing resources – resources that involve putting more transistors onto chips. Other kinds of computing resources improve less rapidly:

❑ Bandwidth of data transmission has increased significantly, but more slowly than the rate of increase of memory
❑ Latency (intermittent delays) in networked connections remain problematic, despite increases elsewhere in computing capabilities
❑ Most important of all, battery power has made only modest increases over the last two decades.

Second, it's all too easy for busy software engineers to use up all the memory benefits from Moore's Law, without the user experiencing any net benefits. At the same time as memory size has increased 10-fold, many applications have expanded in size by similar quantities. As one wag put it, "Moore gives, but Gates takes away". Another common saying in the computer industry is that "software gets slower faster than hardware gets faster".

In concrete terms, this means that for each new product, the same issues keep recurring:

❑ The hardware resources grow, but so do the requirements the software has to meet

❑ The software typically grows in size, in order to meet these new requirements

❑ Therefore software developers still have ROM and RAM budgets that they need to care about

❑ In all these products, there are problems with the speed of the software (for example, how long does the system take to start up, and how long do applications take to start)

❑ In all these products, there are problems with the battery being used up too quickly.

In short, Moore's Law is not enough. Moore's Law is an important *part* of the reasons why smartphones are becoming increasingly ubiquitous – but only part of the reason. If your team neglects efficiency considerations, you'll find that software bloat will eat up the gains of Moore's Law, and more again.

Consider two code constructions, which have the same effect, except that one occupies 30 bytes of code, whereas the other occupies 10 bytes. If the longer one turns out to *look* simpler, you may well be tempted to prefer it (on grounds of it being perhaps easier for humans to read), saying that surely 20 extra bytes won't do any harm. However, in a large ROM, the same choice of construction may be applied literally hundreds of times, resulting in upwards of a kilobyte of code being wasted. Again, in the context of a ROM with some tens of megabytes, you may say that even a kilobyte is nothing. But if everyone in the team takes that attitude, you'll suddenly find yourself exceeding the allocated budget, or frustrating the user on account of delays in response, and/or running down the batteries too quickly.

On the other hand, the principles of "beware suboptimization" and "accept slack", that I mentioned in connection with project planning in Chapter 12, also apply in connection with increased performance. There's no point in applying lots of effort to optimize the performance of one module of the software, in the absence of an overall understanding of how the performance of that one module fits into the bigger picture. You have to approach performance both from top-down and from bottom-up. Starting from bottom-up, you need to train your team members to systematically choose high-performance software constructions instead of low-performance ones. Starting from top-down, you need to decide:

❑ How to avoid having lots of code repeated between different modules
❑ Where the various performance bottlenecks are most likely to occur – and how to address them.

16.3 Causes of code bloat

As just discussed, one of the main causes of code bloat (increased memory requirements, bulkier codesize, sluggish performance, and excess drain on batteries) is the general attitude that efficiency no longer matters, since hardware improvements will take care of things. This is a carefree attitude (which is another way of saying "careless").

I'll now describe some specific examples of this general attitude.

Suppose a developer wants a particular software effect, for example, to find the name of the network to which the phone is connected. A carefree developer may stop as soon as he finds an API that has the required effect. A good developer will check as to the side-effects of that API, and keep looking until one with minimal side-effects has been located. It's possible that the API called by the carefree developer will do all the following:

- Query the phone network for a whole range of network character-istics
- Update on-disk storage of the network characteristics
- Update the screen (the parts displaying information about the network)
- Return the name of the network.

(This is a hypothetical example, but I see the same kind of thing all too often.)

More generally, a good smartphone developer will seek to under-stand the APIs being used, whereas a carefree developer will be content to treat an API as a black box.

Carefree developers often add lines of code to call functions "just in case this is needed". In other words, they're not sure whether the line of code is needed, but they want to guard against all possibilities. The result may be, for example, that the screen gets updated five times during the course of a single atomic transaction. (Efficient screen redrawing code may mean that no one notices the repeated updates. However, the battery will notice it, and the whole operation will take longer than necessary.) Instead of not being sure, good developers will dig into things more deeply, and will document what they find. Then, if need be, they will refactor their code to deal efficiently with all different possibilities.

Next, suppose that the carefree developer cannot find an API that meets his precise requirements, but can find some source code that does something similar. In this case, the carefree developer may proceed to make a copy of this source code, and then to tweak it so that it has the desired effect. This is called "copy-and-tweak". The result is that the overall software ends up having many copies of almost the same code. Depending on just how lazy the developer is, he may end up with tens of copies of some sizable pieces of code. He may be happy, because, after all, the software works – doesn't it?

There are in fact two problems with having multiple copies of essentially the same piece of code:

- It causes code bloat
- It makes the overall software system harder to understand – it becomes impossible to "see the wood for the trees".

So, too much clutter isn't just bad for the ROM budget, it's also bad for the comprehensibility of the software. This software often ends up as out-of-control: a no-go area that's really tough to maintain.

Here's yet another problem with code duplication: if it later turns out to be necessary to apply a bug fix to the original source code, the chances are that no one will remember to apply the same bug fix to the one or more copies of the code made by the carefree developer.

Instead of copy-and-tweak, good developers will prefer one of the following:

❑ They will put in the effort to refactor all the copies of the software under their control, to allow the same software (when called with slightly different parameters) to meet all the different needs; instead of there being one monolithic function, there will be a series of smaller functions, each with a clear purpose

❑ Where the original source code is not under their direct control, they will discuss matters with the owners of that code

❑ In some cases, the owners of that code will be able to suggest a different method for the requirements to be met

❑ In other cases, the owners of that code may be prepared to add a new variant to the existing supported API set (as I discuss below, this is something that is easier to do when using OO methods).

16.4 Designing algorithms

Another cause of sluggish smartphone product performance is poor design of critical algorithms.

In principle, the answer in this case is straightforward – apply the methods and results of computer science. Computer scientists have been studying algorithms for decades. It is well known that the most "obvious" algorithms for tasks such as searching and sorting fare much more poorly, for larger data sets, than more sophisticated ones. For example, an obvious algorithm might take a length of time proportional to the *square* of the amount of data being processed, whereas a more sophisticated one might take a length of time closer to direct proportionality to the amount of data.

If you have the wrong algorithm, merely improving the hardware won't help you. It will disguise the problem, but the problem will return once the data size increases. And funnily enough, when the hardware is more powerful, users tend to store larger amounts of data on it, so that your algorithms fail again.

Throwing extra processing power at a difficult problem is akin to throwing more money at a badly performing enterprise. In both cases, what you need to do first is to sort out the internal performance. So don't rely on hardware to solve software problems. Instead, fix the software.

For smartphones, filing system access is an area that can be particularly problematic. If you are using a relatively new kind of memory chip in your smartphone, take the time to ensure the soundness of the fundamental algorithms in the device drivers for these chips. More generally, check out the data throughput for all peripherals. You face the risk of one of these peripherals unexpectedly becoming the choke on higher speeds of network connectivity. Good stress tests (as mentioned in Chapter 10) will alert you early to problems in these areas, but you'll need good computer science to actually solve these problems.

Ideas that your technical team may want to consider, when improving algorithms, include the following:

❑ Calculate hash values ("digests") of data sets, and do the first level of lookup on the hash value, not the data itself

❑ Make internal copies ("caches") of the results of recent searches, in case subsequent searches are the same (but be sure to update or invalidate the caches when the data itself changes)

❑ Construct indices of data, as a background activity (but be sure not to recalculate indices unnecessarily, and be sure that your algorithms cope well with incomplete indices).

I said that the solution to algorithm problems was "in principle straightforward". The reasons why this solution sometimes fails to be applied in practice are that:

❑ Some teams devalue the importance of software algorithms, mistakenly thinking that the progress of Moore's Law makes this subject an anachronism

❑ Some teams are used to developments in computing environments with more powerful hardware (for example, desktop PCs, or pocket-sized PCs with expensive hardware) where software constraints are less in their minds

❑ Some project managers are unused to software algorithms playing an important role in their projects.

It takes a particular kind of individual to be skilled in algorithm design; make sure that you have some individuals in your team with these skills. On the other hand, don't let these individuals spend their time optimizing each and every piece of code they notice. Make sure that they first work out the areas of code that, if optimized, would make the biggest difference to the overall performance of the system.

16.5 Understanding the compiler

Understanding the compiler is an important special case of the need to understand software algorithms.

Earlier, I distinguished the attitudes of groups of developers I labeled as "carefree" and "good". Somewhere in between these categories comes a group of developers who care a lot about making the source code clean, neat, and short. But what distinguishes this middle group from those I call "good" is the level of their understanding of the difference between source (plain text) code and object (binary) code. Smartphones execute object code, not source code. In some cases, efficient-looking source code actually produces a considerable amount of unexpected bloat in object code.

Back in the days when software developers at Psion often rewrote modules from the C programming language into assembler, to reduce codesize, we developed a keen awareness of the C constructs that the compiler handled well, compared to those which caused the compiler to generate larger amounts of machine code. This understanding was augmented by the amount of time we all spent debugging at the machine code level, when we manually matched up the machine code being debugged with the source code it was generated from.

Compilers have improved a lot over the intervening years. But some cases of compiler-induced code bloat remain. These are not due to defects in the compiler. Instead, they arise from the fact that there are things known to the developer, which the compiler does not know. The main impact of this on present-day Symbian OS is in the area of exception handling.

The C++ programming language defines a native system of exception handling, for directly passing control up many levels of the calling stack in one step, in the event of a lower-level routine encountering a run-time error (such as lack of disk space, or file in use, or weak network connection). As explained in Chapter 17, Symbian fully endorses the idea of exception handling, as a way of:

❑ Streamlining the logic of error handling inside source code

❑ Ensuring that resources which have been partially created, during the current operation, are properly cleaned up, freeing them for usage once the error condition no longer occurs.

However, native exception handling in C++ requires the compiler to generate various hidden tables, containing pointers to resources that may (or may not) require cleaning up, in the event of an exception occurring. Symbian's choice was, instead, to disable native exception handling, and to implement our own exception handling mechanisms (which were derived from a similar system in the SIBO software platform). We had two reasons for doing this:

❑ At the time when Symbian OS was defined, standards for native exception handling were unclear
❑ The implementations of native exception handling all introduced considerable code bloat.

Symbian's implementation of exception handling requires extra source code, compared to native exception handling, but compiles into less object code.

Interestingly, our analysis of code bloat was confirmed in a dramatic way in late 2004, when we finally did throw the compiler switch, to enable native exception handling, as part of the release of version 9 of Symbian OS. The single act of toggling this compiler switch resulted in a 10% increase in codesize. In a ROM with more than 20MB of code (plus considerable amounts of data), this pushed up the ROM budget by 2MB. Several smartphone development teams were, unsurprisingly, taken aback by this increase, as it pushed their projects over the edge of the 32MB boundary.

Another aspect of compiler-generated code bloat is if you let the compiler automatically generate constructors, copy constructors, and destructors. Again, this is a case of more object code being generated than you would imagine, from a brief look at the source code. Finally, beware of inline functions and template classes. If you're not careful, these will end up responsible for much more object code than you expected. Symbian endorses a pattern of using templates known as "thin templates". Make sure that your team understand their pros and cons.

16.6 Adopting OO

My first encounter with OO (Object Orientation) in software engineering was a negative one. It seemed to me that OO was unnecessarily complicated, and would result in less efficient object code.

This was in late 1988, as Huw Barnes and Charles Davies in the Psion development team started talking about the benefits of adopting OO methods for the implementation of the UI layers of the SIBO software platform. The idea was that many parts of the UI code would not know exactly what kinds of control widget they were dealing with (for example, date editor, text editor, list box, or radio buttons) and would instead invoke functionality in each widget by means of an indirect function call. So all the control widgets would be so-called "subclasses" (meaning "specializations", or "derivations") of an archetypal control super-class; the super-class would define various call-back functions, and the different subclasses would each provide their own implementations.

Actually, I didn't mind *that* idea, but I was less keen about extending this notion more widely throughout the software system:

❑ There would be a super-class defining variable arrays (arrays with indeterminate numbers of elements), along with specific subclasses for flat-storage variable arrays and segmented-storage variable arrays

❑ There would be a super-class defining active objects (objects encapsulating event sources), and specific subclasses for each different kind of active object (such as timer, serial port, and keyboard)

❑ Most ambitiously, there would be a kind of ultimate grandfather super-class, defining the common behavior of all objects in the software platform, and all objects in the system would be instances of classes derived from that super-class.

As someone who was focused on "lean and mean", I worried that any global system of super-classes and subclasses would introduce undue overhead. Run-time execution would be marginally slower, and the amount of memory storage allocated to each object would be marginally higher. Extended over every object in the system, that seemed a big price to pay. Within Psion at the time, I was not alone in this view.

However, as we looked further into the matter, we increasingly saw two very important benefits from adopting an OO approach:

❑ OO design allows single individuals to understand a larger software system; the classification system it introduces copes well with rising domain-matter complexity

❑ OO design also allows greater elements of code reuse, especially in the case where two pieces of code have requirements that are similar (but not identical).

So OO provides a good solution to various problems described earlier in this chapter:

❏ It provides an alternative to the dangers of "copy-and-tweak"

❏ It allows significant code reuse across different software components; despite the slight increase in codesize "in the small" (that
is, in a given object), there is a significant decrease in codesize "in
the large" (that is, across all objects).

As I understood this more fully, I switched from being an OO skeptic
to a kind of OO evangelist. Over time, Psion adopted OO methods
for wider parts of the SIBO software system. And when the 32-bit
Symbian OS was designed, we took things further again: lower-level
components such as the window server, file server, and the kernel
itself used OO methods from day one. We continued to benefit
from code reuse across many applications. I seriously doubt whether,
without OO methods, the first Symbian OS device could have fitted
within its tight 6MB ROM budget. With OO methods, we achieved
a system of applications with great uniformity of style and strikingly
small codesize.

I've taken the time to explain this history, because I know that many
people encountering modern-day Symbian OS have a first reaction
that is similar to my first impression of OO. Many people have the
initial hunch that Symbian OS is over-complicated. Symbian OS has
a huge number of APIs, grouped together into extended programming
frameworks. But when your technical teams study it further, they will
appreciate the rationale for these APIs and extended frameworks.
They will realize that the costs of the local complexity result in an
overall system that is extremely powerful indeed.

16.7 Selecting C++

Deciding to be OO was only one of the high-level design decisions
facing the SIBO team in the late 1980s. We also had to decide which
programming language to adopt. It had to be a language based on C,
since that was what the team knew well (and we knew that it allowed
highly efficient programming). That left three main candidates:

❏ Objective C, developed by Brad Cox
❏ C++, developed by Bjarne Stroustrup
❏ An in-house system, built on top of C, with its own "category
translator" and preprocessor.

(See the annotated bibliography, in the appendix, for details of books
we read at the time that influenced our decisions.)

Around this time, Bjarne Stroustrup happened to be giving an
informal lecture at one of the colleges in London close to Psion's

development site. Charles Davies (my boss at the time) suggested I go and listen to him. It was a smallish audience, so I took the opportunity to ask Bjarne some details about the implementation of multiple inheritance (something that hadn't been introduced widely into C++ by that time). Bjarne picked up an A4 piece of paper and sketched a diagram for me of the main points in his solution. To my later regret, I didn't have the presence of mind to ask Bjarne to sign the paper; worse, I've misplaced it (though I do recall briefly seeing it some years later in one of many boxes I have containing paper archives from that time period).

Despite the sophistication of C++, we decided it would be too disruptive for us to change the SIBO system mid-project over to C++. PC compilers for C++ were pretty immature at the time, and the language itself was evolving quite fast. We also worried that C++ was such a big language, that it would be difficult for us to know how best to use it.

Instead, we developed an in-house system that was closer in spirit to Objective C than to C++. Classes were defined in a so-called category file, which was processed by a category translator into a combination of C source code and generated header files. Object oriented function dispatch was via a new library function, `p_send`. Soon there were partners of `p_send` such as `p_supersend` and `p_exactsend`. The implementation of these functions was in highly efficient assembler. We occasionally referred to the whole system as "POOC" (Psion Object-Oriented C), but (unsurprisingly) the name did not stick.

When the time came to create Symbian OS (known at the time as EPOC32), our first thought was to continue to use the same system. We thought this would give us the fastest time-to-market. At one time, we even toyed with the idea of a monster tool (nicknamed "the munger") which would "munge up" (mix together) huge amounts of SIBO 16-bit source code and automatically generate corresponding 32-bit source code for EPOC32. A few months later, we decided that:

❑ The munger was technically far too hard a project

❑ Time-to-market was by no means the only criterion to use, when initially creating EPOC32; other criteria such as longevity and high value were also critical

❑ Revenues from on-going strong sales of Psion's SIBO PDAs would sustain a longer development project for EPOC32 than was initially foreseen.

So at this time, in late 1994, we took the decision to switch over from POOC to C++. This was motivated by the following reasons:

- Compiler support for C++ had greatly improved in the preceding few years

- We wanted to take advantage of other key features and improvements of C++, beyond its OO features; that is, we wanted to use C++ "as a better C"

- We knew we needed to recruit a larger team of first-class software engineers; we believed it would be easier to recruit quality people to work on C++ than on a proprietary system.

However, we remained apprehensive about the sheer size of C++, and the number of different programming styles it supported. To constrain programmers, we evolved our own rules for how C++ should be used inside EPOC32:

- To avoid design complications, we restricted multiple inheritance to cases in which the second base class is a specially designed "mixin" (we were pleasantly surprised to learn that both Taligent and Java imposed similar rules)

- As mentioned above, we disabled the compiler's native C++ exception handling

- We developed a naming convention that distinguished between classes with and without real destructors

- Our rules for templates and inline functions are designed to avoid there being multiple copies of binary versions of the same code in the ROM

- We developed custom classes for some very common operations – such as the "descriptor" class hierarchy for efficient text string and buffer manipulation.

Symbian has never regretted the decision to adopt C++. It was a far-sighted decision at the time. That language has served Symbian OS well. There's an open question about the best language to use to develop add-on applications for Symbian OS (the answer depends on exactly what kind of application you want to write), but there's no question that the bulk of Symbian OS itself will continue to exist in C++ for the foreseeable future.

16.8 Text descriptors

Let me end this chapter with a few comments about text descriptors. Anyone doing any nontrivial amount of Symbian C++ software development quickly encounters the descriptor class hierarchy. First reactions are almost always the same: "Why is this so different from the usual text handling libraries?" The answer is summed up in two words: efficiency and security.

While working on the earliest prerelease versions of EPOC32, Colly Myers searched extensively, on the Internet and elsewhere, for suitable C++ text handling libraries to utilize in the new operating system. In the end, he decided that none of these existing libraries came close to meeting the needs of a mobile operating system as he understood them, so he designed his own. Colly later filed a patent covering descriptors.

It's easy to find C++ text handling libraries where the code *looks* efficient. However, behind the scenes of an innocent-looking line of source code, a great deal of memory allocating and de-allocating often occurs. This consumes CPU bandwidth unnecessarily. It also introduces the possibility of run-time failures, since any of these (hidden) memory allocations could fail, due to lack of memory. For something as fundamental as text handling, it's important that routine operations have maximal efficiency and security.

By the way, Symbian OS descriptors aren't just for text. They handle any kinds of contiguous binary data. Text is just one example. The core definition of a descriptor is that it has a pointer (to where the data is located) and a length (namely the number of text characters – or their binary equivalents). So that's what the root class in the descriptor hierarchy (TDesC) defines: a pointer and a length. That's all that is needed for very many APIs, such as the APIs to search for given characters, to compare two descriptors, and so on. At this level in the class hierarchy, the descriptor is constant – you can read it, but you can't write to it. (The "C" in TDesC stands for "constant".)

It's when you introduce writing to descriptors that the security issues arise. A significant proportion of the security problems with computer systems throughout the world hinge on so-called "buffer over-runs". That's when software is tricked into copying more data into a text buffer than there is room in the buffer to receive. So the excess is copied beyond the end of the buffer, which can often cause alien new code (as copied beyond the end of the buffer) to be executed. The design of Symbian OS descriptors is to prevent this kind of thing from happening. Any descriptor that is modifiable (writable) also keeps an internal record of its maximum length. So at this level of the class hierarchy (a class known as TDes) a descriptor consists of a pointer, a length, *and a maximum length*. All descriptor APIs which write data into the descriptor check whether the maximum length would be exceeded, and if so, the application is immediately terminated (except for a few special cases when the caller of the API is given a chance to deal with the problem). There are two benefits to this:

❑ The above-mentioned security threat is blocked

❑ It allows for much swifter diagnosis of programming errors (especially when using the debugger) – the program flow stops as soon as the maximum length would be exceeded, instead of jumping off in a random direction depending on how badly the other stack variables in the routine have been trashed.

The next phase of learning about descriptors is when the developer decides where the data will be stored. Most C++ text handling libraries take this decision out of the hands of the developer. However, here as in other places, Symbian OS requires the developer to make an explicit decision. There are two choices, with the second choice in turn splitting into two sub-choices:

❑ The "TPtr" variants of descriptors rely on the data already being in existence, in some other object; these descriptors *point* to the data, rather than the data being directly included in the descriptor

❑ The "Buf" variants store the data directly inline, after the header of the descriptor; the "TBuf" sub-variants are designed to exist on the stack of a function (or as simple elements inside another object), whereas the "HBuf" sub-variants are designed to exist as allocated objects from the heap.

(Don't worry if you don't know the difference between the stack and the heap; the point is that these two forms of memory require two different sorts of descriptor.)

Many C++ text handling libraries essentially rely on every text object being of the sort Symbian OS calls HBuf. It's true that you do need classes like this. But for the sake of efficiency, you need all the other ones too. Because security and efficiency are of such importance to smartphone software, you should encourage your team to understand the rationale for descriptors, and learn how to use them thoroughly.

17
Designing for robustness

17.1 Alloc heaven

One unusual turn of phrase I encountered, on joining the software development team at Psion in the late 1980s, was "alloc heaven". The term is still in common use in the development teams in Symbian, two decades later.

"Alloc" is short for "allocator" – the system that allocates cells of memory to pieces of software for their use. The idea is that pieces of software tell the allocator their memory requirements, use the memory cells provided by the system, and then, when finished with them, notify the allocator that the cells are free for reuse. If software neglects to inform the allocator that the cells are free, they remain out of bounds to other use. In Psion-speak, these cells have "died and gone to alloc heaven"; they never return. Even though these memory cells are no longer being used, other applications cannot get their hands on them.

Other companies use the phrase "memory leak" for the same phenomenon. When software misbehaves, memory leaks, and is lost from the main pool. Psion's term is more whimsical and, at the same time, denotes greater passion: it's tragic that the memory is no longer accessible. Because there has been so little memory on Psion mobile computers, Psion was passionate about not wasting that memory. The same is true on smartphones.

A hallmark of a passion, as opposed to a mere intellectual notion, is that it motivates real action. The creators of Symbian OS were sufficiently passionate about not wasting memory that:

❑ The debug variant of the allocator wrote extra tracking information into the headers of all cells allocated

❑ The debug variant of the CControlEnv "control environment" class makes a call to the allocator, on the exit of the application, to check that no memory cells are in alloc heaven; if there is, the application panics (meaning that it terminates abnormally; "panic" is another of the unusual turns of phrase from the Psion development team).

Software developers frequently regard this `CControlEnv` check as an inconvenience. It forces them to add extra code to their applications, ensuring that all the memory structures created during application start-up are freed during application exit. From one point of view, this is wasteful, since the operating system itself frees the entire heap of the application when the application terminates. But from Symbian's point of view, this extra code helps to isolate instances where applications are systematically leaking memory. There are two bad consequences of these leaks:

❑ While the application is still running (that is, before it exits) it gradually puts larger and larger memory demands on the smart-phone as a whole; the application's own heap needs to extend in size, thereby restricting the memory available to other applications (until, before long, there is no system memory left)

❑ Some applications are designed never to exit (unless the smart-phone itself restarts); these include the telephony application and many system servers – memory leaks in these applications are particularly pernicious.

On more than one occasion, I've heard of third-party software authors complaining about the `CControlEnv` memory check call during application shutdown. This check was saying that the application had leaked memory, whereas the authors did not believe it. They told me that the same software had been running fine on other software platforms (such as Microsoft Windows). However, with the help of a debugger, the source of the memory leak could be clearly identified. The third-party authors turned red-faced. Not only were their applications systematically leaking memory, when running on Symbian OS, the same code was also leaking significant amounts of memory on all the other platforms. The difference with Symbian OS, however, is that Symbian cares enough about memory leakages to incorporate checks that noticed the leakages.

There are actually two kinds of memory leakage:

❑ Those that always occur, even when the software (otherwise) works fine
❑ Those that occur only when a run-time error happens.

By their nature, the former are easier to notice. The latter are harder to find, but for long-running software, their effects can be just as bad. Let's take some time to explore more fully the notion of "run-time errors".

17.2 Expecting the unexpected

On a constrained smartphone, it's inevitable that run-time errors will occur from time to time. These include events such as:

❑ *Low battery* – writes to disk cannot be completed
❑ *Low system memory* – lots of other applications are running at the same time
❑ *Loss of communications* – the remainder of an expected message is missing
❑ *Low disk space* – writes to disk cannot be completed
❑ *Password not given* – access to a plug-in memory disk is blocked
❑ *File not found* – perhaps because a plug-in memory disk has been removed
❑ *Server not responding* – which is another cause for broken communications.

To be clear, none of these events are programming errors. Instead, they are facts about the environment. However, software often makes programming errors as it responds to these run-time errors. Here's how.

A run-time error normally occurs partway through a complex series of operations. For example, the user starts installing an application, via Bluetooth, from a nearby PC, but partway through, the smartphone runs out of memory. At this stage, three things need to happen:

❑ Partially constructed resources (including partially written files) need to be undone
❑ The user should be informed, in simple language, about the problem
❑ The user should be given the chance to fix the problem, and then retry the operation.

However, what often happens is that the partially constructed resources remain in place – as alloc heaven, disk-space heaven, or whatever.

Consider another example: the user receives a phone call, and afterwards wants to add the incoming caller's number to an existing record in the contacts list. But suppose the battery fails partway through updating the record. Ideally, the user should be able to connect a nearby mains power lead, and retry the operation, with no ill effects. But in a bad case, that record in the contacts database will be corrupt. And in a very bad case, the whole contacts database will be unusable.

These are not hypothetical cases. Similar events occurred during the early days with Psion organizers. Irate beta testers found they were no longer able to access important personal data that they had entered into the devices. In a couple of cases, members of the development team painstakingly used low-level data recovery tools to rescue the data from the innards of the device. After an experience like that, you become passionate about never again being in that situation. This is the root of Psion's passion for robustness.

As I'll explain in the remainder of this chapter, there are three fundamental aspects to implementing robust software:

- ❑ You need a programming framework that makes it easy to deal with unexpected run-time exceptions

- ❑ You need a powerful testing program that explicitly seeks out failure cases

- ❑ You need a particular attitude towards programming – this includes the nature of your reaction whenever aspects of fragile reasoning are discovered in your software.

17.3 The perils of multitasking

In between any two lines of code in a Symbian OS smartphone application, numerous other things can happen. Because Symbian OS is a preemptive multitasking operating system, other applications or servers can, in general, run at any time, indefinitely suspending your application in the meantime.

This means that code like the following is faulty:

- ❑ Check that there's a certain amount of free space on a disk

- ❑ If there is, then proceed to write out a file to that disk, without checking for any errors; after all, the program has already ascertained that there is sufficient room, right?

However, there are numerous problems with such code:

- ❑ First, other kinds of run-time error could occur, such as the user removing the disk, or the battery becoming too low to write all the data to disk

- ❑ Second, another program could run in the meantime, also writing to that disk, using up the free space that you thought was secure.

Similar considerations apply for memory allocation: unless memory is actually allocated to your program, you cannot assume that it will be made available to you.

These considerations also apply to testing that given servers are already running. Even though you check in one part of your code that a certain server is running, you need to cater, in the very next line, for the possibility that the server has terminated in the meantime.

In practice, what this means is that, for every single line of code that your team writes, you have to consider the possibility that the line of code will fail. If you think that this could be a chore, you're right. That's why it's imperative to come up with an exception handling framework that prevents the error handling code:

❑ Obscuring the central logic of the main algorithms of your software
❑ Taking up a great deal of ROM space in its own right.

In other words, although exception handling is pervasive, it also has to be lean-and-mean.

17.4 Exception handling

Symbian is by no means the first company to have realized the importance of exception handling. For example, the C++ programming language contains support for exception handling, inside the language; likewise for many other modern languages. However, as explained in Chapter 16, it was Psion's observation, at the time when Symbian OS was being created, that the native C++ exception handling system

❑ Was insufficiently standardized or mature
❑ Involved a considerable hit on the size of software binaries (even though the source code looks comparatively tidy).

As a result, we decided to use an evolution of the exception handling system that was present in SIBO, the 16-bit forerunner of Symbian OS. In broad terms, the resulting system:

❑ Requires an additional degree of thinking by developers – they have to understand the system, and know what they're doing

❑ Involves a greater amount of explicit source code than other exception handling systems (though much less source code than not having any exception handling)

❑ Compiles to a smaller amount of binary code

❑ Provides a highly resilient system.

The first of these points looks like a drawback, but it's actually a bonus. Regardless of the system used, correct exception handling requires careful consideration by developers. Anyone who tries to tell you otherwise doesn't know what they're talking about. You can't sleepwalk your way through exception handling – you need to be wide awake. The Symbian system ensures that you are wide awake, and makes it as easy for you as possible (but no easier!).

The basic idea of any exception handling system is to localize error-handling code to a comparatively small number of places in the source code. That is, you avoid testing each line of code explicitly for whether a run-time error occurred. We avoid writing code like

```
err=FunctionCallA();
if (err==KErrNone)
  err=FunctionCallB();
if (err==KErrNone)
  err=FunctionCallC(); // etc.
```

Instead, we simply write

```
FunctionCallAL();
FunctionCallBL();
FunctionCallCL(); // etc.
```

The "L" at the end of the function names in the second code snippet is an important part of Symbian's code-writing conventions. This is a signal to the reader that the function call can "Leave". What this means is that:

❑ Somewhere in that function (or, very commonly, in another function called from inside the first one) a run-time error may be encountered

❑ In that case, the function call does not complete; flow of program execution does *not* return to the next line of code

❑ Instead, flow of program execution jumps ("leaves") to a preceding "trap harness"

❑ There are several well-positioned trap harnesses in Symbian OS framework code, and you will sometimes want to add some to your own code

❑ Before the code resumes at the preceding trap harness, all items that have been placed in the so-called "cleanup stack" in the meantime (i.e. between the trap harness and the leave) will be automatically "cleaned".

The native exception handling system of C++ automatically keeps track of all objects between these two points (which have different names in C++) and automatically calls the destructors of all of them. Symbian's system puts this control instead squarely into the hands of the programmer. As a result, Symbian OS code is peppered with explicit calls to the `CleanupStack` class. Your developers will soon become used to this!

17.5 Common mistakes in destructors

You have to be sure to free resources when you're no longer using them. The C++ terminology for this is that you need to call the destructor of the relevant object – usually by means of a `delete` statement.

But equally, you have to be sure not to attempt to free resources that don't belong to you.

For example, you may, without realizing it, call the destructor of an object *twice* – perhaps once directly, and once indirectly (because the object has been placed onto the cleanup stack). The second call will lead to the memory heap being corrupted. One way to guard against this problem is to change references to the object into NULL when the object is deleted. The general rule is to pay careful attention to which objects own others at any given time. At any one time, an object can only have one owner.

Another common problem is when the destructor of an object assumes that it will only be called when the object has been fully constructed. This leads to bugs where the destructor contains calls such as:

```
iList->ResetList(); // assumes iList non-NULL
iRequest->Cancel(); // assumes iRequest non-NULL
iSession->Close(); // assumes iSession non-NULL
```

However, if a run-time error occurs part-way through the construction of this sub-system, it's perfectly possible for some of the component parts (`iList`, `iRequest`, or `iSession` in this example) not to have been created by this stage. So the above code will cause an access violation. If you point this out to the developer, they may say, "I thought there was bound to be enough memory". That's a bad answer. You have to change the mindset. And you have to ensure there are plenty of tests that seek out failure cases.

17.6 Seeking out failure cases

Here are some ideas for checking that your code is robust:

- Enable simulated heap failures; this is a feature supported by the debug mode of the PC emulator of Symbian OS. Start by noting the number of memory cells in use by your application (there's an emulator hot key for this too). Then subject your application to various failures. Finally, check that the number of memory cells in use is the same at the end of the exercise as at the beginning

- Start saving data to disk, and pull the disk out before the write completes. The application should display an error message, but the data on the file system should always end up in a good state. There should be no corrupt sectors, and user data stored there earlier should remain intact. Repeat this experiment, pulling out the disk at many different times

- Wire up a smartphone to a power supply that allows you to vary the voltage. Slowly turn down the voltage while various operations are happening on the phone. Check that there is no corruption of user data, and no memory lost to alloc heaven

- Put your smartphone in an environment with a test GSM network, which allows you to control the strength of the signal. Start operations on the phone (e.g. data transfer) and gradually reduce the signal. As before, check that there is no corruption of user data, and that no memory is lost to alloc heaven.

You should also subject your product on a regular basis to an organized set of "stress tests" (as mentioned in Chapter 10).

Perhaps even more important than running the above tests, is to discover and cultivate people in your team who are skilled at the above kind of tests. This requires a special kind of mentality – someone who has a gift for constructive vindictiveness. Make sure that you find such people in your team, and that they:

- Spend some of their time, on a regular basis, trying hard to break the software
- Pass on their testing tips and techniques to others in the team.

17.7 Attitudes towards defects

Suppose that you've written some software and someone points out a potential or actual problem with your code. What is your reaction?

One really bad reaction is that of *defect denial* – saying that the problem must lie elsewhere (for example, in the way that another piece of software is interfacing to yours, or in the sequence of operations being carried out by the "dumb user"). Instead, you need to take responsibility for investigating the problem more fully, and proposing a system-wide solution.

Equally, another really bad reaction is that of *defect complacency* – saying that it's no surprise that there's a defect in the code. Actually, if you find people with this kind of attitude in your team, you need to give serious thought to retraining them or assigning them to other responsibilities. Instead, you want to be surrounded by people who have a high quality ethic – people who think hard beforehand about possible defects in their code, and who do their best to remove defects (and potential defects) ahead of submitting it. You *don't* want people in your team who write functionality that only works in ideal operating conditions. And you don't want people in your team with the attitude of "first we write the functionality, and then we remove the bugs". You want people who strive to write the functionality bug-free from day one.

So the correct attitude, when a defect is pointed out in code, is one of *surprise* and *determination*:

❑ *Surprise* – "How can this be? What usage case did I neglect to consider?"
❑ *Determination* – to fix the defect as soon as possible, *and to consider the wider implications.*

It's the consideration of the wider implications of any bug that distinguishes really great developers from merely good ones. A really great developer will think, "Where else in the code could a similar bug be lurking?" Are there any similar usage cases that also need to be considered? How can repetitions of this kind of bug be prevented? In this way, the really great developer proactively hunts down and removes other defects, even before the test team has found them.

Sometimes a bug will stop happening, without the reasons for this being fully understood. For example, many defects are timing-dependent; rearranging code, or introducing small delays, can stop the defect from showing up. However, you must never be satisfied with this kind of outcome. Don't let your developers persuade you that there's no longer a problem. Until you've understood what was going wrong, and how the change in code fixed it, you can't be sure whether the problem will recur. So your team needs to keep on analyzing, until it has a proper grasp of the problem. Be sure that you address the root causes, rather than just the symptoms.

17.8 Protecting the smartphone vital assets

So far in this chapter, I've talked about two kinds of fundamental problem that you need to avoid with your smartphone product:

- Cases when user data is lost or corrupted
- Cases when hardware resources become inaccessible – e.g. chunks of memory lost as alloc heaven.

I've mentioned techniques to avoid these problems. The same techniques have a big role to play in avoiding another kind of fundamental problem – cases when basic functionality of the smartphone fails. Whatever is happening on the smartphone, the following operations should succeed:

- If there is an incoming phone call, the user must be able to take that call
- If it is time for an alarm, the alarm must sound and/or (depending on the profile setting) flash and vibrate
- If there is a system error, the user must be notified of this problem
- The user must always be able to close down selected applications, or take other steps to free up memory or other system resources.

No matter how busy the smartphone is, and no matter how many other applications are running, these critical operations must always take precedence. This requires a certain amount of pre-allocation of memory and other system resources. So Symbian OS has support for pre-allocated "notifiers" and "sleeping dialogs" (dialogs which exist but which are not visible – until the required time). But don't overuse this kind of resource. Any such resource is tied up permanently, preventing other applications from using that memory.

One thing that can damage the vital assets of a smartphone is ill-behaved add-on software. Don't be misled by stylish appearance or a rich menu of functionality in an add-on application – be sure that it won't hinder the fundamental operation of the smartphone. Users won't care about extra functionality if the basic functionality of the smartphone becomes damaged. Press the authors for some indication of quality, such as endorsement from the Symbian Signed program (discussed in Chapter 3).

The need for high quality is particularly significant for software that lives inside one of the central applications on the smartphone, such as customizations or extensions of the telephone application or the standard top-level menu screen. Creators of new smartphones are understandably keen to achieve breakthrough differentiation, as compared to other phones based on the same UI system. Each UI system typically supports a range of "official" customizations. With each new release of the UI systems, the range of official customizations becomes larger. However, smartphone creators quite often want to take advantage of offerings from third parties to customize the UI system in even more radical ways. In some cases, the results are stunning. But since this add-on software lives inside vital system components, the effects of any fragility in this code can be far-reaching. Any smartphone creator in this situation should:

❏ Ensure that the source code for this extension to the system component is carefully reviewed (including, if possible, by automated static code analysis tools)

❏ Obtain independent verification that the authors of this software know what they're doing, and have significant prior experience with Symbian OS

❏ Thoroughly stress-test these extensions.

18
Designing for usability

18.1 "The operation was a success, but the patient died"

Here's a tragic outcome to a smartphone development project:

❑ Your team manages to keep to the requested timescale
❑ You deliver software with low defect count
❑ The software fulfills the specification that was given to you
❑ But the product fails to sell well in the shops.

In summary, the project was a success, but the product was a failure. In medical terms, the operation completed successfully, but the patient died.

As a special case, it's possible that your product appeals to so-called "early adopters" and "technology enthusiasts", who give it good reviews, but this interest fails to translate into mainstream sales.

So, despite what you'll often hear, keeping to the project plan isn't the most important priority. The most important priority is to deeply satisfy customer needs.

In practice, what this means is that you must augment your existing best practice on smartphone project management with the following five principles:

❑ Invest in world-class product managers and account managers, who can accurately distil, and even foresee, customer requirements

❑ Build sufficient slack into your schedule and resourcing plan so that, when your product management team feed late-breaking new market requirements to you, you can accommodate them within the project plan

❑ Pay attention to the importance of cosmetics and other aspects of graphical and emotional appeal – these can make all the difference as to whether a user finds the product enchanting or boring. In particular, pay close attention to all usability defects raised during FUT (Friendly User Testing)

❑ Instill a strong spirit of customer orientation among your development team; make sure that they keep on thinking hard about how their software fits into the larger picture of deeply satisfying customer needs

❑ Develop your software with a platform viewpoint from the beginning, so that you can create many variants from it; that way, even if the first product has limited success, you can quickly make amends and release version 2, with greater market success.

I return to the last of these points in the next chapter. I have already addressed the first two points in Chapter 12. In the present chapter, I'll offer some advice on the issues of enchantment and customer orientation.

18.2 Enchantment

Mainstream customers have no interest in "technology for technology's sake". They don't care whether the software is written in C++, or whether the processor is clocked at 400MHz, or even whether the operating system is Symbian OS (let alone which version of the operating system is used). They certainly don't care to be reminded of many of the computer-like aspects of their smartphone – such as the potential pain of viruses and antivirus scanners, techno-speak system error messages, hourglass icons, and so on. They're not buying a computer. They're buying an incredibly useful appliance, which happens to be a great phone, with a whole lot of additional valuable aspects to it.

Customers rely on various sources of advice when deciding to buy a relatively expensive piece of consumer electronics:

❑ Their own prior experience with products from the same manufacturer or network operator
❑ Marketing brochures and advertisements
❑ Recommendations by sales staff at retail outlets
❑ Reviews in trade journals
❑ Word-of-mouth recommendations by friends, relatives, and colleagues.

Word-of-mouth recommendations can have particular force – both for good and for ill. If people have a bad experience with a product, they tell lots of people about it. Equally, if they are enchanted with a product, they often pass on this enthusiasm to many other people. I regularly met owners of Psion PDAs who told me they had personally recommended these products to literally dozens of their associates. In effect, these owners were evangelists for Psion PDAs. You need owners who will become, in effect, evangelists for your product. In turn, your product needs a sufficient mix of enchantment, to grasp users' enthusiasm.

The two foundations for enchantment are the topics of the preceding two chapters – high performance (efficient use of limited hardware resources) and rock-solid robustness and reliability. Unless you get these characteristics right, you can't even play in this game. But they're only the foundation. Next, you have to provide features and functionality in ways that genuinely delight users. Ideally, users should find that the software anticipates their ideas and aspirations. They should find themselves thinking, "OK, now that I understand this, I guess it would be nice if this also happened ... oh wow, so it does, even better than I expected!"

The key goals your team should keep in mind here are:

❑ External simplicity
❑ Consistency of interface
❑ Responsiveness
❑ Attractive graphics
❑ Support for user experimentation
❑ Easy "cancel" and "undo" operations.

18.3 Designing the user interface

Ideally, your product has no need for a user manual. Users should be able to work out by themselves how to use it.

However, this doesn't mean that you should strive for a user interface that all users will find "immediately intuitive". This is a false goal. An "intuitive UI" depends on users' familiarity with a small set of basic concepts, but sometimes these concepts need to be pointed out beforehand to the user (e.g. by a retail assistant, by a friend or colleague, by a magazine article review, or in a "getting started" leaflet packed with the product). These basic concepts can include items such as:

❑ The difference between a short keypress and a long keypress
❑ The difference between a single click and a double click

- ❏ The difference between clicking on an item that's already selected, and clicking on an item that's not yet selected
- ❏ The possibility for a list to have more items off-screen, whose existence are indicated by scroll arrows or similar
- ❏ An application supporting more than one mode (and more than one view)
- ❏ A special keypress to switch between predictive text input and "triple tap" text input
- ❏ Possible five-way motion of a "jog dial".

Concepts like these need to be learned. But the key point is this: once they've been learned, they are very easy to remember. That's what makes them the basis for a good UI. In turn, this depends upon whether they are used consistently, and whether they are sufficiently simple.

You can receive early feedback on whether your UI choices are correct from the responses from Friendly User Testing (see Chapter 10). You should involve a wide set of people with different backgrounds in your FUT program. And when these users query some aspects of the usability of your product – or when they show signs of disenchantment or frustration – you had better pay close attention to what they say. You need to establish whether:

- ❏ These users misunderstand the intent of the product, or one of the fundamental mechanisms of the UI – in which case, you should consider how to make the design intent clearer

- ❏ These users are wacky individuals whose viewpoints are unrepresentative of mainstream users – but be cautious before reaching such a conclusion

- ❏ These users actually have a good point!

The one thing you should *not* do is to simply answer, "This is how the product is specified to work", or "This is in line with the style guidelines of our company", and therefore, "There is no defect". That way, you may finish your project on time, but find that sales of the product are dismal.

To resolve issues of this type, you need to involve representatives from product management and usability design. See Chapter 6 for more information. In that chapter, I described a five-fold classification for defect priorities: Immediate patch required, Showstopper, High, Medium, and Low. Be sure that you don't always assign so-called 'cosmetic' defects as having low priority. If the text looks wrong on the screen, that's something that will annoy users, and silently turn them against your product. Cosmetic defects should normally be assigned medium or even high priority.

18.4 Multimedia performance

One factor that has a big impact on users' feelings about smartphone products is the multimedia appeal of the device – the quality of the graphics, sounds, and video on the device. This connects to a different part of the user's brain; if you get this right, you are onto a winner.

Good multimedia is partly about good hardware, and a lot about good software. If your multimedia software is poor, don't expect new generations of hardware to miraculously fix things for you. Here are some of the things you need to solve in software:

❑ Dealing appropriately with sound played by applications that are in background

❑ Making sure that "silent" really does mean silent – no part of the phone should emit embarrassing sounds if the user has selected the silent profile

❑ Avoiding audio cracks and pops as the sound system is switched on or off

❑ Avoiding visible flicker when the screen is updated, or, for example, when the user cursors up or down a scrolling list.

Flicker-free redrawing is an art-form in its own right. Make sure that your team learn about the issues here, sufficiently early during your project.

Customers also look for near-instant response to their input. If they press "Play", they expect it to start playing almost at once; if they press "Pause", they expect it to pause almost at once, and so on. The multitasking features of Symbian OS help you to achieve high responsiveness to user input, but you also need to give some careful thought to your use of active objects. Break up lengthy operations into smaller chunks, each handled by a single hit of an active object. (See Chapter 20 for more details about active objects.)

18.5 Understanding the real competition

An important part of understanding your customer is that you under-stand the alternative systems that they might use, in case they find your offering unsatisfactory. Sometimes a development team has a narrow view of the competition. They may say, "This solution is as good as is available on any other smartphone – so it should sell well". This is the recipe for a nasty surprise. It ignores the fact that many users won't use smartphones at all. Instead of smartphones, they may use:

- ❏ Simpler phones, for example, feature phones
- ❏ Pencil and paper diaries
- ❏ Yellow sticky paper for notes and to-dos
- ❏ PC-based PIM and messaging system
- ❏ Standalone MP3 players and/or portable games consoles.

So you can't be satisfied by just being "among the best in your class". You need to be sure that your offering is sufficiently compelling to attract many new users into usage of products of this class.

Ideally, that's something that should be planned before your project has proceeded far. It's something for the product management part of your organization to address. However, be on the lookout for feedback during Friendly User Testing. You may discover that some parts of your product are unexpectedly weak – or unexpectedly strong. Be ready to feed this information into plans for your current product, and into plans for follow-on products. The key point is that you are open to learn from feedback, and that you have the flexibility in your setup to cope with this kind of feedback. There's more about this in the next chapter.

18.6 Customer orientation for developers

One other aspect of customer orientation deserves highlighting. This is something that marks out first-class software developers as opposed to average good developers: it's a passionate concern that their software is ready for use by other developers (who are another kind of customer). Too many developers allow themselves to be satisfied if they think that their software has internal quality. But to my thinking, software has *no* quality unless it is ready for use. Developers have to design their APIs for usability. Two fundamental benchmarks here are the attitudes of your developers towards test code and documentation.

First-class developers have a deep love of test code. They don't see test code as a burden or a nuisance; on the contrary, they work hard to maintain their test code, and to ensure that it is comprehensive and up-to-date. They observe good coding practices with their test code, and keep it all properly backed up in configuration management. When they find a new bug in their code, they add a new case to their test code, to catch any recurrence of this bug. Although their test code is comprehensive, it also has a simple overall structure, making it easier to understand and maintain. In contrast, average developers tend to shirk test code: for them, test code is a kind of "necessary evil" – something to be avoided, if possible. As a software leader, you should reject code submissions that lack evidence of the test code being up-to-date and well maintained.

First-class developers also have a deep love of API documentation:

☐ They write design documentation at the same time as they write the code, ensuring that their APIs are clear; actually, they aim to complete the documentation even before they complete the code

☐ If they find that they can't explain their APIs easily, it means they need to redesign the APIs; the sooner you find this out, the better

☐ They document with both words and pictures: "A picture is worth a thousand words", but words force greater clarity and precision

☐ They update their documentation as often as their main code

☐ They keep their documentation inside configuration management

☐ Finally, they keep their documentation simple and efficient – the same way that their main code is simple and efficient!

18.7 Designing panics

Good API design involves swift penalties in case functions are called with illegal parameters. In such a case, your API should "panic" the caller – which is a Symbian term meaning that you call an operating system function which terminates application execution. (Think of the phrase, "Press the panic button".) You specify a "panic number" when you do this. Be sure that you use a different panic number for each different place in your software where you panic. That way, it's completely clear which internal check has failed.

Sometimes people think that code should avoid panics – that these calls should all be removed, prior to the final shipping version of the software. That's a mistake. If your code doesn't panic, what else should it do? If you've received garbage parameters, the only output you can give is garbage too: "garbage in, garbage out". If you try to muddle along, somehow ignoring the error, the application will almost certainly fail in some other way shortly afterwards – but that failure may be harder to diagnose. That's no help to your immediate customer – the developer who's trying to use your APIs. And it's no help to your ultimate customer, the end-user who doesn't understand why the smartphone occasionally malfunctions. So embrace panics.

To be clear, panics are different from the run-time errors discussed in the previous chapter. Run-time errors involve conditions in the environment of the smartphone, such as shortage of memory, or a broken communication link, or a low battery. These conditions are *not* programming errors. They're circumstances that the software has to deal with. In contrast, panics are when a programmer has lost control of the software. It's like asking for the tenth element in an array where there are only six items, or trying to take the square root of a negative number, or dividing by zero. If so, the best service you can do to your customer (in this case, the other programmer) is to terminate the software immediately, with a clear panic number identifying the reason for the termination. That way, bugs will be identified and fixed more quickly, and the smartphone quality level will increase.

19
Designing for longevity

19.1 Preparing for variants

If you're really lucky, your Symbian OS smartphone product will be a great success, and many millions of users will purchase your software.

More realistically, your product won't get everything quite right. It will appeal to lots of users, but many other users will remain relatively cool to it. You'll satisfy some customer requirements, but you'll leave other customer requirements unmet.

You should foresee that kind of outcome to your project, and plan ahead for it. That is, you should be planning follow-up projects, even while you are still in the midst of an existing project. Plan to build on the software for the existing project, by making innovative additions and changes, to boost your market share.

Actually, even if you are really lucky, and your initial product hits the jackpot of widespread acclaim, you should still be planning to create variants. Even in this situation, you can boost your sales even further by smart differentiation into new market segments. So, both in the situations of modest success and stunning success, you should be considering variants – variants such as:

- ❏ Geographical variants (Chinese, Thai, Arabic, Hindi, US, etc.)
- ❏ Different industrial designs (novel keypads, sliders, folders, rotators, etc.)
- ❏ Different peripherals (attachable full-size keyboard, GPS tracking system, additional data storage, biometric sensors, etc.)
- ❏ Variants for youth or sports markets, or with celebrity endorsement or joint marketing
- ❏ Variants for more intense business use
- ❏ Variants for different network operators
- ❏ Variants with additional functionality (extra built-in middleware and applications)
- ❏ Variants with reduced manufacturing cost

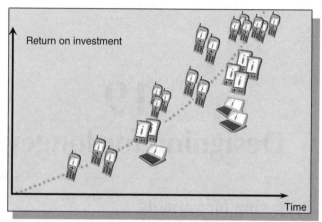

Figure 19.1　Multiple smartphones from a common platform

❏ Variants with madcap innovative ideas, just to see what the market likes (refer to Figure 19.1).

19.2　Be ready to fail fast

The way to succeed is to double your failure rate – so said Thomas Watson senior, the founder of IBM. Just as you can't foretell beforehand the exact course of project execution, you can't foretell beforehand which products will be hits in the marketplace. Just as you need flexibility in your project planning system, you need flexibility in the product creation system. To incorporate scope for change, incorporate the following:

❏ Low-cost experimentation with new concepts and usage models

❏ Early feedback from the marketplace

❏ Rapid termination of ideas which receive discouraging feedback (unless you have reason to believe that, despite appearances, they can become the basis for a new network equilibrium once appropriate market conditions have been established)

❏ Rapid evolution of ideas which receive encouraging feedback

❏ Opportunities for further innovation and differentiation

❏ Rapid adoption of product concepts which continue to receive encouraging feedback.

If you are able to experiment with, say, four times the number of ideas, you can accept a doubling of your failure rate, and still end up with a higher success rate than before. Paradoxically, a business unit with too low a failure rate is probably a failure as a business unit. On the other hand, a business unit that spends too much money discovering that an idea is a market failure is also likely to be a failure. So whilst it's important to fail often, it's also important to fail fast. That way, you'll be more successful.

An important part of rapid experimentation is to make good use of prototyping tools. These include:

- PC emulations of your product concept, based on the PC emulators of Symbian OS
- Macromedia Flash – running either directly on the PC, or running on existing Symbian OS smartphones
- OPL, AppForge Crossfire, or Java.

Another important part of rapid experimentation is to invite third parties to create special demo versions of possible new applications as add-ons for your existing products. If focus groups and research analysts endorse these demos, the third parties can press ahead with the development of fuller versions of these applications, ready for inclusion in your new product releases. The greater the number of different third-party applications you can experiment with in this way, the greater your chances of finding an application with genuine breakthrough potential. That's the striking benefit of an open smartphone operating system and its rich ecosystem of third-party developers.

19.3 Prepare your own SDK

Your smartphone product builds on top of several interlocking platforms – Symbian OS, a silicon platform, and a UI system platform. Each of these platforms supports reuse. These platforms have existing Software Development Kits (SDKs).

However, in many cases, you'll want to create a new platform of your own, which builds further on these existing ones. Your platform will incorporate some additional software from your own company, and may also replace some of the software from the original platforms. Your platform is what distinguishes your range of smartphone products from those of other customers, based on the same original platforms.

If you do create your own smartphone platform, please give careful thought to creating your own specific plug-ins to the existing SDKs. Such SDK plug-ins will augment the original platform SDKs, and will describe any special features (or altered features) on your own smartphone platform, so that third-party developers can take advantage of them. Items you should document include new APIs, your company's style conventions, specialist tools, server-side resources, modifications to the PC emulator, and so on.

This is important, since supporting a developer community is something relatively new to many phone manufacturers. As a smartphone manufacturer you should plan, long before your projects are finished, to produce (and support) SDKs:

❏ So that there is a thriving community of independent software vendors ready to add extra value, quickly, to your phones

❏ So that there is a steady flow of new applications ready for further innovation and inclusion on your next generation smartphone products.

As well as an SDK, you need to plan ahead for providing support to the third parties who create software especially for your smartphones. Don't imagine that the SDK, by itself, will be sufficient to answer all their questions and to provide all the necessary advice. Some of your team will need to spend time with the third parties to provide practical training and consultancy.

19.4 The value of codevelopment

It's been said that you can't tell whether software is usable until it's been used, and that you can't tell whether software is reusable until it's been reused.

One reason why the Symbian OS libraries support such a high degree of reuse by different applications is that the libraries were not developed in isolation, but were co-developed at the same time as the applications. In addition to their own test code, they were also regularly exercised by several different applications:

❏ Whenever applications highlighted areas of weakness in the system libraries, we considered whether we should rewrite some aspects of the libraries in question

❏ Most such rewrites involved a temporary impact on nearly all application writers, since they had to deal with changes in the APIs; so individual application writers took longer to finish their applications

❏ However, as time progressed, application writers were able to take increasing advantage of functionality that was already present in the system libraries – this functionality was available "for free" (as it already existed in the ROM).

You're not able to take that kind of decision if you're always focused just on short-term development issues. Although you want to finish your project as quickly as possible, that doesn't mean that you need to finish each individual task as quickly as possible (that would be another example of "suboptimization").

You're only able to take that kind of decision if the development team has a whole-project attitude. Individual sub-teams can accept slower local development if it contributes to the bigger picture of faster global development – the creation of a long-lived software platform which supports numerous high-quality new products.

19.5 Basic principles for reusable solutions

Here are some key steps you can take, to help you design for reuse:

❑ Base your product upon elements which are applicable across several different situations; don't go too far down the route of software that is tightly optimized for only one niche circumstance

❑ Seek long-term relations with partners and suppliers

❑ Make sure that you are making correct use of configuration management, to maintain the different branches for different variants in the most effective way

❑ Spread your skill base across more than one project team – don't end up in the situation where your entire team is exhausted at the point where the first product is launched

❑ Separate your software into engine modules, view modules, and UI modules (as discussed in Chapter 15)

❑ Avoid hard-wiring too many assumptions into your code. For example, just because a text message fits neatly onto one line of the screen in the English language version, don't imagine that all translations of this message into different languages will still fit easily onto one line

❑ Whenever you have to provide some functionality in your software, consider whether you could, with some forethought, provide it in a more general way, and then specialize your solution for the particular requirement of the present moment. In this way, you end up

with a solution that is more reusable: it meets your present requirements, but should also be future-proof for subsequent similar
requirements.

Designing software in a reusable way is harder than designing one-off
solutions. It may slow you down in the short term. However, once
your team becomes skilled at designing for reuse, the quality of your
designs will rise significantly, and you'll be able to produce a whole
series of new products in quick succession.

19.6 The value of architecture

The skill of being able to see the big picture of a design is called
"software architecture". A good tool of the software architect is a
system for drawing diagrams that show features such as:

❑ Module dependencies
❑ Class hierarchies
❑ Physical decomposition
❑ State transitions
❑ Data and ownership flow.

Something that's even more important than a tool that can draw these
diagrams is the skill in knowing:

❑ The particular diagrams to draw
❑ The aspects of detail that can safely be omitted – this is the so-called
  "accidental complexity"
❑ The aspects of detail that do need to be captured – the so-called
  "essential complexity".

If you skate over the essential complexity, your architecture diagrams
will be feel-good but content-free.
    The real point of an architecture diagram is:

❑ To convey meaning that wouldn't otherwise be so noticeable
❑ To clarify important points of constraint for the design
❑ To clarify important assumptions of the design
❑ To demarcate divisions of responsibility
❑ To raise questions about possible alternative designs.

The best way to develop good skills with software architecture is to
work in close proximity with an existing software architect. If you try

to work at the architecture level from scratch, there's a big risk that you'll succumb to one of two conflicting pressures:

❑ An architecture that is so vacuous ("fluffy blobs") that it adds no real value to the existing, lower-level design information
❑ "Analysis paralysis" – whereby you end up in an endless round of study groups without making any tangible progress.

As with so much in smartphone development, the trick is to proceed iteratively: "design little and often", and build larger architecture designs upon existing smaller architecture designs.

19.7 The value of ignorance

By looking at an architecture diagram, you may realize that some of the functionality in your system is positioned suboptimally in your system. There may be some merit in its present position, because other software is able to take advantage of knowing how it works. That may gain you some efficiency benefits – but at the cost of constraining the future evolution of your design. If you take the short-term view, you'll be happy to keep things in their present state. But if you take a longer-term view, you need to consider future versions of your software. In the future, some of the assumptions of your present design will become invalid. The question is, how painful will that be?

Ideally, when a design assumption is changed, it should impact only a small number of modules. If you realize that an assumption spreads more widely than that, you have two options:

❑ You should change the design (this is sometimes called "refactoring")

❑ You should document the assumption as being of cardinal importance, and make sure that it never changes (or that anyone who wants to change it is prepared to cover all the costs involved).

The basic idea of object orientation is to separate the interface from the implementation. The interface should generally continue to exist in the future, but the implementation can change. The interface defines *what* the software does, but not *how* it does it. So the implementation can have secrets.

When I first came across this concept, I was unimpressed. I thought that, as a smart young programmer, I should be able to discover the secret internal details of other software modules, and take advantage of them in my own code. I thought that, the more knowledge my modules had, the more efficient they could be. But later I realized that, the more knowledge *of a certain type* that my modules had, the more fragile the overall design became. It could no longer tolerate change. So it was suboptimal: it had optimized heavily for one situation, but failed to cope with the requirements of new situations.

The opposite of good modular design is spaghetti (sticky noodles): everything is tangled up. With spaghetti, if you try to remove one small piece, you'll find unexpected connections with lots of other items on the plate. A spaghetti design is fine if you're sure that you've got the design perfect and it will never need to change. But in the real world, there will be lots of change requests – inside projects and between projects. If you want your software to adapt quickly to these changes, you need to practice the virtues of secrecy and ignorance. Don't let the left hand know what the right hand is doing. And don't let the right hand know what the left hand is doing. Or rather, make sure that the interfaces are clear and well known, but that the internal implementation details remain secrets. That way, your software will be much longer-lasting.

In the meantime, you may have to undertake the hit of refactoring your design, so that it can last longer. That's a sign of a healthy software system. Set aside time for it, and make sure that it happens. The more you delay a refactoring, the tougher it will eventually be, and the more likely that it will never happen. And in that case, it's more likely that a competing system will leap-frog you. So instead of your existing system being overtaken by a competitor's system, you should refactor it, to prevent any competitor from catching up. Refactoring will extend the longevity of your system – find out what's involved, and go ahead with it!

20
Designing for smartphones

20.1 The licensing question

Symbian's focus on smartphones arose from the confluence of several strands of events. One of these sequences of events gathered pace in the mid 1990s. In 1995, analysts and journalists seemed to delight in posing the following question to Psion representatives: Would Psion die like Apple, or would Psion die like IBM?

At that time, Psion was widely perceived (in Europe, if not further afield) as having the best PDAs available – the same way as Apple was widely perceived to have the best desktop computers. However, Apple's software system was only available on Apple hardware; likewise, Psion's software system was, at the time, only available on Psion hardware. So, in both cases, third-party developers needed to take a leap of faith before learning how to program for this software system. The leap of faith was that the limited hardware platform would be strong enough, by itself, to drive sufficient volume sales to repay the investment.

In contrast, Microsoft Windows was seen as markedly inferior to Apple's software system, but it was available on an increasing number of different hardware devices. Some of these different hardware manufacturers failed and went out of business, but others brought some additional market distribution and market share, selling PCs to many people who previously hadn't thought of buying such a device. Because of the larger volume sales, Windows was a more attractive proposition for the third-party developers. In turn, the third-party developers created new software for the Microsoft platform, which increased the value of that platform, and diminished the market share for Apple.

Psion's inquisitors, in 1995, wondered whether Psion's software system would follow a similar fate. How could a small UK-based hardware company outperform the likes of Casio, Sharp, HP, and Compaq (not to mention Apple), all of whom were creating PDAs?

So the idea was born of licensing Psion's software system to other manufacturers. That way, third-party developers would have the confidence that, as well as Psion, other companies would be creating devices from the same software system. Psion's software would no longer be proprietary but would become an open standard.

This left the threat of "dying like IBM". IBM developed the original concept of the PC, but left the control of PC software in the hands of a small subcontractor – Microsoft. Microsoft subsequently licensed the same software system to numerous companies who became competitors to IBM. IBM ended up owning a thinner and thinner chunk of the value chain for PCs. Might not the same happen to Psion?

To rigorously examine the pros and cons of external licensing of some or all of the Psion software system, Psion engaged Stephen Randall, formerly founder of Eden Group (who had created, in 1993, what can be called the world's first pen-based PDA, namely the Amstrad PenPad). Discussions continued for many months. One of the key considerations was the fact that the emerging 32-bit software system, Symbian OS (which was in the process of being written at the time) almost certainly had wider potential than Psion itself could directly utilize. External licensing was seen as the best way to realize the greatest value from Symbian OS.

The decision to license the 32-bit software system was linked to a restructuring of Psion. Psion Software was created as a separate division, with its own executive management team meeting on a weekly basis from May 1996 onwards. A formal board of directors was constituted in September, consisting of five executive directors (Colly Myers, Managing Director; Mark Gretton, Technical Director; Bill Batchelor, Development Director; David Wood, Software Director; Stephen Randall, Sales Director) and three nonexecutive directors from Psion Group (David Potter, Marina Wyatt, and Charles Davies). We started talking to potential customers of Psion Software – many of whom were competitors of Psion Computers. It was a weird new world. We quickly adopted new habits and new processes to prevent customer information from filtering back from Psion Software to Psion Group. Suddenly there were a whole lot of things that we could no longer chat about with our former Psion colleagues.

20.2 Focus on strategy

At first, we talked to lots of different kinds of potential companies. I remember going to one meeting with a well-known manufacturer of lifts who was considering licensing Symbian OS. After all, we reasoned to ourselves (only partly in jest), lifts are mobile, and our business is mobile software. We soon had *far* more interest from potential licensees than we could cope with. We knew we had to start making some hard decisions. What kinds of sales leads should we cultivate most carefully, and what kinds of new features should we build into our software system in anticipation of the best sales leads? Instead of taking these decisions piecemeal, we initiated another internal series of strategy discussions.

These meetings culminated in an all-day session at the Clarence Room of the London Metropole Hotel on 13th November 1996. The Psion Software team of executive directors was joined for the day by Nick Healey, our applications and usability guru, and by two recent recruits into our management team:

❏ Simon East, who had transferred from Psion Industrial, bringing huge practical experience of building corporate wireless access systems on top of Psion PDAs

❏ Juha Christensen, who had transferred from Psion Computers; Juha was highly imaginative, extremely well networked, and had a strong entrepreneurial bent.

We candidly discussed five possible markets, weighing up our strengths and weaknesses in each case:

❏ PDAs (Psion's traditional market)
❏ Communicators (such as the recently launched Nokia 9000 Communicator, based on the GEOS operating system from GeoWorks)
❏ Smartphones
❏ Network computers (as popularized by Larry Ellison of Oracle)
❏ WebTV (at the time, the subject of very considerable media attention).

After lots of discussion, the meeting ended with the following unanimous decisions:

❏ We would defend our leadership in the PDA industry segment, but do no more than that in this segment; we resolved that only a small team would do follow-on work specifically for PDAs after the launch of the Series 5

❏ We would prioritize the development of Symbian OS as the leading platform in the emerging smartphone industry segment; to meet that challenge, we would significantly grow our headcount

❏ We foresaw that the smartphone market would be several orders of magnitude larger than that for PDAs; we also foresaw that existing phone operating systems would be hard pressed to scale up to the increasing needs of smartphones, whereas computer operating systems (such as Windows CE) were unsuited to phone requirements – hence the special opportunity for Symbian OS.

At the time of this meeting, the vast majority of our development team was working flat out on the software for the Psion Series 5. Seen in this light, our strategic decisions were remarkable. We were setting a strategic direction at some variance from the primary needs of our then main customer and 100% owner.

From that time on, the strategic needs of smartphones have always been squarely at the forefront of the minds of our management team.

20.3 Smartphone heritage

One factor that gave us the confidence to decide to focus on smartphones was the implementation project that we had just started with Philips – to create the Synergy smartphone clip-on for use in conjunction with their Ilium GSM phone. Even though that product turned out not to be a commercial success, we could see the potential huge fit between the content of Symbian OS and the requirements of smartphone products. Several other major phone companies could also see this potential fit, and were entering into promising discussions with us.

Another factor in our favor was a long history of prior experience of interesting projects that interfaced Psion PDAs to various mobile phones and other wireless devices.

For example, Motorola and Psion carried out a joint project in the early 1990s to create a wireless terminal known (by Motorola) as the PDT200 and (by Psion) as the RWAN. This was based on Psion's HC industrial-use handheld computer, which in turn used the 16-bit SIBO system. Here's some text from a March 1994 Psion Inc. press release:

> Psion utilizes Motorola radio modem for Nation-wide NETS
>
> Psion Inc, US subsidiary of British portable computer group Psion Plc, has launched the world's first hand-held terminal designed for nationwide wide area networks.
>
> Developed in concert with Motorola Inc, and called the RWAN, the system is based on Psion's HC hand-held computer fitted with a built-in Motorola Radio Packet Modem. The RWAN will provide users with nationwide wireless access over the PSDN networks operated by

ARDIS and RAM, allowing mobile workers to communicate with other machines, email gateways and host databases in real time via radio.

To support RWAN, Psion has developed MSIS, a radio communications job management software to run on the system. With over 40 percent of the US workforce operating outside the office, MSIS helps the mobile executive deal with decision support, quotations, manpower management and distribution control on the spot.

Psion was also carrying out joint development projects with Nokia as early as 1995. Here's another press release from the time:

Psion has launched a messaging application for its range of handheld computers. The product, called the Telenote Link, enables users to connect mobile phones to Psion's range of palmtop computers. Users will now be able to send and receive short text messages to and from other people with a digital phone and a Psion via the Vodafone digital mobile phone network which supports SMS (Short Messaging Service).

An intelligent cable, designed by Psion, will connect the Nokia digital phones to the Psion Series 3a. The system will also work on Psion's Workabout range of rugged handheld computers.

From December 1995 customers will be able to buy a Telenote Link package comprising of a SMS cable that connects the Series 3a (or Workabout) to the Nokia 2110 phone, and a messaging application for use on Vodafone's digital GSM network. The product will be priced between £50-70 and will be sold through selected Psion stockists.

The Telenote Link is the ideal pocketable solution for two-way mobile messaging. It provides a low cost, easy to use solution for preparing, viewing, editing, storing, sending and receiving SMS (Short Messaging Service) messages over GSM digital mobile phone networks.

And here's news of a joint project with Ericsson:

March 13, 1997 – Psion Computers PLC – UK

Psion Computers and Ericsson Mobile Communications AB today announce a range of connectivity options for their respective phones and palmtops:

The combination of a Psion Series 3c and an Ericsson Dataphone GS18 provide a compact Internet and messaging solution designed for busy mobile professionals. The system links the phone to the Psion with a cable as portable as a matchbox. It will mean that mobile executives will be able to send and receive email, browse the Internet and send and receive short text messages (SMS messages) whenever they choose, keeping them in touch while they are on the move.

These early joint projects had several important long-term consequences:

❑ The mobile phone companies came to have a high appreciation for the capabilities of the Psion software systems; this predisposed them favorably towards licensing Symbian OS shortly afterwards, and then taking a financial stake in Symbian

❑ The Psion software team saw that, in the context of telephony, parts of the software system worked well, but other parts worked less well. These realizations resulted in significant improvements in the telephony capabilities of Symbian OS.

20.4 Active objects

One of the pieces of Symbian OS that was refined and strengthened through our exposure to telephony systems was our system of "active objects". This remains one of the fundamental design patterns of Symbian OS. All smartphone implementation project teams should have a thorough appreciation of active objects.

Our original implementation of active objects dates from June 1989, when they were invented by Charles Davies, based on some ideas derived from HOOD ("Hierarchical Object Oriented Design Tool") and from the writings of Grady Booch. The role of active objects was to provide a lightweight mechanism for easily introducing new asynchronous event sources into an application. Here, "event sources" include:

❑ Timers
❑ Keyboards and pens
❑ Messages from other applications
❑ Window redraw requests
❑ Client–server interactions
❑ Serial communications
❑ Messages from other devices
❑ Progress from long-running background calculation tasks.

The event sources are "asynchronous" in the sense that the program cannot predict which event source will deliver the next event. The act of "requesting" an event is separated in time (in other words, "asynchronous") from the delivery of that event.

All modern software systems revolve around one or more so-called "get-event loops". The structure of these loops is:

```
do
  {
  get_next_event();
  process_next_event();
  } // repeat forever
```

Different get-event loops differ in the set of event sources that are monitored at any one time. In Symbian OS (as in SIBO before it) there is only one get-event loop. This is in a class known as CActiveScheduler – the class which schedules different active objects. The CActiveScheduler maintains a prioritized list of all active objects that are current in the application, including ones which have been installed by system libraries utilized by the application. In general, software does not know (nor does it care) which active objects are current at any one time. Provided software follows the rules, the whole system works like magic – events are delivered to the appropriate handlers, and the different handlers coexist with minimal interference.

So there are two levels of multitasking in any Symbian OS phones:

❑ *The kernel contains a thread scheduler* – which preemptively multitasks between the various live execution threads on the system, following classic design principles

❑ *Most threads contain a CActiveScheduler* – which *non*-preemptively multitasks between the various live active objects in the thread.

Active objects have minimal overhead, and share (within one thread) the same data space and execution stack. They serve a different need to multi-threading. Both kinds of multitasking are needed. As Symbian designed more and more systems involving telephony interactions, the active object system evolved, and became more and more valuable.

20.5 Power management

One of the cardinal rules of Symbian OS software is: never poll. Do not burn round a tight loop, continuously testing whether something has happened. Instead, you should use the active object system. You should let the system know that you're interested in an event and ... that's all. There's nothing more for your application to do, so the operating system suspends your application until an event of interest occurs. At that moment, the operating system wakens your application, and routes program execution to the relevant active object.

As you'll realize, this has a big influence upon battery usage. The operating system is able to put the processor to sleep the moment that all applications have finished responding to the latest events. This piece of control occurs in the null thread – the thread with the lowest priority. The null thread is always ready to run. Whenever it gets to run, its action is to suspend the processor. It's a stunningly simple design.

Often, software that is designed with a different heritage (for example, desktop software) fails to appreciate the critical importance of battery lifetime and power management. Such software often contains internal busy loops, or it wakens up the smartphone on a regular basis to check for particular events. Make sure that your software follows the rules for good power management. Reflect on the ways that smartphones differ from laptop computers: smartphone batteries are much smaller than on a laptop, but smartphone batteries need to last at least a complete day. This kind of dramatic performance gain can't be implemented in hardware alone – it requires huge software support. Ignore the rules and your software will cause smartphone battery failure. Follow the rules and users will give your software a warm endorsement.

20.6 Beware stray signals

The heart of any Symbian OS application is the get-event loop that is contained in the CActiveScheduler object in the application. The CActiveScheduler object keeps track of all the event sources in the application. For each event source, the CActiveScheduler object knows:

❑ Whether the event source is active
❑ Whether the application is waiting to process an event from that event source
❑ The piece of code to call, when the application gets a chance to run.

The system relies on a small number of rules. For example, for any one active object, the application should have at most one outstanding request at any one time. If you request another event before you process the previous one from that active object, it's a sign that the application is out of control. It's akin to polling for events. It's literally a waste of energy. The system won't allow it.

Each active object implements a `Cancel` function to cope with cases when you have issued a request for an event, but now need to issue another request instead (from the same active object). In general, you can never be sure whether the cancel will take effect before the event source actually delivers the event. For this reason, in Symbian OS, cancel never works as "undo"; it always works as "precipitate completion".

These rules are designed to maintain the integrity of the power management system. The kernel keeps track of the so-called "signal count" of each application. When the signal count becomes negative, the application is suspended. Any piece of software that messes with the signal count is a menace, so Symbian OS performs regular sanity checks. If a signal occurs but no active object can be identified as being responsible for it, `CActiveScheduler` calls panic. This is called a "stray signal panic". Such panics can be a pest to diagnose, but it's still better for your project that the application is terminated. This draws developer attention to the fact that some software has broken the rules for signals, active objects, and/or power management. In Symbian's view, that's definitely something to panic about.

20.7 Final comments on asynchronous events

Because of their openness, smartphones involve an unknown number of event sources running at unpredictable times in an unforeseeable sequence. You can't control the number of applications on the phone; nor can you control the environment that the smartphone finds itself in. Active objects are the foundation to tame this potential anarchy, but there are a couple of other critical aspects of handling asynchronous events that are well worth noting.

First, take care over the lifetimes of objects. Many programming operations on smartphones involve passing the address of an object into an API. If that API is asynchronous, you have to beware the possibility of the object being destroyed before the API completes. If that happens, the API will attempt to access a nonexistent object – with random consequences. One complication here is that C++ may create a temporary object (on the memory stack) without you realizing what's happening. This makes it harder to spot this kind of programming error. On many occasions, your program will survive, because the asynchronous API will complete immediately. But once in a while, the timing will differ, and the object will be destroyed (programmers call this "going out of scope") before the event completes. In a world of synchronous events, there's no problem. But in the world of asynchronous events, you need to be more thoughtful.

Second, respect multitasking priorities. There are priority allocations both for active objects (within a single thread) and for threads (within the overall smartphone). Developers are sometimes tempted to try to fix issues by increasing the priorities of threads and/or active objects in their software. For example, to avoid being interrupted, you can try to set the priority of a thread to the maximum allowed value. However, anything that alters the priority structure risks destabilizing other aspects of the operation of the smartphone. There are good reasons why certain threads and active objects have the priorities that have been assigned to them. So unless you are sure you know what you're doing, stick with the standard priority assignments. Instead of increasing your priority to avoid your software being interrupted, design your software to cope with being interrupted. That's how smartphones work.

Part 4

Human aspects of smartphone projects

21

The essential role of the project manager

21.1 Focus

I now reach the single most important piece of advice in my book. The one factor which, more than any other, determines the success or failure of a smartphone development project is the caliber of the individual assigned to be the full-time leader of that project.

I'm not saying that all the other pieces of advice are unimportant – far from it. However, if you find the right person to run the project, with proper support and backup from the highest levels of senior management in your company, that person will ensure that the team correctly implements the other pieces of advice.

A high-powered project manager will bring repeated laser-focus to the question of what needs to be done to make your project a success. He or she will regularly survey the entire scope of project activities, looking for risks, and searching out the best responses to these risks. Provided the project manager is properly advised (and that's the subject of the next chapter), this survey will cover all the matters raised within the chapters of this book. So finding the right project manager is the key to solving all these other matters.

Different project managers have different styles. There is no one unique correct style. However, there are some fundamental elements that your project manager needs, regardless of personal style:

❑ An understanding of smartphones

❑ An understanding of complex software systems

❑ An understanding of agility and dynamic planning

❑ The ability to motivate all the different players in the team

❑ The ability to communicate clearly with all key parties involved in the project

❑ The ability to "manage up" – to gain the necessary organization support from higher management

❑ The ability to drive completion of contractual issues

❑ The ability to drive completion of the project as a whole

❑ The ability to bring organizational focus to the smartphone project topics that are most important at any one time (as opposed to those that are merely urgent).

Critically, the project manager needs to be dedicated full time to your project – and incentivized entirely by the degree of success of the project. A project manager whose attentions are spread between two or three different projects will be much less effective. It's when your project manager gives full commitment to the one smartphone project that you gain the best returns.

21.2 Project manager vs. technical lead vs. product manager

The project manager is a distinct role from technical lead. Both roles are necessary, but don't confuse them. The technical lead is the person who has overall responsibility for the technical quality of the implementation of the smartphone product. This is the person who:

❑ Understands how all the technology fits together (hardware, software, etc.)

❑ Can deeply analyze individual defects

❑ Can deeply analyze the pros and cons of various proposed defect fixes

❑ Understands the technical strengths and weaknesses of all the software engineers who work on the project.

The reason why the project manager should be a different person from the technical lead is to ensure that the project manager retains a focus on overall project issues. In order to have a good understanding of the day-to-day problems being faced by team members, the project manager needs to have a strong technical background in smartphone development, but he or she must resist being sucked into the solution of individual technical problems. No matter how important an individual technical problem may seem, the project manager must retain a focus on the project as a whole, ready to devote quality mindshare to any of the rapidly changing issues that could affect the overall project well-being.

Another role that should be distinct is that of product manager. Whereas the project manager runs the project as a whole, the product manager is responsible for the company making optimal profits from the product line being served by this project. The project manager is a world expert in "getting things done", whereas the product manager is a world expert in the commercial opportunities of this product line. The product manager has a particular focus on making sure that the product will be well loved by customers. The product manager:

- ❑ Understands the competitive landscape
- ❑ Ensures that appropriate marketing campaigns are organized
- ❑ Decides pricing
- ❑ Owns the specification of the product – which features are in or out, and which quality and performance levels are required.

Just as the project manager needs to be fully comfortable with technical issues, he or she also needs to be fully comfortable with product definition issues. However, neither of these areas defines the primary role of the project manager. The former is handled by the technical lead, and the latter by the product manager. In contrast, the project manager handles the project as a whole:

- ❑ Whatever the project needs, the project manager should anticipate the need, and find a solution

- ❑ Whatever skills or resources are missing from the project team, the project manager should devise ways to cover this gap

- ❑ Whatever obstacles are preventing the team members from working together optimally, the project manager should find ways to repair the working relations

- ❑ Whatever contradictions are contained within the project setup, the project manager should find ways to address them, so that the project can proceed swiftly to commercial success.

All these tasks require support and assistance – the project manager does not act alone. For this reason, one of the core skills of the project manager is the ability to draw on the strengths of the different key players in the team.

21.3 Project review meetings

Project review meetings can be among the most awkward aspects of a project manager's job. The meetings are formal (or semi-formal) occasions where the project leaders report on:

- ❑ Recent decisions about the product spec or design

- ❏ The integration timetable
- ❏ The overall project schedule
- ❏ Progress with testing and verification
- ❏ Customer feedback
- ❏ Current project risks and issues.

Because the project manager tends to know all these issues already, it may seem that the meeting is a waste of time. Instead of talking about project issues, it's more pressing to actually fix these issues. However, you need to resist that pressure. Here are the benefits your team gains from a regular project review meeting:

- ❏ The team members gain a better understanding of the context of their work

- ❏ Although you may think that people already know various pieces of news, it often turns out that they do not (or that they haven't paid much attention to them earlier)

- ❏ You may often hear novel suggestions or feedback from team members during the meeting

- ❏ The meeting can include short periods of brainstorming, as the collective intelligence comes up with new ideas for dealing with project issues.

It's my experience that a significant amount of time can be wasted in projects because of communications failures. For example, sub-team A thinks that sub-team B is working on a particular problem, whereas sub-team B is still waiting for sub-team A to deal with it. Or, sub-team A regards a particular issue as a critical blocker preventing further development work, but sub-team B is planning on getting round to this in several weeks' time, being unaware of any urgency. Regular review meetings are one way to identify these kinds of communication failure.

I sometimes say (half-joking) that although I used to be a software engineer, I have long ago changed into a "meetings engineer". Being a "meetings engineer" is a highly skilled job! You have to ensure that:

- ❏ Meetings have a clear purpose

- ❏ The right people are attending – neither too many nor too few

- ❏ People know the purpose of the meeting in advance

- ❏ The meeting avoids being dominated by a few loud individuals

❑ The meeting has the right mix of formal reports and unstructured open discussion – the right balance between snappiness and thoughtfulness

❑ Minutes are distributed promptly afterwards, clearly stating any decisions reached, and also giving background reasons for these decisions

❑ People follow up the meeting with agreed actions.

Here are some other guidelines to ensure good communications within your project team:

❑ Focus on the successful *reception* of a communication, rather than on the successful *transmission*; it doesn't matter how well you spoke or wrote, if the intended audience can't properly understand the message

❑ The best tool available to a project manager is a good pair of walking shoes; the project manager needs to spend a lot of time walking into different team areas, to meet with team members in the context of their work, and to notice the issues that are occupying their minds

❑ Make sure that you give your team a chance to talk to you, giving their version of the status of work in their team, before you tell them your opinion about this; *seek first to understand, then to be understood.*

21.4 Commercial negotiations with third parties

The project manager is responsible, not just for good working relations between internal team members, but also for good working relations with the third parties who are also working on this project. For each company that is supplying people or intellectual property to your project, you should check that:

❑ There is an account manager (or partner manager) in your company, whose job it is to look after the relationship between your company and this third party; talk regularly to this account manager

❑ You have a contract in place that clearly guarantees prompt support when needed – for example, if you need someone from that company to provide specialist technical support in a hurry

❑ There is clarity about ownership of any intellectual property created during the project; you don't want to end up quarreling at the last minute about whether you need to pay additional fees to include some functionality in a follow-up product

❑ Your payment terms are sufficient to encourage the partner to continue working on your project for longer than the initial expected time (in case there is any change in schedule); you want to avoid the situation that the partner is now giving greater attention to a different customer

❑ You have full access (ideally) to all source code of the partner's software – or, failing this, that the partner guarantees to supply a suitably skilled support engineer on site (with a laptop containing the source code) whenever needed.

The commercial aspects of software integration can be just as challenging as the technical ones. Don't neglect them.

Even before you agree commercial terms with a third party, you have to be confident that they are a good choice to work with. See Chapter 3 for information on various Symbian partner programs, allowing you to understand which partners are endorsed in various ways by Symbian.

21.5 Project manager authority

Sometimes it seems that companies forget their business is to make great products that delight their customers. I see many cases when project managers are held up in their work, not by external obstacles, but by internal blockages (company politics, red-tape, internal rivalry, etc.). At the beginning of this chapter, I said that you need to find the right person to run your project *and* you need to provide proper backup to this person from the highest level of senior management in your company. Senior managers must be ready to support their project manager in any political battles in the company. Because smartphones are more complex than other kinds of phones, it is not appropriate for corporate bureaucrats to insist that exactly the same processes are followed:

❑ The QA processes for smartphones need to be more tolerant than those for feature phones (see Chapter 6)

❑ Since a larger number of third parties tend to be involved in a smartphone project, you need quick turnaround on contractual reviews from legal and supplier management

- ❏ In order to be maximally effective, on-site consultants need good access to their email and other corporate IT systems; this may need special cooperation from your own IT department

- ❏ On-site consultants need to be able to compare individual items of smartphone functionality against those of competing devices; access to these devices may require special cooperation from your security department (who may otherwise insist that no one is allowed to bring any such "alien" technology onto your premises)

- ❏ Although you should have systems that enable distributed working across several different sites, you may also need rapid action to agree co-locating different teams on the same site during critical periods of the project

- ❏ Decisions on investment in your project may require cooperation from people in different budget reporting groups; given the large potential income from timely sales of high-end smartphone devices, you don't want to be held hostage to the ordinary pace of financial approval systems.

In all these cases, be sure that you are adopting agile processes. Agility isn't just a technique for assembling software more reliably – it's an approach that cuts through heavyweight constraints of all sorts, in order to place breakthrough new products more quickly into the hands of eager customers. Don't let it be said that you had a better product that your external competitors, but you were prevented from making it a commercial success by internal obstacles.

22
The essential role of the support network

22.1 Pros and cons of support consultants

One of the hardest things to do – especially for a company that is highly successful – is to ask for help. Asking for help is perceived as an indication of weakness. Companies like to think that they have very smart people working for them, who should be able to figure out, by themselves, everything involved in creating winning smartphones. For this reason, they are reluctant to engage specialist consultancy companies for help with their smartphone projects.

I can well believe that there are lots of bright people working in your company. And, given time, these people will figure out, by themselves, a way of making progress of a sort. However, the harder question is whether that rate of progress will be sufficient to finish the whole project in good time. It won't be at all clear whether your team is paying sufficient attention to all the many hidden variables involved in completing a smartphone development project. And the chances are that the progress you do make is being achieved at far too high a price in terms of resources exerted. With the right guidance, your development team can utilize Symbian OS to create stylish smartphones in leaps and bounds; without the right guidance, your team will make all kinds of unnecessary errors.

Despite their pride, most companies do recognize the advantages of engaging with support consultants. But still they hesitate – for two reasons:

- They are fearful about information leaking from their experience and projects, to benefit their competitors (especially if the consultant also carries out work for competing companies)

- They wish to gain the benefits from consultancy without paying the usual costs for this service.

Both these reasons are false economies. Let's start by looking at the cost argument. Here's a sequence of events that I know has often happened, with a phone manufacturer talking to a consultancy supplier as time progresses:

❑ *Month 1*: "We won't use your people; they are too expensive"

❑ *Month 2*: "We won't use your people for long; they are too expensive"

❑ *Month 4*: "You're too expensive, but please can we have two more of your people"

❑ *Month 6*: "You're too expensive, but we have a very important milestone coming up; we need all of your best people immediately"

❑ *Month 10*: "You're too expensive, but we couldn't have finished the project without you!"

What this exchange shows is that, despite complaining, the phone manufacturer does end up putting a high value on the services made available by the consultancy supplier.

If you delay your project by two months because of haggling over charge rates payable to consultants, you lose two months of revenues from your project. From the rough estimates presented in Chapter 2, that could cost you upwards of 20m USD in lost profits. You may think that your finance department will reward your prudence in lowering the consultancy rates by, say, 15% through two months of tough stop–go negotiation. Instead, your CEO should fire you for losing precious time during the critical start-up phase of your project. (Of course, I'm not saying that you should cave in during pricing negotiations with consultancy houses. But I am saying that you should be negotiating very quickly and constructively.)

The argument about information sharing is more subtle. In broad terms, all consultancy companies operate strict systems of nondisclosure. Specific commercial secrets learned during an engagement can never be passed on to people outside the project team. However, there's also the question of so-called "residuals". These are the ideas and techniques that consultants pick up from working with your team, without giving any conscious thought to the matter. These ideas and techniques then become part of the set of background ideas and techniques which the consultants occasionally utilize in all their work. These ideas and techniques dovetail with the general skill-set the consultants already possess. Afterwards, if you ask a consultant where they learned the idea of doing such-and-such, they may not be able to give you a simple answer. If pressed, they may answer that the idea has many grandfathers – something they learned on a training course once, something they learned from a magazine article, something they learned by talking to colleagues, and, yes, some ideas they picked up while working with various clients.

My advice is that you shouldn't worry about this. Accept that the consultants will pick up a few new tips and tricks from working with your employees. But appreciate, also, the fact that your employees will pick up many tremendously valuable tips and tricks from working with the consultants. Take good advantage of this opportunity.

22.2 Cultivating connections

The best smartphone developers, almost invariably, turn out to be well networked. They don't themselves know all the answers about Symbian OS development, but they know people they can ask for the answers. They know people who will probably be able to answer questions on topic A, another set of people who will probably be able to answer questions on topic B, and so on, for all the possible kinds of questions.

A good starting point for cultivating your own connections with Symbian OS experts is the set of discussion forums hosted by Symbian's website. See *www.symbian.com/developer/support.html*. If you click on the "community links" section of that site, you'll also have the option of looking at newsgroups and forums hosted by third parties. Take the time to explore these sites.

Another invaluable source of information is the set of existing source code published by Symbian and the wider community, including open-source projects.

Whichever sites you end up frequenting, you have to follow the basic etiquette of newsgroups: if you expect to raise new questions on these sites, you should also contribute answers to other people's questions. Instead of just taking knowledge from these discussions, you should also add to it. Instead of just downloading existing open-source projects, consider uploading some of your own source code (from noncritical projects). In this way, you'll develop your own online reputation. Then when you have questions to ask, you'll find that people will be readier to help you out. You may fear that, by answering people's questions and by uploading sample source code, you are helping your competitors. But think, instead, that you are enlarging a support network that will, over time, repay you in many ways.

Even before you ask questions, check out the FAQs that are available. You'll often find these contain the answers to what's on your mind. There are some extensive FAQs on Symbian's developer support website, at *www.symbian.com/developer/techlib/faq.html*.

You should cultivate similar links and networks *inside* your company. People working on Symbian OS smartphone project X should internally exchange questions and answers with people working on Symbian OS smartphone project Y, even though they're based at different sites, or belong to different organizations. Take good advantage of the knowledge that's already inside your company.

Even inside a single team, you'll be surprised at the potential for different team members to be able to help each other, given the chance to do so. If you have a question about an aspect of Symbian OS development, you basically have four options:

- Out of pride, keep the question to yourself, being determined not to show your ignorance
- Ask a few friends – people who you think might know the answer
- Ask the question on a public newsgroup, where it is visible to everyone in the public Symbian OS developer community
- Ask the question on an in-house newsgroup or discussion database.

Apart from the first approach, there are advantages to each of these methods. The last approach is often the most attractive; you'll often get an answer from someone you wouldn't have thought of asking. That's very often how I personally find an answer inside Symbian – I raise the question on our in-house Programming database (or on a more specialized variant of it), and the answer pops up from someone I hadn't thought of asking individually. It takes effort to set up such a database but, in my view, this effort is well worth it. It helps you to get more value from your in-house knowledge. To get even more value from it, make sure that your in-house knowledge systems support state-of-the-art searching.

22.3 Building a team out of nothing

You can't grow a Symbian OS smartphone development team out of thin air. Any successful large team grows from the seeds of previous teams. Here's where you can find these seeds:

- If your company already has a Symbian OS smartphone development project underway, transfer a small number of people from that team into your new team (this decision will require vigorous support from senior management)

❑ Hire new recruits who have proven prior experience with Symbian OS smartphone projects

❑ Involve consultants who have proven prior experience with Symbian OS smartphone projects; assign these consultants as advisors to some of the key roles within your organization

❑ Shortly before the project is due to start, send the entire team on a dedicated training course, such as the ''boot camp training'' available directly from Symbian, and from some of Symbian's training partners

❑ Follow up the initial training with regular training refresher courses.

Remember the basic rule of training: you need to keep on reinforcing the training material, at regular intervals after the course, in order for the attendees to make best use of it.

Remember also that mistakes made in the early phases of a project can take a long time to undo afterwards. It's like the way that childhood traumas can have unexpected effects even into adult life. So right from the beginning of your project, be sure that you're receiving the best possible advice.

22.4 Helping consultants to be effective

Once you've taken the decision to include external consultants on your project team, you need to follow up that decision by providing full support to these consultants. You have to help them to be able to help you. This includes the following measures:

❑ Assign someone in your team to be the ''consultants' uncle'' – someone who constantly tries to find ways for the team to make more effective use of the consultants, and who searches for project tasks that would benefit from assistance from the on-site consultants

❑ Allow the consultants to walk around freely within the project team area. Much of the value they add comes from impromptu discussions with your team members. Don't isolate the consultants in restricted rooms, where they will be much less effective

❑ Allow the consultants to study your source code. That way, they'll often be able to point out problems with it, by doing proactive code reviews. It will also allow them to carry out source code debugging, and to try out experimental modifications to the code. If you prevent the consultants from seeing your source code, out of a misguided attempt to protect the secrecy of that code, don't be surprised if they fail to point out issues with that code

❑ Allow the consultants to access your software configuration management system, so that they can review the history of various changes in the code; this can often be invaluable in shedding light on the causes of unexpected changes

❑ Keep the consultants informed about progress and issues in the project. Don't imagine that they somehow already know these things. Perhaps they will, but perhaps they won't

❑ Allow the consultants to have full access to the IT services in their own companies, so that they can quickly consult their colleagues and knowledge-base systems regarding questions arising on the project. If you are overly paranoid about information leaking from your project back to the HQ of the consultancy company, don't be surprised if you get less value from the consultants.

As is well known in our industry, a really good software developer can be up to ten times as productive as an average developer. It's the same when you bring really good consultants into your project team: the right consultants can make parts of your project proceed up to ten times more quickly. However, that depends upon the consultants in turn receiving, from you, the support that they need. Don't be tardy.

In short, treat the consultants as partners, not as suppliers. The greater the degree of cooperation, the more likely it is that the engagement will have a truly successful outcome.

23

The essential role of renewal

23.1 The role of the post partum

Whether your smartphone development project meets, or falls short of, your expectations, you owe it to yourself to conduct a formal review of the lessons you can learn from that project:

- ❑ What aspects went well?

- ❑ What aspects went badly?

- ❑ What would you do differently in the future?

- ❑ What immediate changes should you make to your organization to increase the chances of greater success in future smartphone projects?

Inside Symbian we regularly hold such reviews. In the case of a failed project – for example, if the smartphone was cancelled prior to launch – we call the review a "post mortem". In the case of a successful project, we call the review a "post partum". In either case, we produce a written document, containing both analysis and recommendations. For example, I've just taken a few minutes' break from writing this chapter to read through a 23-page document written within the last month, at the end of a major project support engagement by Symbian technical consultants. The document makes a total of 21 separate recommendations.

Hold these reviews about a month after the end of the project. A month is long enough for the participants to have gained some perspective – they're no longer wrapped up in project minutiae. But it's not so long that people will have forgotten their key experiences.

To get the best value out of a post partum, you should prioritize the recommendations that it makes. Otherwise there's a risk that the recommendations will just gather dust inside the document. It's also worth rereading the output document after two or three months have elapsed, to see what other pearls of wisdom in it need greater promotion.

Investing time in a post partum review is an example of a cardinal principle of long-term fitness to carry out major smartphone development projects. That principle is that you need to take time out of being busy with the project, to review and reflect on your progress.

Some people characterize smartphone development projects as a marathon – requiring sustained high-pressure effort. I disagree. A far better metaphor is to see these projects as a series of hard sprints, interspersed with recovery time. That's why I call this chapter, "The essential role of renewal". For long-term success, you need your people to work hard *and play hard.* Without time devoted to rest and recreation, your team will burn themselves out. Sure, you'll be able to recruit new people to replace those that are burned out, but it will take each new person up to two years (sometimes longer) to reach a similar state of overall system knowledge as the people they are replacing.

23.2 Line management skills

As a software leader, you need to ensure that each person in your team receives a regular performance appraisal. Don't let more than six months pass between these appraisals.

In my experience, a good appraisal from your manager is like a good session with a personal coach:

❑ The coach challenges some of your thinking
❑ The coach helps you to see things in new light
❑ The coach helps you to reevaluate your goals and priorities
❑ Even as you are considering problems and challenges, the coach helps you to conceive solutions
❑ The coach draws out ideas that are already semi-formed in your own thinking.

It takes special skills to deliver a good appraisal. Just because someone is a good software engineer, or a good project manager, does not mean they will (automatically) have the skills required to conduct a good appraisal. These skills include:

❑ Perceptiveness to psychological factors
❑ Ability to detach their own personal feelings

- Knowledge of skills and techniques to aid personal growth
- A thorough understanding of career development opportunities available
- Ability to collect feedback, and to weigh it up dispassionately, separating the substance from the fluff.

That's why it's important that there's good training for line managers, and also why it's important for senior managers to be able to pick out people in their teams with genuine potential for line management roles. (And, where it turns out that someone with line management responsibilities persistently lacks the necessary skills, senior managers need to reassign that person to a different role.)

Another area of some difficulty is that of "management by objective". A lot has been written about the problems here, and about why measurement systems risk being dysfunctional. In short:

- Clarifying goals and objectives is important for everyone; we all need to work out the highest priorities, and we all need to attend to these priorities

- However, *measures* of goals and objectives are notoriously hard to achieve

- Typical measurement schemes may concentrate on measurements of, say, X and Y, where X and Y are two contributors of the overall (unmeasurable) goal G; but frequently X and Y are not the only required causes of G, so too much emphasis on X and Y produces distorted effects

- So, it takes special skill to set metrics for goals and objectives

- It also takes a special commitment to review the continuing effectiveness of these metrics.

Once objectives are set at the beginning of an appraisal period, they need to be regularly reviewed throughout that period, in case the overall priorities need to be changed. Again, this takes special dedication from a line manager to carry out. But individuals can help too: if they judge that conditions have changed, and that previously set objectives may no longer have the highest priority, they should book a one-to-one meeting with their manager to discuss this.

23.3 Circulation of team members

Individual career development includes moving people into situations where they will:

❑ Find new personal challenges
❑ Be able to learn from working with new colleagues
❑ Avoid becoming stale.

This can introduce some tension into management decisions. The course of action that's the best outcome for an individual's career development sometimes fails to match the short-term needs of a project team. As a software leader, you need to balance these needs. You also need to ensure the well-being of one more entity: the team itself, which needs to possess a suitable mix of skills and personalities. So you have to simultaneously look after the needs of the individual, the team, and the project. That's no easy feat. In order to carry it out, you need to:

❑ Avoid thinking of your team members as being some kind of interchangeable resources, who can easily be replaced by one another (or by newcomers to the team). That's a sure way to demotivate your team members, and they'll leave you when the chance arises

❑ Allocate some quality thinking time to all three sets of needs. If your first ideas fail to work out, keep on trying; you may be surprised at the creative solutions you uncover

❑ Keep in mind the longer-term needs of the project, as well as the shorter-term ones; there will be follow-up projects after the first one.

Circulating team members into new areas of responsibility maintains freshness in the organization. It's far better for you that the team members find some new challenges inside your organization, than that they feel they have to leave your organization to stimulate their interest anew.

23.4 Principles of collaboration

I've seen three broad phases of maturity in the development teams at Psion and Symbian:

❑ The first era was an era of "super heroes" – individuals who worked incredibly hard, and who single-handedly created huge amounts of software functionality

❑ Then came an era of "internal teamwork". We realized that it would be better to take the time to hire larger numbers of new developers, and to train these developers. That would slow us down in the short term, but would increase our collective productivity in the medium and long term. We needed to learn how to improve our methods of interviewing, selecting, and mentoring. The outcome, after a considerable culture shift, was a team that could develop software significantly faster than the original, smaller group. One of the greatest strengths of Symbian today is our ability to attract, year after year, large numbers of the brightest and most productive young graduates from all over Europe (and beyond) to join our development teams

❑ Finally we've been living for several years in the era of "extended teamwork". We realized that it would be better to take the time to learn how to work with a large number of external companies. Even though that slowed us down in the short term, there was, again, a medium and long-term boon to our overall productivity. Again, we needed to learn new skills. Extended teamwork was even harder to learn than internal teamwork. But the benefits have been greater, too. Symbian's ecosystem is, today, brim-full of companies who are ready and willing to work on smartphone development projects. If you're ready to collaborate, you'll find very many willing and capable helpers.

To unlock the potential of the Symbian ecosystem to accelerate your own development projects, your organization may need to pass through something of a similar culture change. You need a mindset and processes that favor collaboration:

❑ Treat companies as partners rather than as suppliers

❑ Err on the side of over-communicating rather than of under-communicating

❑ Specify the desired outcomes, not (necessarily) the way of reaching these outcomes

❑ Tolerate creative tension; tolerate differences of approach

❑ Specify principles rather than processes

❑ Focus on the success of the project, rather than the delivery of the individual task

❑ Reward the sharing of ideas, rather than the hiding of them

❑ Reward early reporting of bad news, rather than attempts to hide the trail of responsibility

□ Avoid the culture of blame and antagonism; instead, favor constructive suggestions

□ Realize that, if your collaboration is successful, the overall pie (the smartphone marketplace) will be larger; avoid squabbling over how to divide up the existing pie (thereby risking the destruction of that pie altogether).

23.5 The increasing importance of software

Over the next few years, the importance of software in smartphones will continue to grow. The software in these phones is already so complex that you need an intensely collaborative mindset in order to play in this space. The complexity has already gone far beyond what any one company can handle. And the inner complexity is still growing:

□ Larger screens, with higher resolutions, raise demands for better UIs to guide the users through the rich sets of available options

□ Users learn that they can customize their smartphones, and seek ever fancier ways to carry out this customization

□ Operators insist on phones containing software variations that identify the phones as belonging to their networks, rather than as being "vanilla" phones

□ Companies see how smartphones can plug into corporate data systems, and stipulate that new capabilities are added to the phones to cope with specific application requirements

□ Wide area communications protocols (such as GSM and CDMA networks) are increasingly being supplemented by local area protocols (such as Bluetooth and WiFi) which have different cost structures

□ The advance of Moore's Law allows escalating amounts of software functionality to be packed into the same amount of physical space inside a smartphone, available at the same cost as before

□ Smartphones are gaining increasing acceptance as entertainment devices, camcorders, games units, personal organizers, and the repositories for tickets, vouchers, and even money

□ All this functionality (and lots more) needs coordination, security, and appropriate backup and synchronization with other software stores

❏ Users will move from expecting that they can personally customize smartphones to expecting that they can personally program them; the advent of widespread graphics programming systems will boost renewed interest in user-originated content and applications.

23.6 A guide for software leaders

Because software will become increasingly important, it's vital that we find ways to keep control of it. We don't want to end up with our mobile phones running software systems that no one understands.

Personally, I have a love–hate relationship with my laptop. I discern that I'm not alone in this. We can all frequently hear users of PCs cursing at them. Thankfully, I have a much more positive relationship with my smartphone; again, I'm not alone in this. We need to keep things this way. Otherwise, the remarkable promise of smartphones will stall, before it really starts. Users won't be interested in the potentially huge benefits of the forthcoming new smartphones if they start to experience nasty drawbacks from flaky smartphones – resets, data loss, mind-numbing complexity of the UI, viruses and virus scanners, etc.

In this book, I've systematically outlined one solution for the task of creating successful smartphone products: that of applying smart software development. It's a methodology that requires deep thought as well as copious hard work. And because smartphone development projects take considerable time, your plan needs to include renewal time along the way:

❏ Take the time to discuss your experiences with your team-mates and peers

❏ Take the time to investigate how other people write Symbian OS software – how they structure their APIs, how they write documentation, and how they dovetail their test code with their main code

❏ Take the time to find out people's views on best smartphone development practices

❏ Take the time to work with a variety of different team-mates

❏ Take the time to attend training courses

❏ Take the time to search hard for simplifying principles. The best solution to burgeoning complexity is to find a new way of looking at things, which illuminates an inner simplicity

❏ Take the time to read and reflect. You should find the material in the selected bibliography in the appendix to be helpful. I've listed books that will repay regular rereading, and which can provide the basis of highly beneficial group discussions. In many cases, these books go into more details on the points I've mentioned in my own book. I've chosen these books with care: they are all guides for software leaders to become even more successful.

But don't procrastinate. Make it a guiding principle, in any demanding project situation, to deliver some value quickly. With each new sprint, you deliver extra value. Sprint early, and sprint often.

23.7 Symbian OS renewal

Symbian continues to renew Symbian OS, making minor and major new releases in response to the evolving needs of the marketplace.

We receive regular feedback from multiple parts of the smartphone value chain: from phone manufacturers, network operators, semiconductor vendors, enterprise solution providers, integration specialists, middleware specialists, corporate IT departments, venture capitalists, smartphone retailers, and creators and aggregators of applications, services, and content. We also keep a close eye on what press and analysts say, and on feedback from smartphone end-users. We carefully weigh up all these ideas and suggestions, thereby renewing our own internal ideas about the evolution of Symbian OS.

At the time of writing, phone manufacturers are developing smartphones based on version 9 of Symbian OS. This version contains a number of very powerful upgrades to its predecessors. I wish to highlight two of these:

- ❏ A comprehensive new "platform security" framework builds on previous measures, to defuse the threats of wireless malware (software intentionally or unintentionally written to abuse personal user data, run up large phone bills, or interfere with phone or network performance). This framework is the foundation for increased user and network confidence in the value and reliability of new smartphone services

- ❏ A new version of the kernel of Symbian OS, known as "EKA2", enables a host of new kinds of solution for mobile computing and mobile communications – through enhanced real-time characteristics, improved portability of Symbian OS to new hardware platforms, and revised internal design which makes it easier (among other things) for smartphone vendors to reduce their manufacturing costs by combining the application processor and baseband processor.

Symbian Press is publishing books on both of these topics. They complement the material in this book.

I'll be very interested to hear of your own experiences creating smartphone projects (whichever version of Symbian OS you use). You can reach me at david.wood@symbian.com. Your feedback will influence the creation of future versions of Symbian OS.

Today's smartphones offer only a fleeting glimpse of the potential of the devices we'll all be using in 10 years' time. To create the smartphones of the future, we need to keep on sharing our collective insight and learnings. I look forward to hearing from you, and to hearing about the breakthrough smartphone products you create.

Appendix 1
Annotated glossary of abbreviations

AI   Artificial Intelligence – as found in games on smartphones, in smart messages, and in numerous other aspects of smartphones

AP   Applications Processor – one of the main silicon chips on a smartphone, which runs the applications visible to the user

API   Application Programming Interface. In the narrow sense, this is the set of functions provided by a platform available to be used by applications writers. In the broad sense, the API includes the HAI and the SPI

AQA   Any Question Answered – a service available through many network operators, whereby mobile users SMS a question to a predefined number (63336) and receive an answer by return, again by SMS. This service is provided by the company IssueBits, founded by Colly Myers (Symbian's first CEO) after leaving Symbian. Another of Symbian's EVP cofounders, Bill Batchelor, is the Technical Director at IssueBits

ARM   Advanced RISC Machines – the company based at Cambridge, UK, that designs the silicon architectures (also called ARM) that are used in most smartphones in the world. Symbian OS has been specially optimized for aspects of ARM architecture

BAT   Basic Acceptance Tests – a set of tests covering all functionality in a product, that should be run on every candidate release of the product

BC   Binary Compatibility – where the APIs of two platform versions are such that executable code built on one version will successfully run on the other without being rebuilt

BP   Baseband Processor. Another name for this is CP, the Communications Processor, referring to the communications between the phone and the wireless network, but I prefer the name BP, since there are many other kinds of communication in the smartphone as a whole

BR   Break Request – a request for approval of a software change that will cause a break in interface compatibility

CBR   Component Based Release tools – which make it easy to incrementally update the large sets of files forming the smartphone development environment on developers' PCs

CCB   Change Control Board – a team of software leaders which reviews CRs submitted to a project

CDB   Code Data Base – a tool provided by Symbian to assist in interface management

CDMA   Code-Division Multiple Access – a wireless digital baseband technology that is used in (among other countries) North and South America, Japan, Korea, and China

CM   Configuration Management – a system allowing software teams to keep track of multiple changes in the source code of the software being developed. Another name for CM is SCM

CP   Communications Processor. See BP

CPU   Central Processing Unit. When someone says "this consumes CPU" they mean that the processor(s) on the smartphone (AP and/or BP) are being made to work hard, potentially reducing battery life

CR   Change Request – a request for the product to meet an additional requirement, or for a change in an existing requirement. (Occasionally, there are CRs to *remove* functionality)

C++   Pronounced "C plus plus". The programming language in which the vast majority of Symbian OS is written. It is an OO extension of the C programming language, and was adopted by Psion in late 1994 in a key early design decision regarding EPOC32

DKL Dev Kit License – a license from Symbian entitling a partner company to have access to APIs and source code that are not part of public SDKs

DLL Dynamic Link Library – the format of many smartphone software components, supporting dynamic (run-time) linking from other software components

EKA2 EPOC Kernel Architecture v2 – as available in Symbian OS v8.1b forwards

EPOC EPOC was an early name for the software system now known as Symbian OS. Before that, EPOC was at one time the name of the 16-bit precursor to Symbian OS (which is itself a 32-bit operating system). As the 32-bit version was being created, we started to differentiate between "EPOC16" and "EPOC32". After a while, the older name "SIBO" was generally readopted in place of "EPOC16", and "EPOC" came just to mean "EPOC32". For a long time (until our Marketing department advised us otherwise), we only capitalized the initial letter, "Epoc", since it was a name, not an acronym. The origins of the name are a matter of some controversy. David Potter (Psion's chairman) has variously joked that "EPOC" stands for "Eat Plenty Of Carrots" and "Electronic Piece Of Cheese". Colly Myers, the primary author of both EPOC16 and EPOC32, has stated that the name was chosen out of reference to "epoch" (as in "epoch-making"), and was restricted to four letters in similarity to both Mach and Unix

ERA EPOC RISC Architecture – another early name for what we now call Symbian OS

EVP Executive Vice President – the job title used in Symbian for executive managers who report direct to the CEO (Chief Executive Officer)

F2F Face To Face – a meeting where people are present in the same room, as opposed to a telephone or electronic discussion

FAQ Frequently Asked Question. Any team committed to the principle of reuse should consider creating a database of FAQs, to speed up general learning

FOMA Freedom Of Multimedia Access – the name given by NTT DoCoMo in Japan for the UI system (and associated platform) that runs on their smartphones

FTE Full Time Equivalent. This is used in the context of resource estimates, as in "10 FTE", meaning that there could be 20 people assigned to the project, each working half-time on it (or 5 people working on it full-time, and another 10 people each working half-time, etc.)

FUT Friendly User Tests – a system of beta testing in which selected users agree to provide helpful feedback on their usage of the smartphone product as their main phone

GSM Originally (in French language) Groupe Spéciale Mobile; then anglicized to Global System for Mobile [Communications]. A wireless digital baseband technology that is in use in virtually every country in the world

HAI Hardware Adaptation Interface – the set of functions expected by a platform to be provided by hardware-dependent lower-level plug-ins such as device drivers

IDE Integrated Development Environment – a core development tool with multiple features, including support for plug-ins with extra functionality, providing developers with a unified dashboard for editing code, compiling it, debugging it, and (usually) a whole lot more. Most of Symbian OS was developed using Microsoft's Visual Studio IDE

IOT Inter Operability Tests – to confirm that the product inter-operates well with other products on the market; this is sometimes also abbreviated to IOP (Inter OPerability)

ISC Inter Systems Communications – referring to the communications between the applications processor and the baseband processor

ISV Independent Software Vendor – a company (or person) who writes software intended to be added into smartphones

IT Information Technology – the department in a company that looks after corporate email, computing resources, and other information systems; this is also often called IS (standing for Information Systems)

MMS Multimedia Messaging Service – in which mobile phones can exchange messages that include multimedia elements, such as pictures, audio, and video

OO Object Oriented (or Object Orientation, etc.) – a design system for large software systems that is in almost universal usage

OPL   Organizer Programming Language – a programming language invented by Psion, with some features of Basic and others of C. It was supported on the Organiser II, then on SIBO, then on Symbian OS, and allowed users to create surprisingly powerful applications on the devices themselves. Recently OPL has been rechristened as "Open Programming Language"

OS   Operating System

OTA   Over The Air – a way of sending messages, updating applications, or patching the operating system, etc., using the telephony networks, rather than a local connection to a PC or storage disk

PDA   Personal Digital Assistant – one of many names for a smart handheld computer

POOC   Psion Object Oriented C – the proprietary in-house system used to create SIBO software

PSD   Partner Solution Directory – a directory listing from Symbian, available to phone manufacturers, that lists solutions from device creation partners that are known to be available for incorporation into current smartphone projects

QA   Quality Assurance – the group with responsibility for determining whether the product has high enough quality to allow it to be released

RA   Requirements Analyst – someone assigned to write and review requirements documents, checking for clarity, proposing measurable outcomes, and unearthing implicit assumptions

RAM   Random Access Memory. More generally, the "RAM" usage of a product is the amount of working memory it needs

RISC   Reduced Instruction Set Computer. The opposite of RISC is CISC – Complex Instruction Set Computer, such as those based on the ×86 architectures. Smartphones typically have RISC hardware, for reasons of cost, execution speed, and simplicity of design. During 1993 and 1994 Psion considered targeting its forthcoming EPOC32 software to ×86 computers, but decided in the end to target RISC, with a particular focus on the chips designed by ARM

ROM — Read Only Memory. More generally, the term "ROM" often refers to the set of software that is built into a smartphone, or (for an add-on application) the amount of storage space taken up by an application when it is installed onto a smartphone

SC — Source Compatibility – where the APIs of two platform versions are such that source code which compiles on one version will successfully compile on the other without modification

SCB — System Compatibility Board – a team of senior engineers which reviews any BRs submitted to it by engineers on the project team

SCM — Software Configuration Management. See CM

SDK — Software Development Kit – containing descriptions of how developers can use APIs; SDKs are freely available for download from **www.symbian.com**

SIBO — "SIngle Board Organizer" and/or "SIxteen Bit Organizer" – a name often used for the 16-bit precursor to Symbian OS (see EPOC for more details)

SIM — Subscriber Identity Module – the small card that is inserted into GSM phones so that they can talk to the telephone network

SMS — Short Message Service – the technical term for mobile phone text messages

SPI — Service Provider Interface – the equivalent of API for providers of service-enablers

SS — Show Stopper – a defect that will "stop the show" in the sense of preventing product release, rather than the common meaning: something so good the show will stop as the audience applaud

TA — Technical Authority – a senior engineer who is the acknowledged expert for a given area of software functionality

TTM — Time To Market – how long it takes you to create a product and bring it to the market

UI — User Interface – software that includes menus, buttons, lists, edit windows, dialogs, and so on, allowing the user to input data to applications

UIQ	The pen-enabled UI system provided by UIQ Technology. "UIQ" is said to be short for "UI with IQ". The "Q" also refers to "Quartz", the original codename for this UI system, referring in turn to "Quarter VGA", which was the screensize originally targeted
USD	United States Dollars
USP	Unique Selling Point – a reason for someone to buy one product rather than another
XIP	eXecute In Place – a system whereby programs can be run directly from ROM without needing to be loaded into RAM

Appendix 2
Selected bibliography

The best source of information about books on Symbian is the web page of Symbian Press at **www.symbian.com/books**. New books are being publicized on this site on a regular basis.

For more information about the ways smartphones are transforming society, see:

❑ *Smart mobs: the next social revolution,* by Howard Rheingold
❑ *Mobile disruption: the technologies and applications that are driving the mobile internet,* by Jeffrey Lee Funk.

For more about disruptive technologies and network effects for new products, see:

❑ *The innovator's solution: – creating and sustaining successful growth,* by Clayton Christensen and Michael Raynor
❑ *The slow pace of fast change: bringing innovations to market in a connected world,* by Bhaskar Chakravorti.

For general advice about high-quality software engineering, see the following by Steve McConnell:

❑ *Software project survival guide*
❑ *Rapid development*
❑ *Code complete.*

Four books that had a big influence on Psion's emerging understanding of OO and C++ during the 1980s and 1990s, and which are still well worth reading:

❑ *Object-oriented programming: an evolutionary approach,* by Brad Cox
❑ *Object-Oriented software construction,* by Bertrand Meyer

- ❏ *Object-Oriented analysis and design with applications,* by Grady Booch
- ❏ *Taligent's guide to designing programs: well-mannered object-oriented design in C++*
- ❏ *The design and evolution of C++,* by Bjarne Stroustrup.

Other true classics in the field of software engineering management which every software leader should reread every few years:

- ❏ *The mythical man-month: essays on software engineering,* by Frederick P. Brookes
- ❏ *Peopleware: productive projects and teams,* by Tom Demarco and Timothy Lister.

Some books that are, in their various ways, modern classics on software engineering:

- ❏ *Refactoring: improving the design of existing code,* by Martin Fowler et al.
- ❏ *Large-scale C++ software design,* by John Lakos
- ❏ *Software configuration management patterns: effective teamwork, practical integration,* by Stephen Berczuk and Brad Appleton
- ❏ *Joel on software: and on diverse and occasionally related matters that will prove of interest to software developers, designers, and managers...,* by Joel Spolsky.

For the foundational ideas of critical chain project management and avoiding suboptimization, see:

- ❏ *The goal: a process of ongoing improvement,* by Eliyahu Goldratt and Jeff Cox
- ❏ *Critical chain: a business novel,* by Eliyahu Goldratt
- ❏ *Project management in the fast lane: applying the theory of constraints,* by Robert Newbold
- ❏ *Breaking the constraints to world-class performance,* by H. William Dettmer.

For deep insight into combining agility and software process, see:

- ❏ *Lean software development: an agile toolkit for software development managers,* by Mary Poppendieck and Tom Poppendieck
- ❏ *Agile management for software engineering: applying the theory of constraints for business results,* by David J. Anderson.

For outstanding advice on the overall product development process, please read:

☐ *The inmates are running the asylum: why high tech products drive us crazy and how to restore the sanity*, by Alan Cooper

☐ *The invisible computer: why good products can fail, the personal computer is so complex and information appliances are the solution*, by Donald Norman

☐ *Slack: getting past burnout, busywork, and the myth of total efficiency*, by Tom Demarco

☐ *Experimentation matters: unlocking the potential of new technologies for innovation*, by Stefan Thomke

☐ *Managing the design factory*, by Donald G. Reinertsen

☐ *Leading the revolution: how to thrive in troubled times by making innovation a way of life*, by Gary Hamel.

For inspiring ideas on how to take best advantage of collaboration in large teams, I recommend:

☐ *How to make collaboration work: powerful ways to build consensus, solve problems, and make decisions*, by David Strauss and Thomas C. Layton

☐ *King Arthur's round table: how collaborative conversations create smart organizations*, by David Perkins

☐ *The wisdom of crowds: why the many are smarter than the few and how collective wisdom shapes business, economies, societies and nations*, by James Surowiecki.

Some fascinating history books, that have in places more parallels than you might expect with what happened at Psion and Symbian:

☐ *Showstopper: the breakneck race to create Windows NT and the next generation at Microsoft*, by G. Pascal Zachary

☐ *Piloting Palm: the inside story of Palm, Handspring and the birth of the billion dollar handheld industry*, by Andrea Butter and David Pogue

☐ *Just for fun: the story of an accidental revolutionary*, by Linus Torvalds and David Diamond

❏ *Microsoft secrets: how the world's most powerful software company creates technology, shapes markets, and manages people*, by Michael A. Cusumano.

Some other history books, which are also deeply inspiring in their own ways, dealing with companies in or near the smartphone space:

❏ *Sony: the private life*, by John Nathan
❏ *Matsushita leadership: lessons from the 20th century's most remarkable entrepreneur*, by John Kotter
❏ *Breaking Windows: how Bill Gates fumbled the future of Microsoft*, by David Bank.

Four outstanding books about the conditions for companies to become world leaders:

❏ *Good to great: why some companies make the leap. . .and others don't*, by Jim Collins

❏ *Mastering the dynamics of innovation: how companies can seize opportunities in the face of technological change*, by James Utterback

❏ *Crossing the chasm: marketing and selling technology products to mainstream customers*, by Geoffrey Moore

❏ *Will and vision: how latecomers grow to dominate markets*, by Gerard J. Tellis and Peter N. Golder.

Finally, five exceptional books about renewal, line management, and developing true potential:

❏ *First, break all the rules: what the world's greatest managers do differently*, by Marcus Buckingham and Curt Coffman

❏ *The 80/20 principle: the secret to success by achieving more with less*, by Richard Koch

❏ *Artful making: what managers need to know about how artists work*, by Robert Austin and Lee Devin

❏ *The power of full engagement: managing energy, not time, is the key to high performance and personal renewal*, by Jim Loehr and Tony Schwartz

❏ *The 7 habits of highly effective people*, by Stephen R. Covey.

Appendix 3
Acknowledgments

I have been fortunate to have a large number of deeply inspiring teachers and mentors along my path towards smartphone product engineering. On this occasion, I can only mention a small number. I wish to give special thanks to:

❏ My mother and father, Cath and Bill Wood, who gave me the best possible start in life, and who have constantly shown me great kindness and thoughtfulness

❏ Ian Kelman, the brand new mathematics teacher at Turriff Academy, Aberdeenshire, who arrived fresh out of teacher training college in 1972 and proceeded on the as-then unheard of path of providing 13-year-olds (including me) with extra lunchtime classes on programming in Fortran; that was my happy introduction to software engineering

❏ Bill Smith, the head of the mathematics department at Turriff Academy, who let me loose for two weeks solid on the traveling neighborhood mini-computer when it finally arrived at our school in 1977

❏ Richard Harrison and Charles Davies, for offering me the chance to work at Psion, in 1988

❏ My colleagues in all departments in Psion and Symbian over many years, past and present, from whom I have learned innumerable insights

❏ The board of directors of Psion, especially David Potter, Colly Myers, Charles Davies, and Marina Wyatt, for having the great courage and astonishing foresight to create first Psion Software (1996) and then Symbian (1998)

❏ The smartphone visionaries in multiple companies who acted on the conviction that Symbian should be created, including Anders

Waesterlid, Michael Kornby, Hans Wagner, Mikko Terho, Juha Putkiranta, Jerry Upton, Stephen Randall, Bill Batchelor, and Juha Christensen

❑ The members of the Symbian Press team at Symbian for their support while writing this book, especially Phil Northam and Freddie Gjertsen

❑ All members of the Symbian Press team at Wiley, especially Sally Tickner and David Barnard

❑ Everyone at Symbian who provided me with comments on drafts of the material in this book, including Richard Harrison (who tirelessly reviewed every single word in a few short weeks), Freddie Gjertsen, Twm Davies, Kang Hun Lee, Kevin O'Neill, Ben Morris, Peter Jackson, Tony Lofthouse, George Purchase, John Pagonis, Matt Davies, David Mery, Peter Ferguson, Adrian Steward, Christophe Le Coent, and Andrew Margolis. All errors and the numerous stylistic quirks that remain are, of course, my own responsibility

❑ The authors of the books I have listed in the Bibliography, for providing me with incalculable inspiration and instruction. I heartily recommend these books to people wanting to follow up the ideas in my own book: readers will see the origins of some of these ideas, and will find many fine explanations that go into considerably more depth on key points

❑ My incomparable soul-mate, Hyesoon, and our wonderful son, Erroll, for their encouragement and support during my periods of absence while writing this book, and during very many other periods of absence over nearly 20 years as I have attended to one project emergency after another.

Index

Symbian Press Portfolio

Learning Symbian OS C++

Beginner　　　　　　　　　　　　　　　　　　　　　　**Advanced**

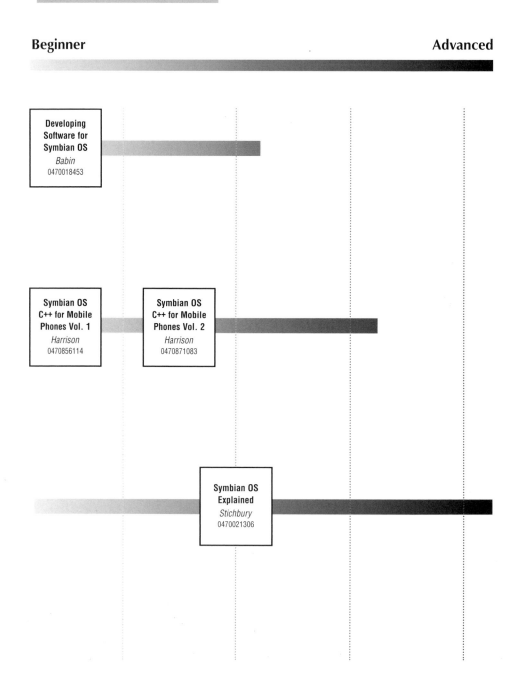

Developing Software for Symbian OS
Babin
0470018453

Symbian OS C++ for Mobile Phones Vol. 1
Harrison
0470856114

Symbian OS C++ for Mobile Phones Vol. 2
Harrison
0470871083

Symbian OS Explained
Stichbury
0470021306